One Way to Get
to Arizona

One Way to Get to Arizona

Mildred de Szendeffy

Writers Club Press
San Jose New York Lincoln Shanghai

One Way to Get to Arizona

Writers Club Press
an imprint of iUniverse.com, Inc.

For information address:
iUniverse.com, Inc.
5220 S 16th, Ste. 200
Lincoln, NE 68512
www.iuniverse.com

ISBN: 0-595-15211-2

Printed in the United States of America

To my Husband, Foster de Szendeffy
Father to my sons—Rodney, Michael, Stephen, Gary and John
and
The Love of My Life

Part I

The Journey

Sooner or later, any female saddled with the name "Mildred" has to wonder whatever possessed her otherwise well-meaning parents to zero in on that particular monicker.

Hundreds and thousands of other names could have been selected for an infant with unfortunately no say in the matter—for instance "Rose Marie" as in Jeanette MacDonald's "Indian Love Call," movie-of-the-year in the 30s. But no. The only possible explanation is, once "Mildred" was suggested, everyone assumed they'd heard some other name and innocently voted Aye for "Mildred." And then it was too late.

My mother Bessie also disliked her own name, but nevertheless named my older sister Bessie. Knowing my grandmother's given name was also, guess-what, I should have been grateful to be forever tagged as "Mildred." I could have been Bessie IV.

Name-wise, my father was much luckier (who could have a problem with "John") and his last name of "Mack" was never a problem. Except of course for those immediately asking "Mack-what?" By profession,

Papa was a mechanical engineer, but unfortunately for "family values," more often than not he was away on some steamship working as chief engineer. In 1921, the year I joined the world, steamships were the only way to go, and my favorite picture of Papa was taken by some obliging sailor out on deck on one of those ships. He was between cruises in Hamburg, Germany, and it wasn't until he returned home three weeks later that he knew he had another daughter.

Snapshots of my father are few and far between, but one I have always treasured is of him walking up and down the hallway of our apartment in Jersey City, holding me on his shoulder, patting my back and saying over and over "Papa's baby, Papa's baby." I have very few actual memories of him—he died when I was ten—but thinking of him at that long-ago moment makes him somehow come alive for me for a few seconds.

The so-called "Roaring Twenties" into which I was born were apparently part of another world. In Jersey City, New Jersey, most parents, including my own, had things pretty much under control. There were no street gangs—there weren't even any neighborhood "bad boys"— and children were literally expected to be seen and not heard. Definitely not heard.

Consequently, as a child my opinions were seldom, if ever, solicited, so I naturally assumed they were unwanted. This resulted in an almost total lack of self-esteem until I was well into my teens. Even kindergarten was a challenge. This is not to say my parents were in the least unkind. Strict, yes, but only in what they deemed my best interests—and in their opinion self-expression was not one of them.

When I was two years old, we moved out of the Jersey City apartment for reasons still unknown to me (who consults a two-year-old?) and wound up in Fairfield, a rural suburb of Caldwell. The house my parents rented there was happily next door to a very large farm, the first one I, a city-born child, had ever seen. Until then I never knew farms existed.

The most important resident over there was Rosie, a girl my own age, who became my very first best friend. She and I knew that particular farm was created for us alone. Whenever Rosie's farmer Dad was busy elsewhere, I would hear Rosie's little voice shrieking, "Millie, the tomatoes are waiting for us!" whereupon, we would deplete yet another crop of the most delicious red tomatoes I had ever seen. New Jersey tomatoes, pride of the state, are justifiably famous. All other tomatoes, even in the finest of restaurants, seem only half-ripe at best.

Fortunately for us, not that we were old enough to care about "figures" anyway, tomatoes were strictly non-fattening, otherwise even at the tender age of two we would have been waddling all over the place, stuffed to the gills with tomatoes.

By the time I was six, we had moved up into Caldwell itself. Along with most other children of that era, I was seldom clued in as to what was really going on with other members of the family, either health-wise, career-wise or emotionally. Consequently, not until some time later did I learn that two years before my father passed away of a kidney ailment at the age of 50, my mother had been informed that Papa had but a few months to live.

For his last two years, how the four of us—my parents, my sister Bessie and I—subsisted financially, I have no idea. I was aware that my mother was borrowing enough funds from my grandmother to keep up payments on a small insurance policy, but a certain bitterness Mom carried with her for the rest of her life was probably due to whatever she had to go through for those two years of what must have been pure hell.

After school closed that June, my mother and Bessie and I moved in temporarily with Mom's sister and her family in Bloomfield, a nearby town where I had a very enlightening experience at the local grammar school. In those days, children knew "their place" in school as well as in their home, consequently no one in my class—certainly not I—ever questioned why the entire class was suddenly marched one day into an empty auditorium, seated several feet away from each other, and handed what turned out to be that particular school's version of an IQ test. After obediently filling in our answers, we were duly returned to the classroom. A few days later, the teacher told me—and only me—to accompany her back to the auditorium. There, she sat me down and handed me yet another IQ test. While I recall nothing whatsoever of the questions, I do remember they were an entirely different set. As soon as I finished, the teacher snatched the paper from me, and we were on our way back to the classroom.

Still dying of curiosity as to why I alone had been selected for what to me was a senseless retaking of a test, I finally got up enough nerve to ask the teacher, in effect, "Why me?"

She actually replied, saying, "Well, since your first test produced the highest score we've seen yet in this school district, we wanted to make sure it wasn't just a fluke," (her term). Thereupon all concerned decided I should take another test by myself.

That teacher came close to turning my life around that day. While I never did learn the results of Test #2, and wasn't about to push my luck by asking, I felt as if a brand-new door had been opened for me. Evidently I wasn't the dumbest kid in school, and from that day on, whenever I wanted to ask a question or make a comment, I could hold up my hand as fast as anybody else.

The Christmas before my father passed away (he had been pretty much housebound), my mother had presented him with an Airedale puppy, Laddie. The gift of a dog from Mom to anybody at all was in itself highly unusual—she was anything but an animal lover—but Papa, Bessie and I loved that puppy on sight. Laddie was instantly a bona fide member of the family. After Papa died, and we moved temporarily to my aunt's house in Bloomfield, Laddie was duly installed in her back yard. One of the saddest days I experienced as a child was one afternoon after school when I, as usual, immediately rushed around to the back yard to play with Laddie and he was nowhere in sight.

My mother, who had evidently been watching out the window, opened the back door and came out. I can still hear her saying, "You won't be seeing Laddie any more. I've given him to some people out in the country where he'll have more room to run around."

My entire ten-year-old world fell apart. No matter how I pleaded, Mom would not say another word. I finally rushed up to the attic, crying my heart out, as only a child can cry when his or her heart is broken for the very first time. Later that afternoon, my sister returned home from work, looked all over the house for me, and finally located me in the attic. She comforted me as best she could but had surprisingly little to say. Years later, she finally came out with "I felt so sorry for you that day, what with Papa having died and you being moved away to another town, another school. At least you could have had your beloved Laddie to cling to, but now he was gone."

For the first few months of living at my aunt's house, all went reasonably well, considering it was a rather stressful period for everyone. Before we moved in, the household had consisted of Auntie (who worked for the Public Service Company in Newark), Uncle George (who was almost totally deaf and only worked around the house), their 24-year-old daughter Alice, and my grandmother, Nannie.

Nannie, to me the model of all time for what grandmothers are supposed to be, sometimes seemed to be my only friend in that house. She was always on my side. Whatever I did, or failed to do, was perfectly understandable to her. Auntie, on the other hand, was exactly the opposite. Encouraging words from Auntie to anyone were yet to be heard. To do her justice, she did bear the brunt of her own family's expenses, but one time I recall all too well, she came down on me like a ton of bricks—and it really wasn't called for.

We were all gathered around the dining room table for dinner. Families in that era assembled automatically every evening, same time, same place. The conversation of the elders, to which I hadn't even been

listening, suddenly apparently had me as the subject. I heard Nannie
say, with considerable pride, "Mildred was a very good girl today."

That compliment, totally unexpected as it was, had me sitting with
my mouth open for a few seconds. The next remark was Auntie's "Well,
it's too bad she can't be like that all the time." For one of the few times I
can recall, my mother actually came to my defense. She stood up, threw
her napkin on the table, grabbed my hand and said, "You never give this
child credit for anything. We're going out for a while."

As I recall, all Mom did was drive us around town for a few minutes,
but it was long enough to calm her down. My only real concern at the
time was my dessert, which was still sitting on the otherwise empty
table when we returned.

That same evening happened to be the night before my Cousin
Alice's 25th birthday. I had been eyeing her across the table as we ate,
with nothing but the deepest sympathy in my heart. All I could think
was, "Poor Alice—she'll be so old tomorrow. She'll be TWENTY-FIVE!"
Fortunately I kept my mouth shut or I would have been in even more
trouble.

A few weeks later, Mom, Bessie and I were watching our furniture
being moved into a nearby apartment. My mother must have been having a few second thoughts about having sent Laddie away, because when
she noticed me playing with a small kitten I found hiding under a bush,
she called me over with a smile.

"Mildred," she said, "how would you like to keep that cat?" I could
hardly believe my ears, but was of course ecstatic. I instantly named the
kitten Puff and rushed into the apartment with him to show him his
new home. The beginning was sweet—it almost made up for Laddie—
but I was still too young to suspect the ending could be otherwise.

Puff grew quite a bit in a few months, fast becoming the center of my
world. He appeared to be no trouble whatsoever to anyone—until the
day Mom told me our landlady was not at all happy having a cat under
her roof. She might possibly ask us to move out, therefore Puff had to

go. (Mom had already called the pound to have him picked up the next morning.)

When the van from the pound pulled up, I was the only one at home. In a matter of seconds, some man was at the door, holding out an empty kitty basket. I will never forget picking up that little cat, giving him a hug, and putting him down inside the basket. With tears running down my face, I asked the man if they would kill him right away. He said, "No," closed the top of the basket, and left.

I don't think my mother had the remotest idea how much Laddie and Puff meant to me, or how I felt knowing I'd never see them again. The apartment was suddenly very empty.

In high school, my least favorite subject was geometry. Arithmetic was comparatively easy, everything there eventually made sense. Algebra was less understandable—I liked to work with words, not figures—but even with borderline grades I finally managed to put algebra behind me.

Then geometry reared its ugly head, and one day, understanding less and less of what the geometry teacher was saying up there in front of the class, I raised my hand.

His response: "What IS IT?"

My question was "Sir, I'd just like to ask why you solved the problem that way." (Teachers were always addressed as Sir or Ma'am. Without that courtesy title they wouldn't even look in your direction, let alone answer.)

His reply was as brief as he could make it, "Because THAT'S the way we do it." With that, my geometry textbook was closed forever. Shortly after class, the Principal's office was kind enough to allow me to drop geometry—much to my relief and undoubtedly that of the teacher.

In 1939, just before graduation, "Gone With the Wind" was about to be premiered in Times Square. My entire family and I considered ourselves experts on the subject, since Alice had been working in New York for the lucky publisher. Not only had it been her sworn duty to keep the family posted on how many pages were printed each and every day, but by the time she got home at night, half the neighborhood would be waiting on the front porch. Overnight, people who had never looked at Alice before were suddenly her best pals. Everyone had to know the "latest"—and Alice was their only source. Reason: each night, she brought home copies of the latest G.W.T.W. chapter spewed out by the printers that day. Chapter by chapter, this once-in-a-lifetime novel was given out to all the neighbors months before it hit the bookstores, and as long as Alice came up with samples she was as popular as Scarlett.

Alice herself, of course, had already read the latest chapters, which was fortunate since there was almost a stampede every time to snatch them up. While we did manage to take turns, day and night someone would still be up reading the latest.

Eventually, when the last words left to read were "The End," we had to settle back with everyone else to await the film itself. But it was fun being able to read ahead of time—and free—what the rest of the country was still panting to read—and buy—at the bookstores.

In school that year, prizes had been offered in English classes for the best essays on Fire Prevention—the first prize being $10, the second, third and fourth each $5. I managed to walk away with a big $5 for the second. While five dollars today is scorned even as a tip, in 1939 five dollars were more than enough for me to take my mother over to New York (via bus, train, subway and tube—the only way to get there), and pay for two orchestra seats to the very first showing of "Gone With The Wind."

Mom and I never forgot that evening, and as a fitting climax we had enough money left over for a snack at one of New York's famous Automats on the way back to said tube, subway, train and bus.

My very first job after graduating in a year in which jobs were few and far between was as secretary to an attorney in the next town. Salary: $12 a week, five-and-a-half days. Just finding that job was an accomplishment. One almost hesitated to bring up the question of salary with a future boss for fear he would say, "Forget it. I'll interview somebody else."

Once I was sure the job was really mine, if I happened to meet a friend on the street and proudly announced I had a job, he or she wouldn't even ask where it was. Or for whom. And certainly not what it paid.

My new salary of $12 a week was enough to pay my mother $5 a week board, put $5 a week in a savings account for whatever my "future" turned out to be—and splurge the remaining $2 on the very next item I saw. Provided it didn't cost more than $2. Unfortunately, my new employer was not the most sought-after attorney in town, leading to a serious shortage of funds—of which I was made aware only after I had been there several weeks. One Saturday, this up-and-coming solicitor was unable to hand me my $12 check, promising to make it up the following week.

The next Saturday's check was also missing. By then, even I finally caught on. My last check was the last I would ever see from him. So, sadder but hopefully wiser, I left. After rushing around frantically, broke as I was, I managed to find another job—this time with a small insurance company in Newark, where at least employees could count on money forthcoming on paydays.

That year—despite Newark's sadly deteriorating reputation ever since—it was a real pleasure to go down there from the suburbs, whether for work or for shopping. There were no scary tales, as yet, of street crime or hold-ups, and you didn't automatically clutch your pocketbook as you passed loiterers on street corners. However, every now and then, my experience with the attorney back in Orange (and I occasionally wondered if he really had a license) still gnawed at me. Had he been honest, and told me he was temporarily broke but eventually would pay what he owed me, that would have been one thing, but the way he nonchalantly told me "not to worry" was something else again. The more I thought about him, the madder I got.

I finally phoned a local Government agency to see if there was any way to retrieve the two weeks' salary of $24 the attorney still owed me. They sent me some papers to fill out, which I did, and they promised to look into the matter. A few days later I had a phone call from that ex-employer. He had been contacted by the Government agency in no uncertain terms, i.e. "Pay what you owe or go to jail." He was actually sobbing on the phone—and finally did a very good job of convincing me he was almost on the verge of suicide. He said that with the big family he had dependent upon him (I later found out he wasn't even married) he could not afford to pay anything. Certainly not a big $24.

I eventually told him to forget the whole thing. He then said that if I didn't call the officials and state the matter had been taken care of, he could be led off in chains at any moment. Still having learned nothing of the ways of the world, I said, "all right, I'll call them."

Just before I hung up, I heard the sound of a refrigerator door being opened. Mr. Lawyer was no doubt pulling out one more bottle of beer to celebrate having put one over again on some unsuspecting fool. If it's true that what doesn't kill you makes you stronger, at the rate I was going I would soon be strong as an ox.

As of June 8, 1942, twenty-one being the magic age for severing all ties, I was finally legally free to leave the nest and head wherever I chose, and having looked forward to that particular day for the past several years, it was high time to celebrate.

Step One was making a Declaration of Independence from all restrictions—mostly parental—and deciding to which "Land of Enchantment" I wanted to escape. In the opinion of the average New Jersey lifetime resident, that particular goal is automatically Florida. Two of my girlfriends and I had been excitedly talking up that idea for some time, and the three of us could think of nothing else.

Jeanne, Grace and I, best friends since the day we all met in junior high, were referred to throughout our school years as the Unholy Trio. Between classes, we were always together, and arguments between us almost never happened. We even traded the same boyfriends back and forth at times, thus illustrating how lightly we all took the whole concept of dating back then.

We were totally different as to looks and personality. Jeanne was 24, tall, Dutch-blond, and very matter-of-fact. Grace was 22, a genuine redhead, with her heart set on becoming an attorney in her father's office, while I, the youngest at 21 (as I occasionally reminded them at appropriate moments), was a brunette, forever on a diet, with crazy dreams enough for all three of us.

We were all high school graduates, and from the day we ran out clutching our diplomas, had been working as secretary/stenos in various offices. Not one of us had given even a random thought to going to college, or upgrading our education in any way. Not too many people in 1942 were focusing on further education. Pearl Harbor had been a fact of life for several months, and little besides the ongoing conflict was on anyone's mind.

At the time of my 21st birthday, I was working for a firm in Hoboken, whose offices, facing the Hudson River, were right alongside the train tracks which ran down to the docks. Every lunchtime we would watch seemingly endless cars filled with troops headed for the war zone, and it was with an odd mixture of pleasure and pain that we waved to them as each car went by.

The boys always waved frantically back, and as they did, everyone watching felt a little guilty. Those boys were all on their way, voluntarily or otherwise, to defend their country at whatever cost—not holding down five-day-a-week, relatively carefree civilian jobs, as we were.

In my own family, my father had been the only college graduate—setting an example that none of us followed. His own father, reputedly an affluent gentleman-farmer in Maine, had tried in vain to actually bribe his son to become a veterinarian. This particular vocation being of no interest whatsoever to my father, he eventually left home and put himself through the University of Maine. There, he acquired his mechanical engineering degree, later taking post-graduate courses at McGill University in Montreal.

Although the two never met, my father had a rather famous cousin, one Clarence Mackay (Mackay being the family's original surname), who in time was the originator of Postal Telegraph. Clarence's daughter Ellin eventually outdid her father, fame-wise, the day she married Irving Berlin.

In Ellin's day, girls coming from prominent families were considered society's treasures. They were overseen very rigidly during their upbringing, and were automatically expected, when the time came, to marry into their own "class." Certainly not to anyone totally unknown to such a privileged generation.

Irving, in his youth, had yet to demonstrate his fantastic talent for songwriting, nevertheless he and Ellin had already fallen deeply in love and were determined to eventually marry, regardless of the wishes of Ellin's parents who were in shock at such an unsuitable prospect for their daughter. It was then the accepted custom for a society girl's parents, who had finally accepted the fact that their daughter was determined to marry a totally unsuitable member of the lower class, to send said daughter on a so-called "Tour of the Continent," hoping that in due time she would realize the error of her ways, return to the States, and marry someone acceptable to all.

Although Ellin did indeed obligingly journey to Europe, her longing for Irving soon inspired him to not only take up songwriting for a career, but to rapidly produce one hit after another, namely "Always," What'll I Do?" and "While You're Away"—all of which were immediate tremendous hits with the American public, making Irving the musical sensation of the decade.

By the time Ellin was allowed to return home, she and Irving—being world-famous celebrities by that time—were permitted to marry, a union not exactly approved by any of the parents but providing many a thrill to all their fans.

Scholastically speaking, my father should have been a real inspiration to me, but the day I graduated from high school, the last thing I wanted was to see the inside of another classroom. Especially one teaching geometry.

Jeanne, Grace and I had forever talked obsessively about our one common goal in life, i.e., to eventually flee the suburbs of New Jersey and discover for ourselves what the rest of the world was really like—starting with Florida. What we soon found out was, taking leave of the only family you know, the people you've lived with all your life, is a day you never forget. No matter how casual everyone tries to be, if one tear is shed the spell is instantly broken, and from then on, it's Kleenex-time for one and all.

While I realized both Jeanne and Grace would have their own leave-taking problems, theirs seemed like nothing compared to the type of opposition I fully expected. Jeanne's parents were already wondering if, at 24, she would ever get married. The average age for wedding bells then was 18 or 19, and the most horrendous fate imaginable was to wind up as an OLD MAID. Jeanne having so far produced no bridegroom in her own home state, her parents were crossing their fingers that Florida might be the answer.

As for Grace, her own parents from the time she was born, had encouraged her to do "her own thing." This attitude was a classic turn-around from the way most parents felt at the time, but giving Grace all due credit, she did defer to their opinion, at least in the beginning. When she eventually decided to leave home, however, her parents were, strangely enough, not all that understanding.

For me, the major hurdle would be just breaking the news to Mom. Conversations between my mother and me never having been casual or relaxed, I was definitely not looking forward to breaking the kind of news she was about to hear. Since my father had died, Mom had not had the easiest of lives—and her problems all seemed to date back to the day she innocently fell for an atrocious real estate scam.

The insurance money from Papa's death, unfortunately for us all, went down the drain almost as soon as the check was in the bank. Mom, who had no experience whatsoever in handling sizable amounts of money (although this was only $10,000) had somehow been induced to invest most of it in a small rooming house in Newark. She had been convinced that rooming house was doing so well financially she would be foolish to pass up such a golden opportunity. (No records were produced, and she didn't know enough to ask for any.)

She was also informed that all rooms were rented out, and to the most reliable of tenants. Again, no records. Eventually she was introduced to so many so-called "tenants" that she fell for the idea and handed over the money. These "tenants" were anything but. They were strictly neighborhood opportunists, actually living elsewhere on "relief" (eventually known as "welfare"), who were paid a few dollars to pose as paying tenants. No crystal ball was needed to foretell what happened next. The "tenants" vacated on the spot with their newfound money (at least this time they'd earned it), and all of Mom's investment funds were history.

From then on, until the day she retired, Mom worked for various agencies of the Government. She probably would have done better to approach one of the many "relief" agencies, hat in hand, along with all the miserable drunks who helped trick her out of her last cent. However, that was not an "escape hatch" my mother, of all people, would have even thought of, let alone taken.

When I finally told my sister, in private, the long-anticipated Miami Escape Plan was actually set for November 1st, she literally shook with fear as to how Mom would take it. However, within minutes of hearing her younger daughter's incredible plan of departing November 1st from the city of East Orange, boarding the Silver Meteor train at Newark along with Jeanne and Grace, and pointing the engineer in the direction of Miami—Mom for some reason did not appear to be all that surprised. She must have known me better than I thought.

She did warn me, however, that "everybody" would immediately assume Jeanne, Grace and I were hightailing it to Miami for one purpose only, namely, to run after each and every member of the armed forces then stationed in the vast Miami area.

Trying to convince my mother that such was not our intention (although visions of SO MANY handsome men in uniform had certainly crossed our minds from time to time), but that we only wanted to find out what it would be like to be on our own for a while; Mom gave me her famous "Look" which, freely translated, said, "Well, I don't buy that, but there's nothing I can do to stop you."

And there wasn't. For a while I did feel somewhat guilty at having upset my mother, but not for very long. Whatever was going to be MY future had to be waiting out there somewhere—and if I couldn't get up enough nerve to take the first giant step, there was no way I would ever know what that future might have been.

Considering all the events that turned my life upside down from that moment on, I would have missed out on one unforgettable lifetime.

Ever since my father passed away, Mom, Bessie and I had lived together under one roof—or rather, a succession of roofs—sometimes getting along extremely well and sometimes, being totally normal human beings, anything but.

Why Mom never looked around eventually for someone to replace my father, I don't know. It's very possible she thought there was no one who could replace him. She was only seventeen when they were married—Bessie was born a year later—and in Mom's day, marriage and children were a woman's whole life. In any case, it's too bad my mother didn't remarry. She was without my father for an unimaginable 51 years.

My sister Bessie was undoubtedly the most generous person I have ever met. If someone were to say to Bessie, "Would you do something for me?" her immediate, almost unthinking response would be "Yes." The same question being put to me, my answer would automatically be, "What is it?" A subtle difference to be sure—and chances are, I would also wind up doing whatever the friend wanted—but it says a lot for the vast difference in our dispositions. It probably also explains why my sister devoted most of her life to putting Mom first. What I did NOT want was to wind up in the same position as Bessie vis-à-vis my mother. Mom had always taken it for granted the three of us would live together, unmarried and sans any "significant other" until the end of time. Or the end of my mother's own life, whichever came first. At that point, my sister and I—assuming we were not already hopelessly old and decrepit— could feel free to go our own way.

Bessie had always gone along with my mother's way of thinking as far as our mutual future was concerned. Not being blessed with my sister's angelic disposition, however, the older I got—and much as I loved both Mom and Bessie—the more I resented the idea of spending the rest of my life with them. I wanted a life of my own. The year 1942 was really the first of all the war years, and with more and more enlistees and draftees disappearing over the high seas, every heart ached for some one, somewhere. No one was immune, and I wanted to be part of the action.

With the Silver Meteor scheduled to leave Newark at 2:30 p.m., Mom, Bessie and I sat down at noon that Sunday to an early dinner, all trying to act as if nothing at all unusual was happening. This façade lasted about as long as it took Bessie and me to reach for napkins. Mom immediately jumped up, ran to the bathroom, locked the door and burst into tears. Bessie and I followed her as far as the door, finally managed to calm her down, and persuaded her to return to the table. The undisputed title of Black Sheep of the Family, however, was still all mine. All that could be considered successful about that particular dinner was, we actually finished it. Of what it consisted, I have no idea. Bessie and I were cramming everything down our throats, trying to forestall any more outbursts from Mom.

Bessie and her current boyfriend Ernie (occasional boyfriends were permitted) had volunteered to drive me to Newark, my mother having already stated she preferred not to accompany us to the station. Standing by Ernie's car, with the three of us debating how to fit my suitcases into the trunk, I suddenly had the oddest sense of freedom. For the first time in my life, I was really out there on my own—a state of affairs I had been daydreaming about for years—but it was still a little scary.

The sheer excitement of the most thrilling day of my life up to then made the entire trip down through the suburbs to Newark go by in a flash. I was literally breathless, and the ride itself I can barely remember, but arriving at the station was something else again. That was the best part, seeing Jeanne and Grace, surrounded by suitcases, waiting for me at the curb—but one look at their faces was all it took to know their goodbye scenes had evidently been on a par with mine.

As I later learned, the parents of both girls had apparently decided at the very last minute that they were being far too lenient, in spite of the fact that each and every one of us was 21 or over, and proceeded to try to talk their daughters out of every plan we had made, eventually attempting, with some success, to at least make their daughters feel as guilty as possible.

That day had been a horrendous experience for us all, however, with the long-anticipated Escape Plan now under way and the train actually pulling out from the station, we no longer felt guilty about anything. On the contrary, we were more and more hysterical with excitement.

Much later in the train, sitting there looking out the window into the darkness, I don't think I was the only one on board still trying to take a deep breath.

From the very beginning, the one thing we had all agreed on was, Florida meant ONLY Miami. As to where we would be staying in that unseen famous city, no one had a clue—no wonder our families were back there climbing the walls. Naive and ever optimistic as we were, just getting to Miami was all that mattered. However, luckily for us, one of Grace's cousins who had been living in Miami for years, had promised to steer us in the right direction. Once arrived, said Cousin Ursula, all we had to do was find her apartment. Fortunately, having no doubt seen many a bewildered tourist, Ursula had already sent reams of directions. Otherwise, fresh from the Garden State, we would have wandered around like so many lost sheep.

Ursula had also warned us that our dreams of finding a gorgeous and cheap furnished apartment in Miami were just that. Dreams. Shortly after Pearl Harbor, all rents, which had previously been fairly reasonable, hit the roof, and from the day troops moved into Miami, all apartments (condos were yet to come) were occupied to the hilt. Vacancies were a thing of he past. Literally thousands of relatives, reluctant to part with their loved ones until the last possible moment, had been rapidly moving into the area. Consequently, knowing we were desperate to just get going, Grace told her cousin we would be happy with whatever she could find for us.

That first magical trip to Florida was like finding ourselves in outer space, and traveling on the Silver Meteor through one southern state after another—states which heretofore existed only on maps as far as we were concerned—gradually made us realize what a tiny part of the country we three girls had been restricted to all our lives.

Upon pulling into the Miami station, certain signs immediately drew my attention. There were signs I'd never seen before anywhere, and I couldn't believe they were actually there in front of me: "Colored Only" and "Whites Only." I was soon apprised of the local prejudices responsible for these signs, and in time I probably annoyed many a Floridian trying to convince them how unfeeling and stupid, to say the least, was their practice of isolating black people. In New Jersey, the color of your skin is simply the color of your skin. While my home state would no longer be my favorite place to live, it's still way out in front where racial equality is concerned.

From the Miami station, we called Cousin Ursula, who had good news. Not only had she found a vacancy in her own complex, she invited us to a party that very night. Also, we were welcome to stay at her place until we moved into our own. Things were moving faster than even we, optimists of all time, had dared to hope. We flagged down the nearest taxi, and the driver located Ursula's own apartment within minutes.

After introducing ourselves to Ursula (not even Grace had met her cousin before), we rushed over to check out the vacant apartment—which was definitely livable, and we even had access to what in New Jersey would have been for millionaires only, i.e. a pool. The rent per month would be $40.

Not $400. $40. This, for the average apartment in Miami in wartime, was actually par for the course. And while this new apartment was hardly the dream penthouse we had pictured, everything looked better by the minute. We each forked over one-third of the first month's rent, signed a month-to-month lease with the speed of light, and arranged to move in.

Before heading for Ursula's party that night, I wanted to send a telegram to my mother. I had promised to let her know where we were and what was going on, and there was a public phone just around the corner.

After only a few seconds of reading to the Western Union operator the message I wanted to send Mom, I heard her giggling to herself. It was safe to guess I'd been overdoing the enthusiasm bit as to the Sunshine State and was no doubt coming across as some kind of a nut, but I really didn't care. I was finally, at long last, exactly where I had wanted to be for ages, and my mother had probably been waiting all day to hear from me. Who cared what some operator thought?

The next morning it was time to explore our new apartment and see what we had there—which turned out to be a living room, kitchen, bath, one bedroom with twin beds—and a so-called "Murphy" bed in the closet.

Number One priority was tossing a coin to see who would wind up with Murphy. Since no one really wanted him, it was the only fair way to go. As soon as the closet door was opened, out fell Murphy—literally— and getting out of the way fast was crucial. Anybody who got in Murphy's way only did it once.

Grace and I won the toss for the twin beds. How delighted Jeanne really was at "winning" Murphy, we couldn't tell—she was always a good sport, anyway—but when she eventually pointed out that Murphy was several inches wider than any twin bed, Grace and I decided Jeanne was probably the winner after all.

Our new kitchen was devoid of a table, but it did have considerable counter space. However, the room itself was barely large enough to accommodate one cook, let alone three—but no one would be cooking, anyway. We could set up the coffeepot the night before, being addicted to our morning Java, and coffee in the morning was enough to get us to our (future) jobs. And hopefully our (future) dates would soon be taking us out to dinner.

Although becoming permanent Miami residents right away usually means finding a job even sooner, that was not for us. Still oblivious to the facts of life, we made our first stop the nearest Government Employment Office to apply for UN-employment compensation checks, figuring that a little help from Uncle Sam would keep us going till our funds ran out. Job-hunting could wait for later, once we'd had our fill of lying for hours on those golden beaches soaking up all that beautiful sunshine. Coming from a state where sunny days were doled out about twice a month, the famous Floridian beaches to us represented sheer paradise. We couldn't wait to get over there, sunglasses in place and UN-employment checks in our pockets.

We were soon painfully enlightened by Government personnel. The most we could hope for, once our applications were approved, was $18 per week for each of us, a grand total of $54, or $216 a month. Cheap though prices were for almost everything at the time, $216 a month would pay for next to nothing in the way of utilities, clothing and groceries. Without jobs, we would also soon be without food.

Sunning-at-the-beach ideas were shelved on the spot. What we needed—and fast—were addresses of all employment agencies in town.

The very next morning, the three of us were knee-deep in classified ads spread out all over the living-room floor, but before I could even decide on which agency to approach first, some kind soul in the apartment complex gave me a tip. There were reportedly vacancies for secretary-stenos at the United States Engineering Department, which turned out to be my first stop. I had everything to gain and nothing to lose—a job with Uncle Sam, reportedly about as secure as they came at the time, would mean no agency would be looking for a commission.

Although we had yet to make it over to Miami Beach's wall-to-wall sunshine, there had to have been **something** shining down on me that morning. The application I filled out for U.S.E.D. was approved within the hour—and for their very newest employee, the most intriguing future anyone could have imagined was right around the corner.

That same week, Jeanne and Grace were also now employed. Grace was secretary to an attorney, and although her first week's paycheck would be snatched up by an agency, she was thrilled with the idea of being part of a law office. Her own father, who was an attorney back in New Jersey, had originally taken a very dim view of Grace's leaving home at all—let alone moving with two other "flakes" (his term) to Florida—but he was sure to approve of this new development.

Jeanne, the day after the U.S.E.D. took me on, applied to a Government agency as well. For a "job-with-a-future" also, since it ultimately led to her winding up in the Bahamas. The Duke and Duchess of Windsor were at that time chief V.I.P.s of the Bahamas—i.e. the Governor and his Lady—and Jeanne was eventually introduced to them. Presented at court, so to speak.

No one was ever known to record the Windsors' reactions to Jeanne on that particular occasion, but Jeanne herself was definitely not impressed. The Saturday night following Jeanne's formal "presentation," a dance—actually a ball—was to be held at the Windsor residence. All ladies favored with invitations were advised only floor-length, formal gowns were acceptable to the royal couple, however Jeanne—never one to meekly follow ANY crowd, let alone a group of Americans paying homage to a long-lost British crown—decided to appear at the ball in exactly what she **felt** like wearing.

On the arm of a decidedly embarrassed British subject, Jeanne smilingly entered the ballroom. Her chosen attire for the evening was a knee-length, skin-tight, bright red cocktail dress, complete with sequins, a feather boa—and a stunningly regal **tiara**. Every head in the room turned as one and all conversations died a sudden death. There was absolute silence throughout the ballroom, but Jeanne, as only Jeanne could, went on regardless to have a ball at the ball.

While it was only a rumor that the royal couple left the ballroom unusually early that evening, no invitations to future semi-royal affairs were ever again issued in Jeanne's name.

In November 1942, at least half the eligible bachelors in the country, uniformed and otherwise, were crammed into the Miami Beach area, where all females under 90 looked to be in their 30s—at least to the oncoming hordes of draftees, enlistees and officers, who were closely followed by all the office workers required for the inevitable paperwork.

Dates in those days were the least of any girl's problems. Previously shunned females almost overnight had joined the list of desirables.

Other girls, popular with the opposite sex since kindergarten, suddenly had to learn techniques they never expected to need. What took some doing for them was learning how to **decline** dates.

While the average male tends to take turndowns very personally, what was ironical was that these female newcomers-to-the-scene would rather have **accepted** each and every request for a date, not **decline** it.

In no time, the male/female ratio was heavily in our favor. Officers, enlisted men and civilian office personnel took turns cutting in every few seconds at every dance, and it was exciting to feel that popular, no matter how undeserved. The plainest girl in Miami, if there was ever one so designated, could almost overnight feel like Miss America.

Not only my mother, but Jeanne's and Grace's as well, had gloomily predicted we would be chasing after every soldier, sailor and marine in sight—but WE were the main attraction, the ones sought after, not the guys. If only our mothers could have been flies-on-the-wall at some of our dances, they would have loved it.

The ultimate star-of-stars, Clark Gable, had previously been temporarily stationed in the Miami area, however, (unfortunately for future tales to our future grandchildren), that was slightly prior to November 2 when Jeanne, Grace and I actually arrived in Florida. Clark was now overseas, and we would never be able to tell anyone a few untruths about how we had met this all-time legend, and how Clark had naturally immediately fallen in love with each and every one of us. (In any case, our grandchildren's first question would probably have been, "But who was Clark Gable?")

On weeknights, Jeanne and I usually double-dated. It was more fun—and also precluded the usual front-door hassle when all of us returned to the apartment. The guys would want IN, we would want them OUT—but we, being in the driver's seat, could call the shots.

Whoever our dates of the moment were, they could always be written off. They were well aware they had plenty of competition, the Miami status quo being what it was. Besides, we had to decide on what to wear for our next dates. (Talk about a wonderful, wonderful world!)

As for Grace, double dating was never for her. Grace's mission in life was to get married as soon as possible. It didn't seem to particularly matter very much who her current boyfriend was, what he might have to offer by way of a future, or even if she really cared about the guy. Grace fell head over heels in love on the average of once a week. The question was not so much **who** she would marry, but how soon. Fortunately for Grace, Walt—the staff sergeant she met one evening at a dance and of course immediately adored—turned out to be the ideal future husband for her. By sheer chance, Walt was the nicest of them all.

Three weeks to the day from their very first date, Grace and Walt smiled happily at each other throughout their "I Do"s. Jeanne and I stood by, shedding appropriate tears, and wearing the hastily-ordered bridesmaid gowns provided by the bride's parents.

With Grace officially married, and fast settling down into the life of wedded bliss she'd been aiming at as far back as we could remember, Jeanne and I opted to move to an apartment we discovered in Miami Beach. Although somewhat smaller, our new home made up for it by the location—only a block from the beach. The total rent was a little kinder to our wallets—$35 per month—except this time it had to be split between only two of us. Financially, we were not ahead, but loved the idea of finally being close to the ocean. Commuting to our jobs in Miami via the local "jitney" (a miniature bus unique to Florida at that time) took only a few minutes longer than when we lived in Miami itself. And fares via jitneys were not exactly prohibitive: a one-way trip cost five cents.

The first Saturday after moving into the Miami Beach apartment, Jeanne and I headed for a swim (the Atlantic Ocean being practically in our front yard), and when we noticed one certain part of the beach, we had to laugh, remembering what happened on our first excursion to that particular spot. Shortly after arriving in Miami, one weekend

Jeanne, Grace and I went across the "causeway" (a direct route connecting Miami to Miami Beach) in a jitney, to see for ourselves whether those golden sands of the beach we'd heard so much about were really all that great.

That afternoon, Miami Beach had more to offer than sunshine, seashells and golden sand. Most of the armed forces assigned to the area were there ahead of us—and they had already staked out prior claims all over the beach. For some time, we wandered around with our beach blanket, trying to find a reasonably vacant spot. Cameras were being aimed at us from every direction—and that had started the moment we showed up. Ignoring them was almost impossible—although naturally, the more photo-clicks we heard, the more gorgeous we assumed we looked.

Bikinis were still far in the future, but remembering the skimpy one-piece bathing suits we were all wearing began making us a little nervous, and we finally decided against lying down anywhere, blanket or no blanket. We somewhat reluctantly walked away from what was definitely the most interesting part of the beach- and possibly the most dangerous. Later, we estimated a thousand photos must have been taken of the three of us that day. It was a lot of fun and, in a way, a standing ovation.

The entire month of April, 1943 turned out to be like no other period of time I had ever known. On April 1st—and not someone's idea of an April Fool's Day joke as everyone at first suspected—a certain almost incredible rumor was flying around the office

Word from the front office was, any and all employees interested in transferring to the U.S.E.D. office located in Brazil (specifically in Recife, a city not one of us had ever heard of before and could not even find on a map) would be permitted to file their applications.

"Recife" being an unknown quantity to me as well, the only word I really picked up on was "Brazil." But that did it. I was literally first in line, waiting to fill out whatever forms it took to transport me, as if on a cloud—all expenses paid—to this unheard-of city in BRAZIL.

A brief explanation was finally given as to why and how a whole new world was suddenly opening up. Pan American Airlines (in Brazil, formally known as "Pan-Air do Brazil") was, under the supervision of Uncle Sam, constructing airports outside various Brazilian cities for the future use of armed forces personnel. One of the cities was Recife.

Inasmuch as all Government-related procedures are traditionally double-checked to the nth degree, white-collar employees for the inevitable paper work were suddenly a priority. Official permission had been granted to transfer a certain number of them from the Miami area.

As a rule, filling out applications can be somewhat of a drag, but not this time. The totally unexpected prospect of a trip abroad—a freebie coming and going—had my fingers flying through the papers. No one was leaving ME out of this trip. Not if I could help it.

The rest of that day I walked around in a complete fog. I fulfilled my usual duties and turned in the normal amount of paper work—but for all the attention I paid to what I was doing, I would have been of more use on the moon. I was totally lost in a dream of flying to a city I'd never heard of, in a foreign country I never expected to see.

Later that day, back in the apartment, Jeanne took one look at my face and shrieked, "What HAPPENED?" Telling her took forever—I was still so excited I probably wasn't making much sense—but when Jeanne finally understood what I was saying, she also had news.

Some time ago, Jeanne had put in for a transfer from her own Government office to its Nassau branch in the Bahamas. Neither of us had taken the matter very seriously at the time. There couldn't be too many vacancies coming up in Nassau, and even if there were, everyone in Jeanne's office had already put in for such a transfer, just in case.

Against all odds, however, the names of the TWO lucky acceptees had just been announced—and Jeanne's was one of them. She of course went more or less berserk immediately, and the rest of her day at the office was probably no more productive than mine.

One week from the day I filled out the application for Brazil, I was given first the good news, then the bad. The good news was, my application for the transfer had passed with flying colors. Everything was great. The bad news was, practically overnight, Washington had decreed NO employees from the **Miami** office, for reasons known only to the Government, could be considered for transfer to Brazil. Only those from other parts of the country. ANY other part.

In other words, if you happened to be working for any other Government office—in Nantucket, Massachusetts for instance—you were automatically eligible for a transfer to Brazil. If you worked in Miami, forget it. The application of my dreams was now lying shredded in the nearest trash basket.

Talk about falling from the heights to the depths in a matter of seconds! For the remainder of that miserable week, I wasn't even fit to talk to. Nor was anyone else who had filled out applications with unusually high hopes. After a few days, however, with the world obviously not coming to an end on my behalf, I started telling myself they can't DO this to me. Not to ME. I decided to at least put up a fight.

From then on, there was not a day I wasn't trying to figure out some way to get myself back in the running. Who could pull some strings for me?—Who should I talk to?—Was there anybody in public office or even a newspaper columnist I should write to with my tale of woe, etc?

Day after day, I was lost in some kind of trance, and those around me suffering the same disappointment weren't faring much better. It was anything but a happy office. In time, however, since no one had requested either my resignation or theirs, and because that state of affairs could hardly last forever, my co-workers and I finally got back to our normal routines. At the same time, I was interviewing several people in my quest for the Recife job. One was a local representative of Pan

American, the firm involved in constructing all Brazilian airports. I told this gentleman my problem; he took notes galore, promised to check with his upper echelon, and the next day called back. If I'd like to work for Pan American, there was definitely an opening in Brazil for me—only not in Recife.

By that time, I was all but obsessed with this city I had never heard of before and had yet to see, so I could only thank him and start looking around for a few more doors to knock on.

Fortunately the day did come when **somebody up there** decided to come to the rescue. Overnight, I was advised that the U.S.E.D. **could** send me to Brazil. Only NOT to Recife. Belem, a coastal city north of Recife, would be my new destination.

I finally knew better than to push my luck, so I informed my superiors I was delighted. I naturally did not mention I still had my sights on Recife. But the magic spell was still working, and only three days later, the news was even better. I raced home that afternoon, all set to tell Jeanne that plans had been completely turned around and that my new destination was indeed **finally** Recife.

I didn't have to open my mouth. The minute Jeanne saw me, she said "Recife, right?" RIGHT.

From that moment on, it was a race against time. Jeanne and I couldn't wait (although it was obvious we had no choice) to see who got to take off first for parts unknown. She and I were working for two different Government departments, but because of the upcoming transfers, we were both now considered "wartime employees." Our passports were pushed through in record time, so our score was even so far.

The next challenge coming up, however, to which we were not looking forward, was a series of inoculations, and we'd been hearing horror stories about those ever since getting the go-ahead as to transfers. Most of the shots were fairly routine, but a few were truly "The Pits." Out of three tetanus shots in a row—although they were administered a week or so apart, the second shot virtually knocked me out for the rest of that day.

When I woke up, it was noon of the following day and I was definitely not looking forward to shot #3. That last one, however, was like the first—a big nothing.

All we had to do now was wait, and that was the hardest part. The nearer the day approached when either one of us could be getting word to rush to the airport, the more we reminisced about the good times we'd had since moving to the Miami Beach apartment

Jeanne and I were still double dating at times, though not always, but before actually walking back through the front door later in the evening, certain precautions HAD to be observed. First of all, while still standing outside the door, we would reach inside, turn on the light switch, and wait. Rushing in without thinking was not a good idea, unless you happened to be a fan of palmetto bugs and couldn't wait to see one or two heading in your direction.

In a matter of seconds, one or more fat ugly palmetto bugs would appear, literally scuttling across the room. The floor was tiled, and there was no carpeting anywhere, so we could always hear as well as see—but hearing them was the worst part. At the very first "scuttle," all you wanted to do was back out the door and run.

Unfortunately, palmetto bugs were standard equipment in the average Miami Beach apartment at that time. Included in the lease, so to speak. We eventually just resigned ourselves to escorting them out the door.

One weekend there was one memorable near-disaster—not involving palmetto bugs, but just as bad. One of Jeanne's boyfriends had stopped by with a huge bunch of bananas. She and I were both out at the time, so our landlord helpfully opened the door for him, and the fruit was left in the kitchen. Although "a bunch of bananas" sounds fairly innocuous, this one was gigantic. There must have been at least 60 or 70 absolutely perfect bananas clinging to the main stalk, and when we first saw them we couldn't wait. Bananas were our favorite fruit. Jeanne and I both rushed over for a feast—and immediately skidded to a halt. One more species of horrible bugs were happily climbing all over the fruit. It was almost, but not quite, enough to destroy our banana-appetites forever.

Hauling that really heavy, crawling-bug-laden banana bunch over to our landlord's door took us forever. We later learned he simply removed all the bugs and enjoyed all the bananas. Had Jeanne and I been a little less squeamish, we could have wound up as fat, dumb and happy as our landlord.

One date forever circled in red ink in MY book was June 30. I arrived at work that morning to find something very strange had been going on. The entire office was so decorated with banners, ribbons and crazy signs, you would never have recognized it as a place of business, let alone a Government office.

In the middle of the room was a long table sometimes used for holiday buffets. Trays of food covered not only that table but every other flat surface in sight. And, all those wonderful people stood around awaiting my reaction to all this madness. Since I immediately became even more excited than they were, I don't think they were disappointed. That was one party thoroughly enjoyed by all—it started far in advance of the noon hour and nobody was watching the clock.

This sudden celebration could mean only one thing—and as soon as I saw what was going on, it was easy to guess. The afternoon before, I had left early, and no sooner was I out of sight than official word came through: my flight to South America was set for July 1st at 4 a.m., which was the **next** morning. My co-workers had spent the rest of the Government's time that day transforming the office into a party room. Since as far as we knew, I was the only one from Miami as yet to actually wind up with a bona fide transfer and plane ticket to South America, the whole office was in a mood to celebrate—and yours truly was the honored guest. I couldn't remember ever feeling so flattered.

Later that afternoon, back at the apartment, trying to sleep even one minute before 4 o'clock the next morning would be a waste of time. After packing suitcases half the night, however, 4 a.m. didn't seem that far away. Jeanne hadn't slept either, and freely admitted she was green with envy at my getting to leave first.

The boyfriend I was to have a date with the next evening had to settle for taking me to the airport at 3 o'clock in the morning—but from the instant I got a look at MY very first plane, sitting there on the runway waiting for ME, that boyfriend could have disappeared into thin air and I wouldn't have even known he was gone. With the flight scheduled to take off within the hour, I could only hope the pilot was a lot calmer than his newest passenger.

The plane was a converted C-54, updated with a view to the sheer comfort of its passengers, and it had big, deep leather sets. (Not even generals could have found fault.) Seat reservations were not yet part of the game, and the girl I happened to sit down next to naturally had the window seat. I would have given anything for it, especially since not once did she so much as glance out the window. This being my first flight, I would have been glued to it from the moment I sat down.

We were friends right away. Trudy later became one of my room-mates, and eventually, of course, I had to tell her I would have loved to look out that window and couldn't understand why she hadn't. Trudy said, "I was just too nervous to look down at the ground—it was my first flight also, and I would have been only too happy to switch seats." If only we could have known. On the other hand, if I'd had the window seat to begin with, we might never have even started a conversation, let alone become best friends.

Jet planes were still far in the future as far as taken-for-granted use was concerned, but for me the speed of our particular plane was more than fast enough. It did, however, take several hours to reach the very first stop, Port-au-Prince in Haiti. By then, Trudy and I had been awake so long we'd almost forgotten what it was like to sleep.

The walk from the plane to the airport at Port-au-Prince wasn't all that far, so I may have—in my sleep-starved state—made a hasty judgment, but Haiti felt like the hottest place I have ever been in my life. (Since then, I have lived many years in Arizona, and Haiti no longer holds the record.)

The second stop was far more interesting than the first. We were finally, officially, **really** in South America—at a military base in Georgetown, British Guiana.

However, wartime security being what it had to be, we were also totally unexpected. Officers meeting the plane hurriedly advised us (it seemed like more of a warning) that military personnel on the base had not had the pleasure of seeing females of any description for what to them probably seemed like years.

Actually, it had been only a few weeks, but every girl stepping out of that plane looked better by the minute to all those watching. The girls were shown immediately to the officers' quarters, some of which had obviously been very hastily cleaned up and vacated within minutes.

Outside, with hundreds of ecstatic service personnel running around in a frenzy, arrangements for a dance party were already under way, a party wisely declared open to both officers and servicemen, presumably to avoid a riot.

In the meantime, several of the officers, pulling rank as per custom, took all female visitors out in their jeeps for a brief tour of the Georgetown base. Unfortunately, unaccustomed as we were to the British custom of driving on what we considered the "wrong side" of the road, that ride made us more nervous by the minute. Everyone was having second thoughts about ever visiting London if that was the way they would have to drive in England.

Hastily organized though it was, that dance/party/get-together was well worth all the trouble to which the men had gone—and at times it was hilarious. Every guy, whether officer or enlisted, wanted to dance with every gal, and it didn't seem to matter diddlysquat (an expression of my Southern friends I've always found fascinating), what the gal looked like, gorgeous or gruesome. To them we ALL looked good.

Everyone present thoroughly enjoyed himself—or herself—up to the very last minute, when the party ended. It HAD to end because the plane was about to take off again. It was 2 a.m. when we all reentered the plane, and there would be two more stops before we got anywhere near Recife. Both Trudy and I collapsed in our seats, half-asleep even as we fastened our seat belts. Before the plane took off, everyone aboard appeared to be out like a light—with the exception, apparently, of the pilot and crew since we arrived intact at our next port of call: Belem.

Belem was the city to which I had **almost** been assigned. All I could see from the plane was the airfield itself—but oddly enough, I had no desire whatsoever to get out and walk around this airport. Subconsciously, I was afraid of being accidentally left behind in Belem—in which case Recife, my dream city, would remain exactly that—just a dream.

Flying over the jungles of Brazil was an experience I never expected to have, and one I can never forget. From time to time, the plane was so low in the air—lower than I would have liked—the ground seemed to be only a few feet away. The foliage was unbelievably dense, and one crew member told us that opening up one square foot into the jungle would take an hour's chopping away with an axe.

From horizon to horizon, that emerald-green jungle was a solid mass. It looked so deceptively soft, you could almost picture the plane, if it were forced to land, simply perching on top of all the trees, as if on a cushion. Fortunately for us all, the pilot had no such wild fantasies and continued to fly on course.

The next and last stop before Recife was to be Natal, also a coastal city, and about a thousand miles north of Recife. Being once again on terra firma would feel good, even though none of us had been able to take our eyes off the jungle down there. Brazil is about as foreign a country as you can get, and knowing we were actually flying over the continent of South America was a genuine thrill.

Only when the plane finally set down at the Natal military base, to be once again greeted by smiling and surprised faces on all sides, did we feel we were back in the real world. By this time, each and every passenger was a real pro at leaving the plane ASAP. Starved though we all were for sleep, none of us had any way of knowing what we'd find at the next port of call. So, hour by hour, the entire trip was growing more and more exciting—and Natal was to be no letdown. Not for me, anyway.

Trudy and I left our seats in the plane at about the same time, but lost track of each other while at the base. Only much later, when we returned to the plane (which was beginning to feel like our second home), could we compare notes. (Trudy decided my story far outdid hers. **She** had met no one **she** found really interesting.)

A very good-looking Air Force Captain—Bob—who appeared to be running the whole show at Natal, made himself instantly available. He escorted me all over the base—only this time the grand tour was in a jeep which, I was relieved to see, kept to the **right** side of the road. At the same time, he had preparations under way for something no one was really all that surprised to see: another welcome-to-the base party.

Not one girl was ever heard to complain for one second about the almost ceaseless attention we were all getting everywhere we went. It was becoming easier and easier to take it all for granted—and more fun by the minute.

(Luckily for those of us brought up in the real world, we could remember all too well what things were like in more normal times. We realized we would all too soon return to our beginnings, where we were no more important than anybody else—but that was something way out there in the unforeseeable future.)

In the meantime we were all having the time of our lives—which, even knowing it can't go on forever, isn't exactly hard to take. But that evening in Natal, I think everyone at the party was wishing, as I was, that it **could**.

The plane was to be at Natal only a few hours for refueling, but in the comparatively short time we'd had together, Bob and I knew we'd each found someone pretty special. There was a very strong mutual attraction there from which neither of us could walk away—and we didn't want to. Bob was convinced, as was I, that this first meeting should not be our last, that he could definitely, as often as possible, hop a Recife-bound plane and visit me down there. Obviously, we had hit it off right from the start—and all this with a very attentive, and most appreciative, stag line standing by. At the time, I don't think I even looked them over.

At Bob's suggestion, I had briefly toyed with the idea of at least waiting over until the next flight. In normal times, this would have been no problem, but in wartime none of the officials were allowed to predict, even if they knew, when the next plane could even be expected. So, it would be back to the C-54 for me, but Bob had already come up with plans for flying down to Recife the following weekend.

At almost the last minute, Bob, apparently from out of nowhere, had produced a native Natal shoemaker, who proceeded to measure my feet. Hand-made alligator boots were the current craze in Brazil that season, and almost everybody I met appeared to be clad in alligator. It was practically a status symbol—and Bob promised faithfully to deliver MY boots to me in Recife when he flew down.

Back once more on the plane, the nearer we got to Recife the harder it was for me to believe I was still the same wide-eyed New Jerseyite who climbed aboard that Silver Meteor so many moons ago, hoping to (without a clue as to how) eventually explore the entire world and find out what made it run. Well, at least I now had one foot in the door. Anyone trying to shut that door on me would be in big trouble.

When the now familiar C-54 actually rolled to a stop at Recife—really and truly RECIFE—it was a wonderful moment. Seeing a long-cherished dream come true is something that happens, if it happens at all, only once in a lifetime.

Once inside the airport, the real world took over immediately. Brazilian officials were coming at us from all sides. No smiling welcoming committee, no frantic waving of American flags, no excited officers and servicemen running around setting up another "party to end all parties." Just forms to fill out, questions to answer, papers to sign. The Miami-to-Recife trip of a lifetime was indeed over—but no one on that plane would ever forget it.

Thanks to the Miami office looking ahead for accommodations, Trudy and I soon found ourselves in a room at what was then, and probably still is, the best in the city—the Hotel Grande. What came as a very welcome surprise was the fact that room rates as well as food prices were extremely low. Ever the optimists, we could see ourselves, even on Government salaries, becoming rich overnight—and immediately reached for the room-service phone.

The prices in Recife made sense, however. We soon learned the native populace worked—when there were any jobs at all—for next to nothing. We did both manage to save **some** money in Brazil (which for me was a first), but it would have been hard not to.

Our very first evening in Recife, Trudy and I treated ourselves to dinner at Leite's, a very popular local restaurant which came highly recommended. We started out with the most delicious chicken soup I have ever tasted—almost a stew, it was so loaded with goodies—but so filling, we decided against ordering the rest of the meal.

The price of an entire soup-to-nuts dinner at Leite's, which several days later we did manage to consume, was the equivalent of $1.35. Not $13.50—one dollar and thirty-five cents. Prices like that certainly made cooking at home—which we couldn't have done anyway in a hotel—out of the question—at least it was for transient Americans. However most native Brazilians (or Brazzies, as they referred to themselves), had no choice but to do their own cooking. The going wage then was the equivalent of 35 cents a day.

Since Trudy and I would have to report to the local U.S.E.D.office in Recife on Monday, Sunday morning we decided to get in touch with a few of the people we'd flown down with, to catch up on what everyone was doing. One of the girls, Phyllis, who later became our roommate, had **already** been referred to a locally popular dressmaker. Phyllis being a shop-till-you-drop gal, it would have taken a lot more than just finding herself in a foreign country to slow her down. This same dressmaker, whom Trudy and I met soon afterwards, spoke barely enough English to even get her point across—which was fortunate because my knowledge of Portuguese at the time was even less than hers of English. Consequently, at times in sheer desperation, we both resorted to sign language, which oddly enough worked every single time. (Had video cameras been available in those days, any bystander would have snatched one up ASAP.) That dressmaker and I out-did Chaplin.

Weeks later, Suzanne—the dressmaker—made my all-time favorite evening gown, a gorgeous black lace over a black satin slip. No matter how I really looked, I felt gorgeous. No one would believe how little this Brazilian lady charged for **anything** she made. Her styles were almost timeless, and she did spectacular work. If only I'd had sense enough to have her make me every type of garment imaginable, I could have been in style any month of the year.

Work in the Recife office turned out to be the usual take-a-million-notes routine, but the office personnel—many of whom were bilingual—repeatedly went out of their way encouraging me to try what little Portuguese I had learned. (At least we didn't have to depend on sign language.)

Bob arrived the following Saturday morning—complete with alligator boots, as promised. His little Natal shoemaker had done a super job. My new boots looked great, and were even a perfect fit. I was dying to show them off, but we had already been invited to a dance that evening, and a dance floor is hardly the place for clumping around in boots— even alligator boots—so we agreed sandals were the way to go.

This was Bob's very first visit to Recife. Compared to Natal, whose only newsworthy feature was the military base, Recife was a big city— and having been born and raised in New York City, Bob seemed to feel at home right away. There were certainly no subways in Recife, no "El"s, and nothing even remotely resembling a skyscraper, yet Bob was still somehow reminded of his "home town."

That weekend we had one glorious time, and both knew without a doubt this would be only the first of many such visits. Thereafter, Bob managed to catch some kind of a flight down from Natal almost every weekend.

One time when I wasn't even expecting him, he called at the last minute to say he could make it after all, so I caught a fast ride to the airport. Bob, grinning from ear to ear, stepped out of what looked to be the very first plane off the very first assembly line (it was that ancient), saying, "See the chances I take for you?"

More rapidly than probably either of us realized at the time, we were beginning to mean a great deal to each other—until one memorable evening, that is.

Bob's plane had just taken off for Natal. One of Bob's friends happened to be passing through the airport terminal as Bob and I were saying good-bye. This friend later came back, apparently on the spur of the moment, to where I was still standing. He told me there was something he thought I should know.

Bob was married. He had a wife back in New York. The marriage was reportedly most unhappy—according to the "friend" dropping this bombshell—but married he was, nevertheless.

Naive as I was, that was naturally the last thing I thought I'd ever hear. When Bob called from Natal later that evening, he said yes, he was indeed married, but things were not working out between him and his wife. That he had planned all along to tell me himself, and he was going to ask for a divorce on his next leave, etc., etc. Probably the oldest line in history. At that point, I said it was immaterial to me whether he obtained a divorce or not. I was no longer interested in him either way, and told him not to call me again. I hung up the phone, knowing it would ring again in a matter of seconds. Which it did, and I took it off the hook for the rest of the night.

Bob and I had had some really great times together, and while shutting the door on them forever was not going to be any easier than hanging up the phone, even I had to realize he was definitely not for me.

Not too long after Bob had faded into the sunset, Trudy and I were wondering how it would feel to live in a real house, rather than the admittedly very comfortable **and** inexpensive (but also somehow very impersonal), Hotel Grande.

Just mentioning this idea to a few of our friends was enough to have them offering all kinds of suggestions. One of them we soon acted upon.

Phyllis, our fashion-conscious friend, told us she had recently heard of a house on the beach in Olinda—a small, mostly residential town slightly north of Recife—which was available for rent. She had an idea—and after inspecting the house, Trudy and I took her up on it—that the three of us could share the house and split the rent.

While none of us had ever employed so much as one servant, a total of three servants—a cook, a maid, and a **gardener**—came with the house. And, their services were only part of the deal. They would also live there. (The garden was non-existent, as far as we could see).

Each servant was to be paid the equivalent of five dollars a month, the average wage in those parts in that era. Their own living quarters consisted of two small rooms attached to the rear of the house, and three meals per day for them went along with the wages. We soon learned our new-found servants consumed more food than we did—they were secretly shipping out what they considered excess food to members of their own families, all of whom lived in the vicinity. However, since a great deal of food at that time was being supplied to us from various friends in the service, either gratis or at very low cost, financially speaking everything came out even.

All things considered, it sounded like a pretty good deal. No lease was required, and renting the house as well as paying the servants would be on a month-to-month basis. As a matter of fact, the total cost for the three of us would be cheaper than what we were paying at the hotel. In a matter of seconds, we decided to take the Big Step and try living in a real house.

Sometime before we all moved to our Olinda beach house, I had acquired a brand-new boyfriend—this time, one certifiably not married. There was never a shortage of eligible, willing and able males in Recife, any more than there had been in Miami. My instinctive desire, once having arrived in Miami, to then get to Recife as soon as possible, was certainly paying off.

Skeeter and I had met at one of the many dances held all over Recife every weekend. He was a C.P.O in the Navy, and we hit it off from the very first dance—naturally, a Brazilian samba—and became an "item" to both my friends and his from that evening on.

Skeeter was from Georgia, with an accent totally different from any I'd ever heard before. (He sounded exactly like Elvis, long before Elvis-time.) From Skeeter's very first "May Ah have the pleasure of this dance, ma'am?," it was fascinating to listen to him. I never did find out what he really thought of my totally foreign New Jerseyese—being a typical Southern gentleman, he never said.

As a C.P.O., Skeeter was in charge not only of his own men but also (a point which later became most significant) every ounce of food and drink on his ship, then currently anchored in Recife's harbor.

Along with two of Trudy's and Phyllis' current beaux, Skeeter helped move us out to Olinda, and on our first evening there, the six us sat down to enjoy a delicious dinner prepared by our new staff of three. As hostesses—for as long as we could keep our faces straight—Trudy, Phyllis and I did our very best to resemble bona fide, top-drawer members of society—not only born to the purple but long accustomed to servants on all sides, bowing to our slightest wish. All those present having grown up in strictly middle-class circumstances, we weren't even fooling ourselves, but that evening was a lot of fun.

We soon discovered that our new gardener, besides tending to the invisible garden, had other, far more important talents, which in our opinion definitely outweighed whatever he could have been doing with seeds and soil.

Pedro was in charge of making our coffee, both morning and night. He appeared to be brewing it almost like tea, but for some reason it turned out to be the best-tasting coffee of all time. As a confirmed coffee-addict from the age of eighteen, once I'd had my first taste of Pedro's brew, I personally didn't care if Pedro never so much as picked up a rake for the so-called garden. Pedro could do no wrong, not as long as he made that coffee.

For the only time in my experience—and literally overnight—food supplies became something we never had to worry about. (Skeeter's fine Italian hand, so to speak, was behind it all.) Our first morning as bona fide householders in Olinda, a Navy truck appeared at the door—and everything on it was free.

Two sailors jumped out, and proceeded to unload every imaginable kind of meat, fruit, vegetables and assorted pastries into the kitchen—enough to feed half the town, which we probably eventually did. We couldn't believe the amount of food being carried in. That same truck reappeared almost daily with **something**, not in the same quantity as the first lavish delivery, but more than enough to keep us going, to put it mildly. The kitchen was looking more and more like a storehouse.

I often wished I could ship a sizable amount of all this food home to share with my family. Back in the States, daily menus were less and less anything to which one could look forward, what with rationing, coupon-hoarding, and the total absence of many favorite foods. Unfortunately, we knew of no way to ship perishable food anywhere. Consequently, Americans temporarily stationed in Brazil never mentioned in letters to folks back home the over-supply of goodies available to them seven days a week in South America.

There were innumerable T-bone steaks stacked in the icebox. (Refrigerators were yet to come, at least in Brazil, but the presence of iceboxes was much appreciated.) Gigantic jars of huge stuffed luscious olives, enough to outlast the war, filled every cabinet. All canned goods seemed to come in sets of six, and finding where to squeeze them in **somewhere** was a daily challenge. (For our new staff, that is.) Our "horn of plenty" was spilling all over the place.

Nevertheless, several weeks later, although we had really enjoyed having our own house-on-the-beach, we decided for several reasons it was best to return to the hotel. For one thing, Phyllis, who had allergies galore to begin with, had picked up yet another. Being a native of Kansas, she had never been anywhere near an ocean before, and we could only attribute these new sniffing-and-sneezing attacks to the sudden nearness of salt water. We were only about 50 feet from the waves lapping at the shore.

In addition—although this was something we probably should have foreseen—Phyllis sorely missed the non-stop shopping orgies she had been enjoying in Recife. For all three of us, the long, long rides back and forth to work, even via incredibly cheap taxis, left little time for much of anything else, and shopping had taken a back seat.

The day we left Olinda, our well-fed staff and their many relatives happily inherited all the leftover food. This same staff, however, appeared to be a little sad as they waved good-bye to us. Three meals a day were also disappearing from their lives, and we could only wish them a speedy replacement of tenants for the beach house.

Pedro, coffee maker of all time, was the only one we would have gladly taken along.

Skeeter and I had been seeing each other almost daily, as well as dating every weekend. He had been an enormous help in getting us settled in Olinda, not to mention supplying 98% of the food. We had become very close in a relatively short time.

One of the things I most appreciated about Skeeter—aside from the fact that he was an extremely attractive escort in his Navy uniform—was that, in a rather old-fashioned way, he was always very considerate of women's feelings. A trait no doubt due to his upbringing, but, in wartime, one fast becoming all but obsolete.

The most endearing example occurred one evening, in one of our favorite restaurants. We were still sitting at a small table after dinner, when Skeeter suddenly, with no explanation, got up and walked over to an adjoining table.

Several newly-enlisted sailors, whom Skeeter seemed to recognize but whom I hadn't even noticed until then, had been sitting there after dinner, having a great time laughing and joking among themselves. They had also, according to Skeeter, been voicing some fairly loud and offensive expletives to which Skeeter eventually objected, considering (his term) "the presence of a lady."

Quietly but firmly, he then advised the sailors (who shut up immediately upon seeing they were being addressed by a C.P.O.) that if they knew what was good for them, they would start watching their language—FAST.

No sooner said than done. The sailors were out of there in record time, meanwhile mumbling some rather confused apologies as they passed our table. It all made me feel, at the advanced age now of twenty-two, like a thousand-year-old crone who cannot abide naughty words. I hadn't even been listening to the boys, and I was now almost as embarrassed as they were, although I knew Skeeter had only the best of intentions.

A few weeks after Trudy and I returned to the hotel—Phyllis having moved in with a co-worker whose apartment, by no doubt sheer coincidence, was in the same block as Phyllis' favorite dress shop—there were rumors no one wanted to hear, least of all me: Skeeter's ship might be pulling out in the near future.

If these rumors were indeed true, anyone with so much as a clue as to the exact date kept this very touchy wartime information to himself. Or herself. How Skeeter found out as much as he did was a miracle.

Unfortunately, having known more than one ship to exit the harbor overnight without the slightest prior hint, there was a very strong chance that once Skeeter's ship also found itself back on the high seas, we would not be seeing each other for a long time.

Skeeter and I had seen the writing on the wall some time ago, and I had already been in touch with my former pals still in the Miami office. Much as I loved Recife, I had no desire whatsoever to remain there without Skeeter. The word from Miami was, my old job, if I wanted it, was currently available back there.

The day I had arrived in Recife, back in July, I took it for granted I would be working in Brazil from then on, or at least until the end of the war. But then I met Skeeter, and once again my life started turning itself around. I could not now envision any future anywhere without him somewhere in it.

Although Skeeter admitted it was only a hunch, he still had a feeling his ship would be heading for the States, and soon. Whatever the Navy had in mind, we were each, in our own way, getting ready to leave Recife.

Only five short months had gone by since my first day in that never-to-be-forgotten city. I could not believe how many things had happened, or how full my life had become, since the day that C-54—a plane to be forever my favorite, jets or no jets—took off from Miami.

Back then, I sincerely believed I was only interested in getting to see as many foreign places as possible, to just get an idea of what the rest of the world was really like. Without realizing it, I had also been instinctively searching for a little adventure—of which I had clearly already had more than a little.

Skeeter's ship sailed during the night for an unknown harbor. No one on board—with the exception, presumably, of the pilot and crew—had had a moment's notice, nor any clue whatsoever as to their destination. The long, tearful farewell my sweetheart and I had been dreading to face never got to happen.

From wherever Skeeter would be at the time, he would know how and where to contact me, once I was officially back working in Miami. In the meantime, we could only keep our fingers crossed, and slowly count the days.

Flying back to the States, I was not this time on a Government plane, though luckily for me the flight **was** subsidized. What few funds I had managed to save in Brazil probably wouldn't have covered a plane flight for more than twenty miles. Pan-Air do Brazil, a.k.a. Pan American, whom I had interviewed in an early attempt to get to Recife, was the carrier, and the atmosphere aboard the plane was far more organized than that of my first flight. Even so—and predictably—I would have preferred **my** C-54.

Our last stop before reaching Miami (planes really took their time in those days) would be overnight at Trinidad. One more foreign port I had never expected to see. However, it was only thanks to the alertness of certain hotel personnel in Trinidad that I was able to board the plane at all the following morning. Prior to **that** totally unexpected near-crisis, I was again finding it hard to believe where I was **this** time—actually flying into the exotic-sounding Trinidad of the British West Indies. (Except that "exotic" is not the word for the accents heard all over Trinidad. They were strictly British. Veddy, veddy British. Every native worker at the hotel sounded as if he, or she, came straight from Liverpool.)

My hotel room itself was nice enough, but for me what was absolutely amazing was the size of the bed. It was huge—an entire

family could have lost themselves in it—with the first feather mattress
I had ever seen. All of which, unfortunately, turned out to be far more
restful than I really needed.

Another first for me—and something which could have been used to
great advantage in New Jersey during the summer months—was the
overhead "mosquito canopy." The name really said it all, since it effec-
tively protected sleepers from the ever present and apparently starving
mosquitoes.

This canopy surrounded the entire bed from floor to ceiling. Since
chances were nil for invading the canopy, mosquitoes could only eat
their hearts out, looking through the net at all the humans they could
be making miserable in there.

The plane was scheduled to take off eight o'clock the next morning,
so I had asked the desk clerks to call me at six. They assured me they
would. Eventually I parted the mosquito canopy, climbed first on top
of, and then floated as if on a cloud several inches down into, a veritable
feather heaven. My last waking thought was, everyone in the world
should have a bed like this.

Promptly at 6 a.m. the phone rang. It was time to get up. I thanked
whoever was calling—and at 6:01 a.m. floated back down into the
feathers and fell asleep again.

At 7 a.m., again the phone rang. Thinking this was the first time and
that it was only 6 a.m., I sleepily reached over and picked it up. A split-
second later, as wide awake as if I'd never gone to bed, I was throwing
everything frantically into suitcases, and trying to get dressed at the
same time. I never thought I'd make it.

Back once more on the plane, I was still out of breath, but at least
among those present. All the other passengers had spent the last hour
leisurely consuming their delicious breakfasts in the hotel dining room,
without a care in the world. (When leaving the hotel, I'd had to race
right on by the dining room, without so much as a passing glance, but

on the plane some Good Samaritan brought me a breakfast "snack" and, best of all, some life-saving coffee.)

The City of Miami looked the same, but the person looking it over— me—was anything but. In a way, I was simply back at the starting gate, except that my own country now seemed almost as foreign to me as Brazil had the first few days. I did have a job to go to, and two old friends to move in with until I could find my own apartment, but I felt like someone still waiting for a push to get started.

Even in Miami, I missed Skeeter—and yet we'd never been in that city together. Nothing there should have reminded me of him, but I thought of him all the time. I knew he would be getting in touch with me as soon as it was humanly possible—and safe—but in the meantime the days were not exactly racing by.

At the Miami office, there were very few new faces—most were familiar. And those people were now eyeing me as having come from outer space. I was well aware many of them had also high hopes for see-ing South America, and doubtless as many dreams as I about going there, but since I left, no one else had won the so-called "Recife Jackpot."

As far as I could tell, not one of them appeared to resent the fact that I had gone and they hadn't. In fact, all they really seemed to want to hear was what Recife was like, what did I think of Brazil, and how impressed I was with what I had seen of the rest of South America. It was always the #1 topic of conversation, and not one person—certainly not I—ever tired of it.

Via the ever-reliable office grapevine, I learned of a vacant apartment in the same complex where Jeanne and I had stayed, and within days, I was once again a resident of Miami Beach. And again, very close to the shore—which may or may not have been the wisest choice for me. Every time I looked out across the water, I automatically wondered, where is Skeeter now?

Just about the time the office routine was beginning to feel the way it used to, my sister called. My mother had not been feeling well for some time for a variety of reasons—and was currently under a doctor's care. According to Bessie, Mom was seeing this physician once or twice a week—which would be highly unusual for my mother, who normally insisted she didn't have a health care in the world. As far back as I could remember, Mom had always been determined to stay as far away from doctors as possible. My sister went into some detail, however, as to all the current symptoms, and then I began to worry.

As it later turned out, causing me to be upset and to start worrying about Mom was why Bessie had called in the first place. My sister had only one real concern in life—Mom's welfare. Mom had always been able to completely intimidate my sister, with no apparent resistance on Bessie's part. Consequently, when Bessie finally decided I had been away a little too long for Mom's peace of mind, she picked up the phone and called me.

From that day on, it was more and more difficult to concentrate on my office job, which up to then I had really liked. How my mother was doing seemed to be all I could think about. I finally decided to make a clean break with all things Floridian, and go back home. But, not to play the daughter-in-the-household role again. That was not for me. Not after feeling free as a bird ever since I'd left over a year ago. But she **was** my mother, she was ill (as far as I knew then), and I just wanted to get back there and find out for myself what was going on.

There being nothing to celebrate this time such as a trip to Recife, the good-bye party at the office a few days later was small. The next morning, I would be back on the same old Silver Meteor, heading for the same old Garden State (and, in a way, although I tried not to think of it as such, the same old captivity).

Back once more in East Orange, if I thought I'd felt like a different person in Miami after living even a short while in South America, that was nothing compared to the way I reacted to being back in the old apartment again. I was still trying to convince myself I wouldn't be there forever. Walking into the same rooms I had shared for so long with my mother and sister, the whole place suddenly seemed smaller, even a little cramped. It never had before. Even the neighborhood had changed—there were strange faces looking back at me all over the place. Nothing looked the same; it didn't feel right to even be there. The minute I walked in the door, I knew I didn't want to stay.

My mother was in surprisingly better health, which I was very relieved to see. Also, according to Bessie, she had recently even given up seeing her doctor. Naturally I flattered myself all this was just because Mom knew I was coming back home again—but at least worrying about her no longer had to be uppermost in my mind.

Unfortunately, however, for any plans I might have then come up with for my immediate future, my finances at that point could only be described as a disaster. The savings I'd so proudly kept running to the bank with in Brazil had dwindled to almost nothing since my return to the States. My recent salary in Miami had been much less than the "adjusted amount" I'd been paid in Recife. (The extra money we were all paid in Brazil was considered a wartime "bonus," i.e. compensation for being out of one's own country.) The fact I'd had enough money left to buy even a one-way railroad ticket home was amazing.

Although just about the last thing I wanted to do with the rest of my life was to once again live and work in New Jersey, at the moment there did not appear to be any option. If I wanted to at least continue eating, it looked like bite-the-bullet time. Fortunately, there were several places near enough to walk to (which was important, since I had no car) where I knew I could find a job. One of the few positive things the war had done for people like me was, finding work was easier than it had ever been before. Personnel offices statewide had the "Welcome" sign out at all times for new applicants.

Two months to the day after I once again became a New Jerseyite, an overseas call came to the apartment one evening. While not Skeeter himself, it was the next best thing. At whatever mysterious port his ship had then reached, some official he'd become acquainted with there was apparently able to place such a call.

This person made no attempt to identify himself nor wherever he was calling from—and I at least knew better than to ask—but he somehow managed to get a most interesting message across. The ship of "someone we both know" had not made the States her first stop, but I could count on hearing from that certain someone in the not too distant future. This voice out of nowhere ended with "Don't worry, you'll see our friend soon,"—at which point I heard the phone being hung up.

Several days later, the ship of "someone we both know" finally docked at New London, Connecticut, and Skeeter phoned from there. Since he and I had been completely out of touch ever since we both left Recife, the individual who had called on his behalf had first attempted to reach me in Miami. Where I'd gone to from Miami, Skeeter had no idea, but took a chance on trying the New Jersey number. This was one of several I had written down for him, just in case.

It was wonderful to hear his voice again (one of the deepest I think I've ever heard and still sounding like the future Elvis), but this time, for once, we could talk to each other without fear of being cut off by some over-zealous censor. This had happened once or twice before—and that was in Recife, not exactly a combat zone of the war. I promised Skeeter the following Friday I would take the train up to New London from New York.

My mother, needless to say, was far from delighted at the prospect of her errant daughter's suddenly rushing off to what could only be a most joyous reunion—a reunion with someone Mom had never even met—but for once she had nothing to say, realizing at long last it would probably be a total waste of time.

Mom had that part right. But, still saying nothing, she could not resist giving me the famous "Look" (an expression of hers more eloquent than words; you could tell exactly what she was thinking—and it was never good). This same "Look" had often caused me to rethink my evil ways in the past, but not this time.

After almost three months, Skeeter and I were once more at least in the same country, and that Friday afternoon on the train, only a few more hours separated us. I couldn't wait to see him again—and I knew the feeling was mutual.

All smiles, Skeeter was waiting for me at the station. Fortunately for us, the following Monday happened to be a holiday, so we knew we'd have three whole days together—and after the first few seconds in each other's arms, it would be as if we'd never been apart. When Skeeter finally all but lifted me off my feet, a group of sailors passing by laughed and applauded. They looked happy for us, and a little envious.

At that moment, for some reason I found myself thinking, if only my mother could have just once felt that happy for me. Which was, of course, out of the question. Mom had grown up in an era which, at least on the surface, strongly disapproved of any and all public expressions of any emotion whatsoever.

Even in the 40s, all-too-obvious love affairs were decidedly unacceptable. Your own friends would more or less look the other way, at first pretending not to notice, but hoping you would soon return to your senses. While it was a rather two-faced attitude back then, it was also somehow equally innocent. Whether or not the current mode of "let-it-all-hang out" and "doing what you want to do is the way to go" makes more sense in the long run, is a moot question. What is significant is, the term "affair" today is almost never preceded by the word "love". There just might be a clue there.

Sadly enough for both Skeeter and me, that three-day weekend in New London turned out to be our very last time together—but there is no way either Skeeter or I could ever forget it. Or each other. For me, in a way, it was a part of growing up. Predictably, in New Jersey stony silences were once again the order of the day, but this time it didn't really bother me. My only real concern was when I would see Skeeter again, but I eventually learned his ship had taken off again the day after I left New London. (Many years later, I heard through a mutual friend that Skeeter had never married, which I had, but I always wished him well. He was a great guy, a big part of my life in Recife, and I could have done a lot worse.)

In New Jersey, history seemed to be repeating itself. I had found a full-time office job in the very next town. Several of my friends had caught up with me, and we were beginning to see more of each other. Even Mom and Bessie were giving me less and less advice about everything and anything—which in itself was a novelty. But something was missing. No longer did I feel a part of what to me had been the **real** world. A world I could only wonder and speculate about until a comparatively short time ago—and then I was suddenly out there on my own. I had certainly "been there and done that"—but it wasn't enough. Now that I'd had a taste, I wanted more. And Mom had been right in a way. She had foreseen a life as carefree as possible, along with dates galore, starting the day Jeanne, Grace and I had left—all of which predictions did come true, and none of which had been hard to take. Now in New Jersey again, I had been dating occasionally, but since everything else seemed dull, the dates did, too.

One day, on a sudden impulse, I sent in an application to the Government personnel office in Miami, just to see what would happen—telling myself that if nothing did, at least I wouldn't be any worse off. In view of the fact their very friendly response was postmarked the same day they received my letter, I could only assume current applicants were few and far between.

Basically, what they replied was yes, there were quite a few secretary/steno positions available. Only not in Miami. If I happened to be interested in, for instance, **Panama**, all I had to do was fill in the enclosed, more detailed application forms and return them as soon as possible.

Working in Panama, or even going there for any reason whatsoever, had never once crossed my mind. But, it did sound interesting.

Deciding all I had to lose was a currently boring existence in the Garden State, surrounded escort-wise by either draft-rejects or able-bodied citizens currently eluding (but not for long) any branch of the armed forces, I filled out the new application forms and sent them in.

Once again, the Government was holding out the welcome mat—only this time with a proviso that the job would be in Panama. And there were, of course, a few other stipulations. For instance, I would have to pay my own fare to Miami—but once there, and on the payroll, Uncle Sam would keep me busy at some local district office pending my official transfer to the Canal Zone. Specifically, to a certain Panamanian Air Force base by the name of Quarry Heights. My original announcement, back in November, 1942, about going to Florida with two other girls, had produced a stunned reaction from the entire family—aunts, uncles, cousins and grandmother Nannie included—but THIS one was a bombshell.

I might as well have been outlining my plans for a voyage to outer space. By myself. I had the distinct impression they were all simultaneously washing their hands of me, and they probably were. Joined, needless to say, by my long-suffering mother and sister.

Now back once more in Miami, I kept running across so many old friends, even casual acquaintances I hadn't seen since my first job with U.S.E.D., I began to feel more at home there than anywhere else. Checking on my mother's health was the only reason I ever left Miami—I could only wonder now how I managed to leave there at all.

With barely a week before I would have to leave for Panama, I got to stay for that length of time with my ex-housemate Phyllis. This shop-till-you-drop gal had recently also returned to Miami, and we had a ball catching up on each other's recent history. True to form, even as we spoke, Phyllis was busily making out shopping lists for the following day. Each and every store in Miami must have tossed balloons in the air upon seeing her back.

At the Miami airport, when **this** particular Big Day arrived, I now at least felt like a seasoned traveler. An old pro at checking suitcases in and out, and finding the best seats. (It was still first-come, first-served as far as seats were concerned. The days of reservations were still far in the future.)

This plane was a C-47, and definitely not converted in ANY way as far as the comfort of its passengers was concerned. We were all lined up on benches along the sides of the plane, facing each other with our backs to the windows. Or what passed for windows—so little could be seen from them, it was seldom worth making the effort. This unexpected lack not only of leather seats but any real niceties whatsoever was giving me a few second thoughts.

A little late, of course. I was already on the plane, and the doors were closing. However, considering how fast the Panama offer had come up, and how little time I had spent thinking about what the pros and cons might be, it was par for the course. Anyway, there I was on a plane headed for the Canal Zone—people and places unknown—so I might as well enjoy the flight.

A few minutes before touching down at the Panama airport, we were able to briefly view the famed Canal. Had I at that moment known that within days I would be commuting across it twice a day, to and from work, I might not have been as impressed as I was. But I hadn't seen that many famous places as yet, and knowing I was actually looking down at the Panama Canal was a real experience. As for Panama City itself, a few minutes later that was no longer just a name on a map. It was right there in front of me.

At the airport, we were met with more ceremony than the occasion really called for (there being no VIPs whatsoever aboard) by a rather pompous individual. A second lieutenant who, as we later learned, had been commissioned only hours before and was still obviously impressed with the glory of it all—and with himself.

This still-wet-behind-the-ears officer proceeded to collect all incoming civilian employees of the Sixth Air Force to be stationed at Quarry Heights—including me—and escorted his new charges to the waiting bus.

On the way to our new quarters—which were temporarily the Hotel Tivoli in Panama City—he was busily indoctrinating one and all as to proper procedures in working for, and thus representing, the United States Government in Panama.

Few of us heard a word he said. We were riding in what appeared to be an army bus, the windows were all wide open (a year-round way of life in Panama except for the relatively short rainy season), and most of us were literally hanging out those windows, trying to see everything at once. There was a lot to see.

The streets of Panama City at that time, as compared to streets in almost any city of any size whatsoever in the United States, were like country lanes. They were indeed paved—but they might as well have been country lanes. Reason: there were animals all over the place, all of whom assumed theirs was the only right-of-way, and were therefore granted same. Naturally, this continually brought all traffic to one complete halt after another. And it wasn't just the usual dogs and cats out there.

There was actually a cow standing at the curb, presumably waiting for the traffic light to change. Three goats, one after another, were starting to cross the street. You might miss seeing one goat, thereby running into him, or her—but it would be hard to miss three. And maybe they knew that. These three were sauntering across without a care in the world—and with only some old barn out there as a final destination, why should they hurry? It was a scene not to be believed—and it happened every day. Had video cameras been within everyone's reach in those days, we could have all made a fortune.

Meanwhile, all traffic screeched to a stop, not for the first time and not for the last. Just again and again. A most interesting ride, to say the least, and assuredly not one to have drivers dozing off at the wheel.

And the animals were not the only ones to keep you awake. Every so often we would see native Panamanians, both men and women, proudly walking along balancing unbelievably heavy objects on their **heads**. And as a rule, it was—I kid you not—FURNITURE. The worst I ever saw, some time after my very first day in Panama, was a little old man, with a skull apparently made out of steel, transporting a **sewing machine** on his poor little old head. True, it was not the largest of models, but it was nevertheless, a sewing machine.

From then on, I tried not to look whenever anyone carrying anything on his or head was heading in my direction. But I still got out of the way.

The first quarters to which I was assigned (only in the armed forces does one live in "quarters") was at the Hotel Tivoli, which at that time was the pride of Panama City. This hotel was extremely well run, with all employees, in whatever capacity, seemingly acquainted with every known language. My guess is, the Tivoli to this day would be among the most popular in that area.

This time, however, the mattress in my room boasted not a single feather. Which did nothing for the comfort factor, but was probably just as well. The memory of almost missing my plane because of that **too-comfortable** bed down in Trinidad was all too painful. Nor was any mosquito canopy provided—which led to a forlorn hope. Surely this was a sign there was no mosquito problem.

Early the next morning, as per schedule, I was driven over the Canal for the very first time in one of the jeeps assigned to the Quarry Heights base. Our destination was a house belonging to the base, the rent of which I would share with two other girls whom I yet to meet. While at the Tivoli, I had seen not a single person I knew, and was really looking forward to getting together with some girls my own age.

A flight of stairs leading to the second floor, three-bedroom apartment I was to share with these two girls was located on the outside of the two-story house. These same stairs also led me to two unsmiling, definitely non-welcoming faces—Helene and Mandy. My new roommates-to-be.

The total rent for the house, including the services of a maid, would now be split three ways. However, judging by the extremely cool reception I was getting at the door (they never once said "Come in," and the door was only half-open during our entire conversation), apparently not even a reduction in rent was worth having an intruder in "their" home.

My new housemates, having been informed I would be joining them, had most reluctantly moved all their excess belongings out of the third bedroom. A further inconvenience for them—and obviously all my fault. If ever there was a fifth, unwanted wheel at that residence, I was it. I felt like running back down the stairs. Unfortunately, my driver had already left, so I was stuck with the situation—and Helene and Mandy were stuck with ME.

Helene and Mandy, likewise civilian employees at Quarry Heights, from that very first meeting always seemed to be in a bad mood, for whatever reason. In time, I could hardly fail to notice that neither appeared to have any friends, male or female. If there were any, I never saw them. Helene and Mandy didn't even get along with each other. This was a house I was more and more reluctant to return to after work, and every evening I delayed it as long as possible.

There had to be somewhere else for me to stay—**anywhere** else could only be an improvement. I'd had no idea until then that living arrangements between three presumably civilized persons could be such a hassle.

At the Quarry Heights office, however, my first day was a real turn-around. These people were normal, average human beings, and everyone was friendly. Three of them had actually greeted me at the door to welcome me to the office, and then showed me all around the place. A most appreciated change, to put it mildly, from the day before.

Several of my new co-workers, who had occasionally worked with my less-than-charming housemates, strongly advised me to move out, and the sooner the better. Having already spoken to the Personnel office that very morning as to different living quarters, I was way ahead of them—and Personnel had promised to check it out.

The Quarry Heights offices were almost a compound (even in that pre-Kennedy era) of separate, one-story buildings. Due to the awesome climate, a permanently screened open-air style of architecture was standard equipment.

Everyone I met had also, prior to their own arrival in Panama, understandably been a little apprehensive about its well-publicized heat. No one here, however, seemed to be paying it that much attention. As for me, having come from the cloudiest of states, just being able to walk out into the Panamanian sunshine day after day, never having to look up at the sky and wonder if the sun would **ever** shine again, was something only a fellow New Jerseyite could have appreciated. I often wished I could share some of it with my family and friends back home.

At 12 o'clock noon every day, everything Government-related came to a halt. Officers, servicemen and civilians alike met for lunch at the smallest but most popular building, inevitably designated as the "mess." A less than appealing term, considering it was where you went for food.

For civilians in that era, those lunches every day at the "mess" were a rare treat. Back in the States, with the exception of very plentiful chicken and seemingly no end of fish, the choicest foods, such as beef, had been rationed almost out of sight. They were just a memory. A real steak on your plate in Panama almost every day looked and tasted like a slice of heaven.

Not one person eating at the "mess" was ever known to stand up and announce he or she was a vegetarian, or even look askance at the meat-eaters. Whoever they were—and they remained anonymous—they were right there shoveling down the steaks with the rest of us. Certain convictions appeared to be on hold till the end of the war.

After one LONG week in the company of Helene and Mandy, Personnel came up with good news. One more rental house, also on the outskirts of the base, was finished and ready for civilian occupancy—and I was free to move in.

This time I wound up with real people—Doris and Virginia—and although we had met only briefly at the office, we all knew immediately that sharing a house together was going to be a lot of fun.

That house was a little different from others on the same street which had been built before it. Ours was a two-story duplex. There was a driveway under each side, and between the two driveways was a basement for the maid. Although Doris, Virginia and I probably wouldn't have recognized this particular maid if we saw her on the street (she was never around when we were home), somehow between the time we all left for work in the morning and whenever we returned home, she had managed to work miracles with every room. Once again, the whole place would be as spotless and immaculate as the first day we saw it. Suddenly having a maid do all the work for you, and then become more or less invisible, was very easy to get used to.

One Saturday morning by sheer chance I happened to glance out the kitchen window at exactly the right time. (The back of the house was literally no more than 50 feet from the jungle itself—an area we would never under any circumstances approach.) What I saw out there was the most beautiful deer ever created. He was absolutely motionless, like a statue, standing just a few feet from the edge of the undergrowth.

As I watched, not even breathing for fear he'd look up and see me at the window, the deer just vanished. One second he was there, the next he was gone. It was hard to believe he'd been there at all. That gorgeous creature must have had a path, hopefully known only to deer, back through the jungle—and I hope it's still hidden from anyone with a rifle.

Somewhere in the process of moving from the Helene/Mandy menage to the house I really looked forward to living in, I almost missed a call from Jeanne. She was still working at Nassau in the Bahamas (somewhat irreverently known as Duke-and-Duchess-Land), and our letters hadn't been all that frequent lately.

But Jeanne, liking all she'd been hearing from me about Panama, had come up with a few ideas of her own. She apparently managed to pull all the right strings with the Personnel office in Nassau, and they eventually gave her carte blanche to apply long-distance for a job in Panama. Which she did—AND my old friend would soon be on her way to join me in Quarry Heights.

It was incredible news and I don't know how she did it. In the heart of the Bahamas—until Jeanne came along, that is—no employee ever even considered requesting a transfer to any place as far away as Panama. All I could figure out was, she must have just taken them so by surprise that they granted the request without checking the rulebook. Nassau authorities are no doubt still wondering how Jeanne put that one over.

For ordinary civilians, being stationed on an air force base was worlds apart from living in any stateside regular town. In Quarry Heights, for example, one problem Virginia, Doris and I never had to face was commuting from our house to the office every day. To begin with, it was free—and it was fun—although from time to time a little more challenging than we were looking for.

Walking out the door in the morning and standing in front of the house was all it took. Immediately, the first passing vehicle—jeep, truck, staff car, anything on wheels—took this as a signal to stop. The first driver to spot us would slam on the brakes, pull over with a grin—and our ride for that morning was waiting.

Most of the time, jeeps would show up first. Occasionally, the three of us were crowded into the cab of a truck—but the most interesting free ride of all took place on what also turned out to be the most terrifying vehicle to ever stop for us. It was a bomb-carrier.

The driver himself, as were most of the enlisted men, was delighted to have female passengers for a change, most polite, and also very helpful. Helpful in the sense that before we got on, he repeatedly assured us this particular bomb-carrier was not loaded with the normal lethal cargo that day. It was indeed totally empty, but because of the food cartons stacked all over the passenger seat, the only places for us to sit were out in back, on so-called benches running lengthwise on the **outsides** of the carrier.

Speed limits were not posted anywhere on the base—they apparently didn't even exist—so as the driver took off at close to the speed of sound, we began hanging on frantically to the rails in back of us.

Inside the cab, our driver was happily singing away at the top of his lungs. He would never have heard us anyway, but that didn't prevent all three of us out in back from screaming at the top of OUR lungs. For some reason, we suddenly did not believe that every single bomb had been removed. There was probably SOME little bomb hiding in there somewhere, and it could go off at any moment. With all the noise everyone, including the driver, was making, if one HAD exploded, no one in the vicinity would have noticed, anyway.

The end of that ride, with everyone still intact, couldn't have come too soon. As politely as we could under the circumstances (all of us **knowing** we had just escaped sudden death), we thanked the driver and walked shakily into the office.

There, we warned everyone in sight to turn and run if ever a bomb-carrier stopped for them. Better to pay for a taxi.

Although the dating market in Panama was, predictably, very happily outbalanced in our favor (about fifty males to each suddenly-very-choosy female), there was still only one person who from Day One had strongly appealed to me. That was Jimmy, a tall good-looking warrant officer from the Northwest, and originally from Canada before joining up with the United States Air Force.

Jimmy had been assigned to our office as chief aide to the resident Colonel for several months before I arrived on the scene. Very close proximity to each other, every day and all day, during the week was not turning either of us off, so we were beginning to date on weekends. The more I saw of Jimmy, the more I realized that to say I was interested would be putting it mildly, and at that point, I decided to enlist the aid of my two roommates, Doris and Virginia.

This hastily called top-level conference came to a unanimous conclusion—which was, a little more aggressive action was called for here. After all, few of the Americans then in Panama for whatever reason would be there forever. We could all be gone tomorrow, so to speak. Including Jimmy. And including me. Therefore, since Jimmy was MY kind of guy, time was of the essence. The plot began to thicken.

All over the Quarry Heights base, parties were pretty much routine. Every weekend there was one **somewhere** around. There was one rule, however—allegedly unwritten but strictly observed. When you invited officers to your party, you did not at the same time invite servicemen. And vice versa.

This pain-in-the-neck rule could make for a very awkward situation if, for example, your roommates' boyfriends happened to be officers, while yours was a serviceman. The friendliest solution was to literally toss a coin, with the understanding the loser would make other plans elsewhere for the evening.

In Jimmy's case, my co-conspirators and I suddenly remembered something that made all the difference. Warrant officers were apparently considered exceptions to the rule. A warrant officer was considered an "officer", in that all servicemen would automatically give him a salute. Yet that same warrant officer could also mingle socially with the same enlisted men, any time and anywhere, with no problem to any one. He was the "man in the middle", acceptable to all. We decided to take a chance and rearrange our party lists.

As far as civilians were concerned, the rule itself did not make a lot of sense, but to keep everybody happy and not have anyone going into a panic, we decided to experiment. We would throw two parties in a row, on two successive Saturday nights. For the first party, we would invite only officers. For the second, only servicemen. And, Jimmy could come to BOTH.

Up until the night of each party, Virginia, Doris and I were more than a little nervous about trying out this somewhat unique idea. We actually worried about winding up in the local brig for insubordination or something equally horrendous. The way things turned out, we had worried for nothing.

Jimmy was there for the first party, surrounded by officers, all on a first-name basis. Also for the second, with wall-to-wall servicemen obviously more than delighted to be there with anybody. Both parties were a huge success. (The first party did break up a little early, however, as the number of guests outlasted the supply of liquid refreshments. Steps were immediately taken to insure this social catastrophe would not reoccur at Party #2.)

After the first party, Jimmy and I took an office friend, Kara, over to her house in a taxi (Kara's boyfriend was out of town at the moment), and then went on into Panama City to see what was happening.

Not much was. The city was fairly quiet, and for the first time that I could remember, the streets were completely devoid of animals. Cows, goats, dogs and cats had evidently all found whatever it was they were looking for. We stopped by a supper club, and even that was almost deserted, so eventually we went on back to the house.

With the exception of a night-light left on in the living room by my thoughtful housemates, all the lights in the house were out, but we were at least able to walk in without falling over some remnants of the part.

I didn't want Jimmy to leave. I also didn't want to push him. He knew very well how I felt about him, but whatever happened at that moment, and from then on, was strictly up to him.

As if he'd read my mind, which he very probably had, Jimmy very tenderly took me in his arms, and we were finally together in the best way of all. It was the very first night for Jimmy and me, and definitely not the last—but that first time is the one time I will never ever forget.

One morning, there was a message waiting on my desk from Personnel, requesting me to stop by as soon as possible. The minute I saw it, I knew it had to be Jeanne.

And there she was—normally the world's most **impatient** person— waiting patiently inside the Personnel Office. We hadn't seen each other since the day I'd left Miami Beach for Brazil, and then a few days later, Jeanne had taken off for the Bahamas

So many things, **so much** had happened in both our lives in the meantime. We were so excited, we couldn't even sit down, and were all but dancing around the Personnel room. It would take us just about forever to catch upon everything—except for a grouchy Lieutenant Colonel, sitting back in a corner of the office and taking in this noisy grand reunion. He had other ideas.

Highly annoyed glares from His Nibs finally got through to us, and we got the message. All this foolishness must end at once. Everybody else in the area was cheering us on, but for Grumpy's sake, we pretended to calm down. I took Jeanne back to my office, where the atmosphere was a lot friendlier.

Jeanne had already been moved into a house on the base not too far from mine, so we knew we'd at least be neighbors. Then, the day after I met her at Personnel, she was assigned to the very same office I was working in. There having been one such coincidence after another since the day she, Grace and I all left New Jersey, Jeanne and I had to agree on one thing. We were obviously meant to be the best of friends till the end of time.

According to Jeanne, the Bahamas, over which the famous Duke and Duchess currently presided—and particularly Nassau, where Jeanne herself had stayed—had been a really interesting place to work. According to her, mostly because of the people she worked with.

Chances are, all the British government employees there were every bit as fascinated by Jeanne as she was with them. She loved their English accent, and they must have been equally intrigued by Jeanne's much-maligned New Jerseyese—which to British ears sounds like a foreign language.

Oddly enough, in the twenty-one years I grew up in the Garden State, I could not recall a single instance of one of its residents even noticing, let alone ridiculing, accents Jerseyites themselves hear constantly on all sides—accents not only from other parts of the United States but from foreign countries. The crossroads-of-the-world location of the New York/New Jersey area makes their widely known tolerance of how the world about them sounds to their own ears even more significant. New Jersey, as a state, may have no greater claim to sainthood than the other 49, but at least it has a little class in that respect.

On Jeanne's first day at work, I walked her all around the office and introduced her. First of all, of course, to Jimmy (I had already informed her Jimmy was off-limits) and then to everybody else. As I fully expected, Jeanne made a hit with one and all. She was a very tall, beautiful Nordic-style blonde who never seemed to count on her looks alone to put her over. She just had a great personality, and people took to her on sight.

Jeanne even managed to make a hit with our own Lieutenant Colonel, who as a rule neither associated with nor approved of anyone in the office. It was just the way he was—but this time he broke all his own rules to sit her down to question her quite extensively about life in the Bahamas. We later told Jeanne she should go down in office history after that feat.

This particular officer's nickname throughout the entire base was "Blubberpuss". As far as anyone knew, he was totally unaware of this moniker the entire three years he was assigned there, and no one in his right mind—whether officer or enlisted—was about to enlighten "Blubberpuss" as to the profound disregard, to put it mildly, in which he was held by one and all.

Jeanne pretended to be utterly charmed by this infamous Lieutenant Colonel when introduced to him, but later admitted that was the biggest put-on of her life.

One of my very favorite people in that office was Johnny, a sergeant whose desk was directly in back of mine. He was of Italian descent, had a very slight build, and was a born artist. The name we actually called him was "Jno"—the reason being, he always insisted the abbreviation for John was actually Jno, which he liked better. That's what it took to make him happy, so that's what we called him. Anything for a peaceful office.

Jno, from time to time (when not under Blubberpuss' eye) would draw one caricature after another of every one in the office. Even of people he recalled passing by in the street. Somehow every one of those office sketches looked more like the originals than any bona fide photo could have. A great sketch Jno drew of Blubberpuss—which is still in one of my albums—is an absolute work of art. (Should the Smithsonian be interested, my number's in the book.)

Jno was also gay. Another sergeant, who also worked in our office, was his designated "significant other", referred to in that era as "special companion". Before Jno, I hadn't known gays existed, but everyone seemed to take this particular couple for granted. Panama was a little ahead of its time in that respect. Both Jno and his friend were extremely well liked, and incidentally also the two very best dancers I have ever had the pleasure of dancing with. Out on the dance floor with either one, you could have three feet and still dance like Pavlova.

Jimmy and I had been an "item" now for some time. Not necessarily in society columns of the local Panama gazette, but at least on all our friends' social lists. We were automatically invited to parties as a couple. Several people had mentioned to me from time to time that Jimmy had been somewhat of a loner before I showed up, but those days seemed to be long gone, and I thought he was happy. I really cared about him, as he well knew, and I thought I had every reason to believe the feeling was mutual. There were a few surprises ahead.

A few months after I started dating Jimmy, I missed two periods. With the first, I naively decided it was probably the change of climate, possibly even all the traveling I'd been doing. The second time around, I knew better.

Jimmy managed to locate a native doctor in Panama City who could check me out, and made an appointment for the next morning. Upon returning to the office that afternoon, I sat down at my desk and looked over at Jimmy. His desk was on the other side of the room, alongside the window, but directly facing mine. I nodded. The test was positive.

All I could think of at that point was, I'm going to have Jimmy's baby. Obviously unplanned, and certainly as yet unsanctified by any church, I was nevertheless expecting his baby. Jimmy's and mine. And I was absolutely thrilled. More than a little scared, for many reasons, but thrilled.

How the future father felt at that moment, I couldn't even guess. The office was, as usual, noisily taking sides in the latest crisis, so any conversation then and there between us was clearly impossible. A few minutes later, therefore, we met at the door and walked over to the PX, ostensibly for coffee.

When we finally got off in a corner by ourselves, I said "What do you think?"

Jimmy's reply was, "Well, he's got to have a name," obviously taking it for granted it was a boy. (No ultra-sound findings in the 40s, but he had that right.)

Jimmy, having already assumed while waiting for me to return from the doctor's office that the test would be positive, then told me of an idea he had come up with. The idea was this: on September 23rd, Jimmy was scheduled to leave Panama for the States, where, for two months, he would be attending an Adjutant General's School in Texas. (He had applied, and been accepted, for this particular course sometime before I arrived in Panama.)

Following his two-month stay in Texas, he suggested that I fly out of Panama late in November and meet him on December 1st at a certain hotel in Miami—following which we would find a local justice of the peace to marry us. Again he said "My son's got to have my name."

This was in August. After September 23rd, with Jimmy gone, possibly never to return for all I knew, for me there would be eight long weeks to get through. Jimmy would be thousands of miles away, somewhere in Texas, while I remained in Panama—with both of us, no doubt, trying to act as if nothing at all unusual was going on.

While I naturally would rather have had Jimmy committed to me— and the sooner the better—than to some school in Texas for two months, Jimmy had no other suggestion. However, as this somewhat involved arrangement would at least result in our baby's being legitimate, I decided to go along with it.

Jeanne was the only person I had confided in, a few days before Jimmy was to leave for Texas, so she at least knew what was going on. She also was the only one I could really trust not to say anything.

Although Jimmy and I had said our own goodbyes the night before, the morning of September 23rd he stopped by the office to pick up a few papers before heading for the airport. As he walked out the door with a casual wave of his hand for the entire office, Jeanne was looking over at me as if to say, "I can just imagine how you feel."

There was no way anyone could. My own feelings were indescribable. I sat there watching my baby's father walk out the door—and for all I knew, I might never see him again.

Over the next two months, both Jimmy and I had more than enough time to think. We had known each other only a comparatively short time, but creating a child together had turned both our lives around. And yet it was still anyone's guess as to what might happen from then on.

As far as I was concerned, what was really unsettling was, I still wasn't sure how Jimmy really felt about me. He had never been one to pay idle compliments. When we first started going together, he told me I was the first girl he "liked" since he came to Panama. On more than one occasion, he did say I was "pretty smart", (I would have settled for "pretty").

There was one other time. It was my 23rd birthday, and I was wearing a beautiful, peasant-type blouse my mother had sent me. Jimmy looked over at me from across the office and said "You look about sixteen."

And that was about it. It never made me think any less of him— nothing could have done that, since to me he was Mr. Perfect—but I couldn't help wishing he would once in a while be a little more demonstrative, at least verbally. Physically, I had no complaints—and it was only at those times that I could make myself believe he really loved me.

My own schedule for leaving the base late in November was already known to the long-suffering Personnel office. Supposedly, they had already booked me on a flight to Miami on November 30th. Then, about ten days before that date, they had no choice but to call me—and from that day on, it was a brand-new ball game.

My November 30th plane reservation had just been reassigned to some obviously important general—who naturally had priority over all. And there was nothing they could do about that. They further advised there was no seat available on any other Miami-bound plane. Not until the middle of December.

They finally came up with a solution which saved the day technically—I would still get to Miami eventually—but it was a complete turn-around. It was not even a plane trip, but a **boat** trip, via the USS

Cuba. The USS Cuba was currently docked at Colon, on the northern end of the Canal.

From the day I arrived in Panama, what was always hard to realize was, Quarry Heights and Panama City are both on the southern end of the Canal, yet they face the Pacific Ocean. Colon faces the Atlantic. Looking at a map, it appears to be just the opposite.

Having grown up on the East Coast, near the Atlantic Ocean, I was naturally accustomed to looking east and seeing the Atlantic. Now, in Panama, I was actually on the West Coast—but looking **East**, I saw the Pacific. What really blew everyone's mind in Panama was seeing the sun set in what appeared to be the Atlantic. I can't recall how many times all the Statesiders sat around trying to explain just how that Canal worked.

The new schedule Personnel had worked out for me was far more involved than merely walking onto a plane in Panama and walking off in Miami. In two days, I was to take the train from Panama City to Colon, and then somehow (a not too encouraging term) get over to the ship.

There was one more obstacle, which finally occurred to me. Colon being actually on the Caribbean part of the Atlantic meant the USS Cuba would be headed for **New Orleans**. NOT Miami. At that point, all my previous plans went right out the window. All I knew of New Orleans was that it was in Louisiana. Personnel seemed to have no idea either as to when the ship would leave Colon, or when it would arrive at New Orleans—ships' wartime schedules always being a tightly-guarded secret—but I assumed I could take a train from New Orleans to Miami and **hope** to make it by December 1st.

That fifty-mile train trip to Colon across the Isthmus was a unique experience—one that almost made me forget why I was on that particular train in the first place. Just looking out the window, I realized what a truly historic area I was going through, with the Isthmus itself connecting two great continents and the famed Canal connecting the

Atlantic to the Pacific. There was very little time left for wondering about whatever might happen next. Which was just as well.

The train pulled into Colon sooner than I expected. It had not been a particularly lengthy trip, and was certainly anything but boring, so as a result I had not been watching the clock. Fortunately for my peace of mind, however, since I really had no idea what to expect now that I was actually in Colon, there were quite a few taxis waiting. I took the first one in line over to the ship.

Exactly five minutes after I walked up the gangplank, the ship pulled away from the dock. At that point, it would not have been unreasonable to conclude the captain had been hanging out the window waiting for ME to show up.

I couldn't have made it much closer, but since no one would ever admit to knowing the precise sailing time—least of all the Quarry Heights Personnel department—I might as well flatter myself this was NOT sheer coincidence.

To make matters even more confusing, I hadn't had time to locate the cabin I was to share with another girl—which, half an hour later, turned out to be at the opposite end of the ship. All things considered, no part of that experience did much for my nerves.

All the way up to New Orleans, the USS Cuba had a destroyer escort on each side, so we were presumably safe from whatever, or whoever, was out there waiting to do us in. What to many of us was really scary, because we couldn't see any real reason for it at the time, was that at night we would go at least twice as fast as in the daytime. Having been assured there were no lights on the ship which were visible from the outside, we kept telling each other we were still all perfectly safe. And we all did our best to believe it.

As far as the meals on board were concerned, they were deemed delicious. Strictly hearsay—confirmed only by those lucky enough to remain in the dining room long enough to consume same. Unfortunately for me in my newly **enceinte** condition (which completely revolutionizes the workings of any woman's stomach), staying there in my seat even long enough to see the food coming in from the galleys was impossible. Within minutes, I would be on my way out the door. Still hungry.

Although I never actually became sick, a few short minutes in that totally airless dining room almost did me in every time. Not to mention the periodic listing of the ship first to one side and then the other, which just added insult to injury. I exited ASAP.

Back on deck again, everything was fine. All I needed was air. Luckily for me, my new cabin-mate Nancy was most sympathetic, cutting her own meals short to bring something edible back to the cabin for me. And oddly enough, there in the cabin it WAS possible to eat, even with the ship still rolling around.

We finally reached New Orleans, as safe and unharmed by unseen hostile forces as we had been promised. Only then, starting to go through customs, was an interesting if somewhat mindless question put to me. The official in charge, after only briefly glancing over at my suit-cases, which were stacked a considerable distance away, asked "Anything in there I should look at?"

I replied, "Of course not." I was immediately allowed to proceed, along with my unopened luggage which did not, as it happened, contain anything this guardian of the state should have looked at. (If it had, and I'd been a smuggler tipped off ahead of time about this open-door policy, I could have made a fortune.)

Upon leaving the ship, all passengers were informed New Orleans was being invaded by a huge convention that particular weekend. Consequently, rates for hotel rooms of any description, if rooms were available at all, would be at a premium. I called the railroad station to see if I could possibly get on a train for Miami that very day. Answer: No Miami-bound trains were scheduled to leave until the next morning.

The Jung Hotel having been recommended to me by some friends originally from New Orleans, I took a cab over there, fully expecting to hear all rooms were either taken or reserved, but hoping against hope for the best. They did check my suitcases, and took my name in case of a possible cancellation, but did not hold out much hope. With nothing better to do to kill time, and not wanting to become a fixture of the lobby for endless hours, I decided to take a bus tour of the city.

One of the more memorable stops was at a locally-famous ancient cemetery where, according to our driver, all bodies had to be buried in aboveground tombs, presumably due to the lower-than-sea-level altitude. (As to the hazards of alternate locations, no one cared to speculate.)

We also toured the equally historic French Quarter which, along with its many famous restaurants, was somewhat larger than I had pictured—not to mention a most refreshing change from the last point-of-interest. At least the residents were walking around.

Once again back at the Jung, there was still no prospect of a vacancy. Not knowing what else to do, I sat in the lobby until quite late in the evening, at which point an Army sergeant walked over.

Holding out some hotel keys, he politely offered me the use of his room for the night, saying he himself would be out with friends until dawn. It wasn't much of a temptation. Half the armed forces in town probably had keys for the same room. I thanked him for the offer, anyway, and as he turned away, he winked at the group of servicemen he had apparently just left. They all then trooped out of the hotel, presumably in search of greener pastures. And more desperate females.

The sergeant wasn't the only person to take pity on me that night. My guardian angel must have been keeping his/her eye on me, because one of the women clerks at the desk soon came over with a suggestion. If I wanted, I could use the couch in a room adjoining the ladies' room. She assured me no one would bother me there, and I could stay until morning.

By that time of night, I could have curled up on a picket fence, so the idea of a real couch sounded like heaven. I walked over to the room, clutching my pocketbook, and all but collapsed on the couch. I spent the rest of the night there, undisturbed.

The next morning, I was **finally** on a Miami-bound train. I couldn't wait to get down there, yet for some reason I was a little apprehensive. Something just didn't feel right. When I arrived in Miami the next day, however, at least I was on schedule. It was November 30th.

That night, I stayed with Phyllis again, offering no real explanation as to why I was suddenly back in Miami. The next day, December 1st, was the day I was to meet Jimmy at the hotel he had specified.

By 10 o'clock that morning, I had located the hotel. The room clerk advised me she had no record of any reservation in Jimmy's name. Or in mine—while she was rechecking her lists, I suddenly thought he might have made the reservation in my name instead—but there was nothing. I sat down to wait in the lobby.

By 5 o'clock that afternoon, thinking perhaps I had come to the wrong hotel in the first place, I had made calls to several others. There was no Jimmy registered at any of them. Nor were there any reservations in either name. I went back to Phyllis' apartment for the night, hoping she wouldn't ask too many questions.

The next morning, back at the same hotel, once again there was no sign of Jimmy. Nor were there any messages. I had no idea where to contact him. As far as I could figure, he would have been en route to Miami from Texas about the same time I was traveling down from New Orleans. He should have reached the hotel about the same time I did.

For the benefit of the desk clerks, I'd been trying to pretend all along this was probably just a casual misunderstanding. Having no doubt already seen everything and anything while dealing with the public, they saw through that act in no time. However, they did tell me they were extremely concerned for me, and asked what they could do.

At that point, I could only tell them where they could contact me—either at my friend Phyllis' place in Miami or my mother's in New Jersey—but with no real hope of ever hearing from them.

Having finally looked up and read the handwriting on the wall, I was trying to get used to the idea that I would also, in all probability, not be hearing from Jimmy, either.

Once again, there was no other place to go but home. One more time back to New Jersey, to my mother and sister, and the rest of the family. I was just glad there *was* some place for me to go. Before boarding the same old Silver Meteor the next morning, I took enough time out to stop by the nearest jewelry store. There, I picked out a wedding ring for me. I was going to need it. My entire family had been advised in August, via telegram, that Jimmy and I had eloped. In those days, not only were weddings themselves all-important but the correct amount of time between wedding dates and subsequent birth dates was positively crucial. Everyone I knew would naturally be expecting to see a ring on my finger, and if I could display what indeed appeared to be a wedding ring, that was the least I could do.

I boarded the train a few minutes early, and before finding my seat, stepped aside into a little alcove, took the ring out of the box and placed it on my finger.

Somehow, I always thought my wedding day would be a little different.

First on the agenda back in New Jersey was, naturally, finding a job. And there was no longer only **me** to think about. A few months down the line, my little son (even I now assumed the baby was a boy) would be very much present.

While at the moment it seemed highly unlikely his father would be standing by to say "Welcome to the World," every single other person I knew couldn't wait to see my baby, to pick him up and cuddle him, and assure themselves he was **really** there. This would be the first baby in my family since I was born, so they'd had twenty-three long years to wait.

Looking for a job in December, 1944 was still almost a cinch. More and more female office workers had been switching over to defense factories to snap up jobs—and wages—previously available only to men.

Since this obviously left fewer people still interested in office work, salaries in the white-collar field were also going up.

Another consequence was the improvement in office working hours. The traditional five-and-a-half-day work week was scaled down to five days—and no one except employers shed any tears about that. Secretary/stenos in particular were on the Most Wanted lists, and within two days I was again working as secretary to an attorney in the next town. Since I had no car, and couldn't drive anyway, the fact that his offices were at least within walking distance was a big plus.

The only car in the family was, of course, Mom's. The only time she had ever offered to share it was with the stipulation that whoever wanted to drive would pay for the car insurance. There were no takers. Bessie used a bus which dropped her off right in front of her office building in Newark, while I, with a baby on the way, was already looking at every nickel twice. So I either walked to work or, in case of rain, took a bus.

In my new job, the last secretary had quit one lunchtime, without notice, to work in a defense plant, leaving behind an unbelievable amount of work on the desk. Once I got a look at it, I could well understand why the factory job must have looked better and better. Not one record was up to date, there were pages and pages of untranscribed notes in her notebook which apparently even she couldn't read—and in the bottom drawer sat the brown-bag lunch she'd left behind, presumably from her last day there. That office was the mess of all time, and for as long as it took for me to straighten it all out, I of course often blessed her memory, whoever and wherever she was. But at least it was a job, and I was collecting a paycheck.

In January—four months after saying goodbye to Jimmy in Panama—I finally got a letter from him. The envelope was postmarked "Panama," and he was back on the base again. He wrote he'd been delayed in Texas for three days before leaving for Miami, and once there, could of course find me nowhere. Picking up a phone somewhere in the meantime had apparently not occurred to him. He had addressed the letter to New Jersey, assuming I would wind up at my mother's apartment sooner or later—and if not, my mother would certainly know where I was and his letter would then be forwarded. He concluded with, "the Texas school was okay, as schools go. Good to be back at the base. Best of luck to you"—followed, not by his signature, but his initials. Luck appeared to be exactly what I would be needing. Soon, and lots of it. I finally told my mother the whole story.

Mom seemed to be more concerned than surprised—she had always had a kind of sixth sense, anyway. She gave me a big hug, and simply said, "Well, don't worry, everything will be all right. We'll all just take care of each other somehow." That was my Mom.

A few weeks later, my boss, aware of the fact I was not only pregnant but definitely starting to show, said he was really sorry but I would have to leave. At least for a few months. Once the baby was born, he said, the job was mine as long as I wanted it. He was just afraid that if anything happened to me while I was still in his employ, he might somehow be considered liable. In short, he was afraid of finding himself on the wrong end of a lawsuit. In that era, "discrimination" charges were unheard of. If you were fired, you were fired, and that was the end of it. There was no legal recourse.

This was early in March, and the baby was due April 27. Anxious though I was to work, I still had to wonder where I would find anyone brave enough to hire a seven-months-pregnant female. At that moment, my spirits—which as a rule, fortunately for me, were fairly high—were about as low as they would ever get.

As I walked in the door of the apartment that day, the phone was ringing. It was Jimmy.

He was calling from New York City, and had just finished applying for a marriage license. If I could get over to City Hall the next day, March 13, he would have by then obtained all the necessary waivers as to time. And, we could be married.

Not exactly the answer to a maiden's prayer—but it wasn't far from it. In spite of everything that had happened since the day Jimmy walked out the office door in Panama, my spirits immediately rose to the sky. I finally knew how it felt to be happy again—and more than anything else, happy for my baby. He was not only going to have his father's name, but he would have a real live father. And I would have a real live husband.

The next morning, via bus, train, "tube" (under the Hudson River), and subway, I traveled to New York City. Coming from anywhere in New Jersey (unless you drive a car or fly a plane), that exact sequence of transports is unfortunately the only way to arrive in New York the same day.

We met at City Hall. Jimmy didn't kiss me; for a moment I actually thought he was going to shake my hand. He was in uniform, and looked just about the same, but had very little to say. To me, all that really mattered was that we were finally together once again, and everything was going to be all right. How naive I still was.

My husband-to-be did have all the necessary waivers, we both signed all the right papers, and in what seemed like a very short time we were ushered into the Judge's chambers.

His Honor looked somewhat askance at me, all of seven months pregnant, sighed a little, and proceeded with the very brief ceremony.

At exactly 2:20p.m, March 13, 1945, as per the immediately-stamped certificate, we were officially husband and wife. The Judge shook hands with both of us, very cordially wished us well, and escorted us to the door.

As soon as we were outside in the hall, Jimmy said, "Well, I've got a train to catch."

I asked, "To where?"

Jimmy: "What does it matter?"

That was the entire conversation. Not more than sixty seconds of this "marriage," legal though it was, had gone by. I suddenly thought, I must be dreaming, this is some horrible nightmare.

Jimmy started to turn away, still not looking at me, so I said, "Well, take care of yourself."

His reply was, "Bye."

That was the last time we ever saw each other. Jimmy had done what he considered his duty, and our unborn son now had what was his father's one and only concern: his name.

Returning home to New Jersey via the same involved route must have taken place in some kind of trance. I have no recollection of even walking to the subway, let alone getting on any vehicle after that. All I can remember is telling myself over and over, "I don't care, I just don't care."

Of course I cared. More than I had ever cared about anything in my life. All that kept me from giving up forever at that terrible moment was the thought, I'll go home, I'll have my baby, and maybe **someday** I'll look back and say, well, everything turned out all right after all.

On my next scheduled check-up with the doctor, he glanced over the marriage certificate, nodded, said "Good," and made certain additions to my records, presumably as to marital status.

He then suggested that I try to pay the entire hospital bill in advance. In those days, the bottom line of a hospital bill was no more mind-boggling than any other—but the reason he gave (which should probably go down in history) was, this particular hospital offered a **discount** when the total bill was paid ahead of time. The total amount due would be $80. This covered prenatal care, delivery of the baby, and post-natal care—all of which took place in the course of the TEN-day stay in the hospital, then considered routine for all new mothers and their babies.

In today's world, new mothers keep staring at the new-born babies they bring home, telling themselves they must have been in **some** hospital, some place for this to happen.

Later that day, I did stop by to pay the bill, less the 10% discount. At least this was one headache out of the way. As I turned from the front desk, a nurse passing by glanced over at me, did a double-take and then rushed back, saying, "The elevator is right this way. I'll take you up myself."

I eventually managed to convince her my delivery was not quite that close, but she didn't exactly make my day. If four weeks ahead of time (and the way that nurse acted, she was thinking in terms of minutes), I couldn't even imagine how I'd look when the time came.

Not only was the original bill easy on my wallet, what followed after my eventual return home from the hospital with the baby was even more incredible: on top of the 10% discount I'd been allowed, the hospital sent me a $5 refund. **Tie that.** Today, if a hospital were to return funds, the bookkeeper would be out looking for another job—and the nearest museum bidding for the canceled check.

April 27, the Big Day predicted by my doctor—came and went. Just another day. And in a way, it didn't surprise me. For the past several weeks, with everyone in the country speculating on exactly when the long-anticipated V-E Day would arrive, I had been betting everyone in sight my baby would be born on V-E Day. Whenever it was.

Of course no one took me seriously. What did I know? After all, if no two politicians could agree on the most likely date, who was I to come up with a positive prediction? Everyone just nodded, humoring me, no doubt attributing this wild fantasy to my current "delicate" condition.

My cousin Alice, starting with April 27th when nothing happened, made it a point each and every morning thereafter to phone me with "Anything happen yet?" As soon as I answered, "No, nothing," she would sigh and hang up. After several days of this Q. & A. routine, Alice had me feeling like a complete failure. I also wished she would just quit calling me—and then I began to wonder what was going on.

What was going on was, my as yet unborn son, overhearing the V-E Day prediction made by his mother-to-be, along with the scornful reception given it on all sides, then and there decided his entry to the world WOULD be made on V-E Day. He picked out May 8, 1945.

The night before, my mother and sister and I had all just gone to bed, settled down for the night—as we thought—when I sat up and announced, "I think we'd better go to the hospital." Within seconds, we were running in three different directions.

And this despite all the minute preparations we had made for the eventual mad dash to the hospital. For that exact moment, each of us had certain prescribed duties and checklists—and here we were falling all over each other.

If we had never given a single thought to what we would do when The Time came, it couldn't have been more hectic. Finally, my mother said, "I'll have to call a taxi. I'm so upset, I **cannot** drive that car." So much for organization.

I should have known, as we walked into the hospital, that very same nurse would be in the lobby. She said with a smile, "I knew if I waited long enough, you'd be back. NOW let me take you to the elevator."

We had ALL been waiting—and more than long enough. Rodney Paul was born at 4:55 a.m. on May 8 and weighed in at 8 pounds, 11 ounces. Just as well we didn't have to wait any longer.

(Note: Thanks to the right-on-the-line prediction for the V-E Day birth, all future opinions of the new mother were treated with considerably more respect.)

In those days, new mothers **expected** to nurse their babies. It was not only a wonderful experience, but at that time the only way to go. If for some reason, you couldn't handle it, you would be the object of an enormous amount of sympathy each time your baby's formula was brought in to you.

There were three other girls in the room with me, and every four hours all four newborns were brought into the room. Happily for them—and their new Moms—no formulas were required.

Spending ten whole days relaxing in bed after the ongoing stress of the previous nine months, being waited on hand and foot and treated as some kind of heroine by all visitors, and—best of all—seeing your brand-new gorgeous baby brought in to you periodically, right on schedule, was like living in Never-Never Land.

All four of us being more or less the same age—and certainly with the same interests, having just had our very first babies—we got along famously, talking to our hearts' content half the night, as well as all day. The girl in the bed next to me had an interesting, if somewhat exasperating, experience one night. She had been having considerable trouble sleeping ever since her little baby girl was born, so her doctor had left instructions to the nurses for sleeping pills to be administered "when necessary."

One evening, after she and I had been talking for hours about everything and anything, she finally began feeling sleepy, gratefully curled up, and fell sound asleep. Although the nursing staff was ordinarily most considerate, one particular nurse apparently had not read her written instructions too carefully. She came in that night, WOKE my friend up, and handed over the prescribed medication: **sleeping** pills. My friend was awake the rest of the night.

For certain reasons, visiting hours—even though I loved visitors— were not my favorite time of the day. My roommates' husbands always showed up. Not one of them was in any branch of the service, and I was really envious—not at their being there with their wives, but because I couldn't help wondering how they managed to avoid being drawn in one way or another. The rest of the world was at war with Japan—and they were still peacefully at home with their families.

Although I was certainly not looking for my husband, at least no one wondered at his absence, having been advised he was in the armed forces in Panama. My own family was constantly in and out, but carefully taking turns. Only two visitors were allowed at a time. Every time a nurse came in, she automatically counted heads, and if any of her patients had more than two people at their bedside, somebody had to leave.

One afternoon, my mother came in alone, and without saying a word, she handed me a telegram. Unknown to me, she had wired Jimmy in Panama of the baby's birth. His telegram to her read, "Unable to visit. Glad Mildred is all right." I couldn't say anything, and for the first time since Jimmy walked away from me in New York on our wedding day, I broke down and cried. Up to then, I guess I thought I could handle anything, but that did it.

Mom turned away, looking absolutely helpless, and went over to stand by the window. Not surprisingly, she had tears in her eyes. There was nothing left for either of us to say, anyway. The telegram said it all.

Every one of my relatives, far and near—even two cousins from Long Island I hadn't seen in years—showed up—all of them more than ready to welcome the baby to the family. Especially Nannie, my grandmother. Rodney was her first great-grandchild, the only one she lived long enough to see. I will never forget the look on Nannie's face when I placed **her** great-grandson in her arms for the very first time. Nannie was very English, normally somewhat reserved, but her face lit up like a rainbow when she reached out for Rodney. She looked like an angel, a very happy angel, smiling down at that baby.

On June 1st, a Government check for $80 arrived, and I was advised by Uncle Sam the same amount would be sent monthly, as long as Jimmy was in the armed forces. Two months later, V-J Day had officially written an end to the war. Jimmy had sent a brief note at that time, telling me his service in Panama would soon be over, also advising me the Government's check of October 1st would be the last.

He closed with the not entirely unexpected news that he was going back to Seattle to live. Nothing was mentioned about my getting a divorce in the near future—and this was something of a surprise, as I had taken it for granted he would soon be asking for one. There was no reason whatsoever for getting my hopes up for a future together— somewhere, sometime, somehow—but I couldn't resist a few day- dreams now and then. If nothing else, just pretending that against all odds everything between us might eventually work out, kept me going from one day to the next.

As for what to do when the $80 check from Uncle Sam stopped, the solution was obvious. Just get out there and look for a job. There was no real reason to expect anything from Jimmy in the future.

Late in September, Bessie came up with some good news for me. She knew as well as I did that before going back to work anywhere, I would need a full-time babysitter. She had just found one. As far back as I could remember, Bessie and I had always hashed over our problems together. Each of us, at a very early age, had instinctively known better than to take them to Mom. Not that Mom wouldn't have understood, and even been more or less sympathetic—but reams of advice would have been forthcoming until the end of time. Also, there would be a whole new problem if we didn't go along with whatever she told us to do. It was just easier for my sister and me to confide in each other.

Rodney's brand-new babysitter was Mrs.Tucker, a lady we had already met once or twice, who lived in the apartment house next door. She had assured Bessie she was ready, willing and able to start taking care of Rodney during the day, once I had a job.

Mrs. Tucker, luckily for me, turned out to be a godsend. We were never on a first-name basis. She being in her sixties and I at that time twenty-four, to me she was always "Mrs.Tucker." Working Moms of today would shed many a tear at the amount I paid her per WEEK, **six dollars**. Mrs. Tucker was childless herself, but absolutely adored all babies. She once told me she truly believed God put her on this earth to take care of other people's children. Although at the time she was already taking care of one baby, a little boy about Rodney's age, she was more than agreeable to taking on one more responsibility.

I was trying to get used to the idea of turning over MY baby every morning for the entire day—and to a comparative stranger, at that—but it was almost impossible. Against all odds, I was still hoping some miracle would happen, that some fortune would fall out of the sky—and I could stay home with him by myself.

No miracle came along. No bag of gold was left at my front door. I had to realize I was very, very lucky there *was* someone like Mrs. Tucker to come to the rescue—and after spending several hours with Rodney at Mrs. Tucker's own apartment, where she would be taking care of both babies, I knew she was someone I could absolutely depend upon.

For me, getting back to the working world was just around the corner—and I could thank my ever-helpful big sister for making it possible.

Early in October, I registered with a New York employment agency. Ninety minutes of filling out forms came first, then several interviews as to whether or not I was really all that qualified for what they just might have in mind for me. The job-finding routine used to be a snap—but, the war was now over. The days of hearing "If you want it, the job is yours" were no more.

Deciding I just might make the grade, the agency sent me out to a brokerage firm on Wall Street. Once there it was déjà vu time. I found myself sitting at the desk of a secretary who had left in a hurry—and whether that had been her idea or that of the bosses, no one ever said. It was a very familiar feeling—I couldn't help but recall the first few days of my last brief job in New Jersey. I only hoped this new one would last a little longer. At least they'd need something besides a "coming event" excuse to fire me.

This particular brokerage outfit was among the busiest in New York. Fortunately for me at the time, they were very short-handed and all but desperate for someone to help out, so I had been spared the customary in-and-out interview, along with the usual put-offs of "we'll be getting in touch" and "don't call us, we'll call you." Quite the contrary. I had to sit down then and there and get started on my job.

There was only one problem. I wanted to call Mrs. Tucker at lunchtime, let her know where I was and what was happening, and ask her how my baby was doing. I was never able to get through. There was a very frustrating phone tie-up at the time in that particular calling area, so I had no choice but to put my real life on hold until 5 o'clock.

By the time I finally got home that first night, my sister—who so adored that baby she looked for any excuse, anyway, had picked up Rodney, given him his bottle (he had finally been persuaded to give up nursing), and tucked him in his crib.

Having been away from him all day, I had been literally counting the hours until I could walk in the door, pick him up and just hold him. And there he was, in his crib, sound asleep. Bessie explained she had tried to keep him awake, knowing how anxious I'd be to see him, but he was already out like a light.

In time, I got used to not being home from dawn to dusk, and not seeing my baby for hours at a time—but that first day was a killer.

There was another reason why I had to start making my own money again. Jimmy had finally written to ask for a divorce. Even in those days, divorce lawyers were relatively expensive, whether proceedings were contested or not. As far as Jimmy was concerned, I had sensed for some time what was coming and, at long last, gave up all hope of our ever getting together again.

After reimbursing my mother for all the "extras," I had been depositing whatever was left of my salary in the bank every payday. I had to save as much as I could, and as soon as possible. All things considered, I felt a divorce was something I owed the man who was technically, if in no other way, still my husband. Trying to hold on to someone who obviously wanted nothing more to do with me was pointless, and having had more than enough time to think about it, I finally decided that leaving New Jersey and filing for a divorce else-where would be the best way to go. For many reasons.

For one thing, it would be less upsetting for my family if I were out of the state at the time. Assuming I could accumulate enough funds, I could take Rodney and go to, for instance, Florida—still the Land of Enchantment for me—for three months, that being then the required residence for a divorce. For a while, Baby Rodney and I would be away from everybody we knew. At least we'd be together. And, eventually, both Jimmy and I could get our lives back on track. Separately. Not exactly the way I would have wanted.

Fortunately for finances at the time, plane fares to Florida was a little more affordable. In August of that year, 1946, Jimmy, at my request, had sent a $200 check to help out with the plane fare. Adding that to what I had saved, I made a reservation for Sarasota.

My cousins Alice and Don, upset though they were at what was going on, drove up from their home in East Brunswick and dropped us off at the airport. And—Sarasota was next.

Mary, a girlfriend from my early Miami days (we had both worked for the U.S.E.D. there), hearing I was thinking of moving to Florida for three months, had called some time ago. She had a suggestion—that Rodney and I share a small apartment she was about to move to in Sarasota. It sounded like a good idea—sharing the rent is always a plus, and Mary was always fun to be around, so we made plans accordingly. Mary would arrive in Sarasota the day after Rodney and I.

It was the middle of the night before the baby and I finally got to the apartment. The plane had been delayed four hours in Jacksonville, but our new landlady, with what surely had to be a heart of gold, was still waiting up for us. This kind lady had borrowed a crib, a sight for sore eyes after that long flight. And that wasn't all. She had it set up with a blue (for boys, she explained) blanket, waiting for the little occupant. Who was already asleep and couldn't have cared less where he was, anyway.

It was a most appreciated welcome. Had the whole apartment house been shut up tight as a drum, no lights anywhere and no one answering the door at that time of night, **that** would not have surprised me.

Mary checked in the next day. The last time we had seen each other was the day before I left for Recife, so this was also her very first glimpse of Rodney, the beautiful baby she'd been hearing about for months. We had a lot to catch up on (slight understatement), and after several hours of trying to out-talk each other, it was a wonder we weren't hoarse.

Not one to waste time, early the next morning Mary was out looking for a job. Only in Florida—and possibly at that time only in Sarasota—could I have seen an outfit like the one she wore going out the door. Until she disappeared from sight around the corner, I just stood there, watching from the window with my mouth open. Not believing what I was looking at.

You might have guessed her occupation to be, for instance, that of an exotic dancer somewhere in the so-called "entertainment district" in town. Or, at the other extreme, a demonstrator of exercise equipment at the local gym.

None of the above. Mary wanted a 9-to-5-office job. She trotted down the street with all the confidence in the world, wearing the briefest of red-fringed white shorts, a pair of high-heeled (4-in.) silver slippers, and a skimpy, very tight, pink fuzzy sweater—the hem of which was far above the top of the equally skimpy shorts.

It was a bikini before its time. A once-in-a-lifetime sight to see, as far as I was concerned—yet oddly enough, not one passerby gave her so much as a second glance. Sarasota, in its own way, was almost as nonchalant as New Yorkers walking along a crowded sidewalk who see nothing unusual, or out of the way, in anyone else passing by.

Mary knew exactly what she was doing. I would have fully expected the eyes of anyone advertising for office help to literally glaze over at their first sight of her—but whoever hired her evidently saw beyond the outfit. Mary came home that same day with the first job she applied for—and I never underestimated my friend again.

One afternoon, while pushing baby Rodney around town in the new stroller I had rented for him, and thinking to myself how cute he looked in his white sunsuit and white sailor hat, we were stopped by a reporter from the local gazette. She spent considerable time admiring Rodney, as well as interviewing me as to where we'd come from (she didn't ask why), and what was my impression of Sarasota. Before she left, she took Rodney's picture. Both the interview and photo were published the next day, and a clipping of the article, with that picture, still resides in one of my many albums. My photogenic fifteen-month-old son was not particularly impressed, but I was. I decided it must be the Floridian way of saying "welcome," a nice thing to hear from another state.

The day after we arrived in Sarasota, I had managed to locate a divorce lawyer. With three months to officially "reside" in Florida, there was no time to lose. My new attorney's fees, however, came to quite a bit more than what I had figured on. Already my funds were shrinking, and we'd only been in town 24 hours. Time being of the essence, I was more or less a captive client. I couldn't remain in Sarasota indefinitely, shopping around for a less money-driven attorney, but at least, according to this one, my case could be heard three months to the day it was filed.

Knowing nothing about the legal system at that time, I still had my own doubts about any judge paying that much attention to the calendar on the wall, but I had no choice. I would just have to wait and see what happened.

The highlight of every single day, for Rodney and me during the week and for all three of us on weekends, was being on the beautiful sandy beach at Sarasota. It was my little son's first experience with finding himself in a body of water not completely surrounded by a bathtub. A little awed at first by the size of it all, he soon became as addicted to it as the rest of us. Teaching him to keep himself afloat was easier than I expected, but he was a most willing pupil.

Before the sun rose too high in the sky every day, we were on our way to the beach. Once again via one of Florida's famous jitneys, which in certain areas could take the place of larger buses. The jitneys were relatively small, but they got you where you wanted to go—and they were a lot cheaper than taxis.

For reasons known only to Father Neptune, the hundreds of shells cast up on the Sarasota beaches were the prettiest of all. Visitors were told that particular area was world-famous for that alone, and everybody—interested in shells or not—immediately became a collector. Fortunately for all of us, these shells were also free, so almost every day we roamed around, adding to our own collections. All of which added up to many carefree hours in the Florida sunshine. The hidden perils of too much sun were as yet undiscovered. People were totally unaware of the chances they were taking with possible skin cancer years and years ahead. "Sun blocks" did not exist in 1946. In Sarasota that summer, "ignorance" was indeed "bliss."

As the end of the prescribed three months drew near, those happy hours would be about all I had to show for the entire trip. My lawyer, not entirely to my surprise, claimed he was running into one delay after another, trying to get a court date assigned in the near future. Naturally, each successive delay entailed more time on his part—duly charged for—plus all the additional paper work. Also not free.

I finally told him to just cancel the whole thing. With barely enough money to get home again, waiting around indefinitely for a court date—which at the rate he was going could take months—would in time even eat up the plane fare.

My reasoning at that time was, everybody I knew back home was aware I was down in Florida for a divorce, and just how long it should take. Upon my return, all would naturally assume the deed was done, and that I had the divorce papers in my possession. Not even my mother would be expecting me to walk in the door, waving paper evidence in the air for all to see. Nor would anyone even think to ask if they could see something in writing. As far as the rest of the world was concerned, the next time anyone saw me, I would officially be a divorcee. In any case, I would be on my own, anyway. The chances of people—even relatives—asking for details as to what had actually happened in something as touchy as a divorce, were fairly remote.

It naturally did occur to me that sometime in the distant future I just might want to marry again—in which case all this legal turmoil would have to be gone through again. Also, judging by past experience, by that time a divorce would no doubt be even more expensive. But there was no point in even trying to think about what might, or might not happen in the future. I had more immediate problems.

It was back-to-New-Jersey time **again**. At least I had graduated from the Silver Meteor to air travel. On this trip, the baby slept every minute of every hour. At the advanced age of 18 months, Rodney—like his Mom—was now a seasoned traveler.

In New York, my first stop was the same employment agency. This time, all they had to do was update the application forms they already had. The interviewer was actually friendly, saying what they had in mind for me this time would be a far more interesting job. (They had that right.) What was waiting for me this time was a translation bureau on lower Broadway. And, like every other firm in the city, they were of course in a hurry. Another secretary/steno was needed right away—which in New Yorkese usually means yesterday.

However, the term "translation bureau" was totally new to me, so before leaving the agency's office I had a few questions. In the first place, I told them, I was not qualified to translate **any** foreign language—if that was what they were talking about—and as for taking dictation from someone speaking in a foreign language, that was equally ludicrous.

My two years of Spanish in high school were definitely my favorite course, the teacher being the handsomest male I had ever seen in my life (a combination, unbeatable at the time, of Tyrone Power and Robert Taylor), with an absolutely enchanting Spanish accent.

With God's-gift-to-women up there in front of the class, not one girl student could concentrate on anything besides this dream teacher's looks. However, each of us hoping to somehow impress him, we all studied like mad for the tests. At the time, I took it for granted that when the course was completed, I would then speak Spanish like a native. Not so. Aside from recognizing that uno-dos-tres is an interesting way of saying one-two-three, that was the extent of my linguistic skill. And job or no job, I was not going back to school for any refresher course.

After being calmed down as to the facts of life in translation bureaus, I realized that all they really wanted there was the usual secretary/steno. Who has to wing it half the time, anyway. The next step was my interview at the T-Bureau, as they liked to call themselves—and once again I was among the employed.

The office had been originally established years ago by an elderly German gentleman known as Herr Bertsche—and was still being run by him, five days a week. His Frau was, unfortunately, very much present. In the opinion of every girl in the office, this was mainly to keep an eye on her spouse. Said spouse, however, had anything but a roving eye. Frau Bertsche could just as well have stayed peacefully at home and left the rest of us all in peace.

Herr Bertsche himself was all business. If you did your job, whatever it was—actual translating, stenographic, or clerical—and you did it right, that was all he wanted of you. What mattered to him was the bottom line, i.e. his net profit for the day. Or week. Or month.

My own work there grew more interesting by the day, taking dictation from translators adept at all kinds of oddball languages. Not merely, for instance, French, German, Spanish and Italian—these were all second—nature to them and no challenge whatsoever. They translated aloud as they read whatever documents, letters or newspaper articles they'd been assigned. The accents of the translators themselves often made it a real challenge to understand what they were saying—which was **supposed to** be English—as they stared at the papers in front of them. It all too often sounded like pure Greek—but they were used to being interrupted for what amounted to a request for translation of their own way of speech.

The very concept of an office dealing only in converting all imaginable dialects and languages into English, as compared to the usual hectic business transactions of most offices, was somehow fascinating. The translators themselves, unfortunately, did not get along at all, having rather low opinions of each other's linguistic talents. At that time, all four translators were men. (According to Herr Bertsche, no females had ever even applied for the job.) Dictionaries, not only wall to wall, but literally ceiling to floor, were forever being hauled out—which may account for the fact these four men could translate every imaginable language.

On occasion, they managed to forget their own various personality differences long enough to get together and figure out dialects none of them had ever seen before. At such times, these translators were all, and justifiably, very pleased with themselves. One particular translator who happened to be familiar with certain Scandinavian dialects—which the office was seldom asked to translate, anyway—was forever hinting he should be paid more than the others. The boss, however, had other ideas—and his own unique talent.

Whenever current salaries were ever so casually mentioned, Herr Bertsche would appear to be going into some kind of trance—and from this vantage point he could, of course, hear nothing. Not until the subject was changed, that is.

Raises were a very delicate subject, anyway. If a certain sum had been promised as an inducement for coming to work there, for instance, only when the so-called probation period was over would that money be handed out. And, only after reminding Frau Bertsche, who unfortunately was in charge of all things financial, over and over again. To Frau Bertsche, handing out a larger check than usual, no matter what the reason, seemed to be physically painful. Each time, she would appear to be on the verge of tears—and one was doubtless mean to feel a little guilty. No one did, of course, it was bad enough having to wait.

As it happened, this same office-hausfrau knew both German and French very well—definitely as well as her husband—but Frau Bertsche herself took no part in the translating end of the business. Instead, every minute of every day was spent overseeing the office paperwork. It was her firm belief that everyone in the office—and particularly the four secretary/stenos—should, in order to earn their salaries, work at top speed at all times. As she herself actually did.

Should any desk be occasionally clear of work a little too early in the afternoon, she would become extremely distraught, create something out of thin air, and then insist it be done immediately. Consequently, whenever there came an unavoidable lull, in pure self-defense we learned to prop up our empty notebooks in front of us and simply type away at whatever came to mind—personal letters, shopping lists, or even favorite recipes for our friends. (Meanwhile staring at our notebooks as if shorthand notes actually existed.)

Sharp though this woman was, she never once caught on. All new employees were initiated their very first day (as was I) into this most shameful, but necessary, subterfuge.

Had our boss, whom we actually liked, ever suddenly announced Frau Bertsche would be taking a leave of absence (presumably to prove the office would fall apart without her), resisting the impulse to stand up and cheer en masse would have been almost impossible. I say "almost" since naturally we all wanted to keep our jobs, but it would have been a wonderful day nonetheless. (Herr Bertsche's own cheers, though silent, would have been equally fervent.)

My social life at that time consisted of occasional dates, but for some reason not one of them had appealed to me. The war was indeed over, and whether or not a prospective date had himself been a part of the conflict was no longer that important—and yet when one would call for a second date, I usually made an excuse not to go. I wasn't intentionally putting my life on hold, although it probably looked that way to a lot of people. It was just the way it was.

Baby Rodney at that time was, needless to say, a lifesaver. I counted the hours until I could get home to him, and begrudged every minute I was late. On those rare occasions when Mrs. Tucker was ill, or had some matter to take care of outside her home for a few hours, my sister, who worked for a large insurance company in Newark, always managed to take time off from work to stay with Rodney. She said all she needed was an excuse—and her little nephew was her favorite excuse.

Bessie also told me one time that her own children, if she ever had any, could never mean any more to her than Rodney did. Which was certainly a very generous thing to say, and I know she meant every word of it. (A few years later, however, when my sister finally did have her own two children, needless to say **they** came first.)

One Sunday morning, when Rodney was three and a half years old, we had a surprise visitor. This particular visitor, from that never-to-be-forgotten moment, changed the rest of my life.

I say "surprise" visitor because we hadn't seen each other since we were children. When he was twelve and I was ten-and-a-half, our families lived in the same apartment house in East Orange. He and I were part of the same neighborhood group, which group consisted of all boys—except me. I was a confirmed tomboy, and boys were more fun—but we hadn't seen each other since way back then.

Our mothers, even after both families had moved to other towns, had been best friends ever since. They had always made it a point through the years to keep us updated on each other.

As I came through the dining room toward the kitchen, not knowing we had company, I was wearing my favorite red midriff-style P.J.'s. (This outfit, shocking and scant as it was for those times, I was to hear about most appreciatively many times later on.) Mom was standing with a young man—whom I did not recognize—in the doorway leading to the kitchen.

They were both smiling broadly at me (to this day, I can see them there), and my mother said, "Mildred, do you know who this is?"

I said "No," but when Mom said, "This is Foster," I knew him instantly. Of course he looked different, and naturally a little older—and yet in a way exactly the same. I had never really expected our paths to cross again, even though our mothers were so close. It was wonderful to see him—and for a few seconds I think we both somehow felt like the little kids we used to be.

My mother, for all I knew, had vanished into thin air. Foster and I went into the living room, sat down on the couch, and spent the next few hours catching up on everything that happened in both our lives—or at least since the last time we played baseball on the lot across the street.

Foster kept admiring Rodney, who had been running in and out of the room, and before he finally left, asked if he could take us both out for a picnic the following Saturday at a nearby lake.

The way I answered had to be one of the stupidest things I have ever done—and to this day, I can't imagine why I ever did it that way. I very flippantly replied, "Well, I'll have to check my calendar."

Totally unfazed, Foster simply said, "Okay, I'll call you tonight." He was no sooner out the door, when I was absolutely furious with myself. Also on pins and needles as to whether he'd call at all. I need not have worried.

Promptly at 5 o'clock (he'd left at 3), the phone rang. It was Foster, asking if I'd checked my calendar. I told him Saturday looked great. Fortunately for me, he had taken it for granted I was just being facetious, and we talked on the phone for another two hours.

Foster's stopping by that Sunday morning had been his mother's idea. Strangely enough, she had told him she'd like to borrow some knitting needles from my mother. Neither Foster's mother nor mine had ever been known to knit. Together, they couldn't have identified a knitting needle if they tripped over one. So, it had to be a most devious plot, just to get the two of us together again. Which it was. And it worked.

ANOTHER enormous turn-around in my life—but this time a very happy one. Starting that Sunday, we saw each other every day, and I came to realize Foster wasn't quite the carefree soul we'd both been as not-quite-teenagers. He had also gone through the usual horrendous growing-up process, but, being a product of the most unique wartime period in history, he was also a veteran.

Originally, as a potential draftee, he'd been turned down for service because of nearsightedness—a type of vision problem which at that time was enough for Uncle Sam to pass him by. The first time they checked him out, that is. A few days later, deciding that nearsighted or not, he wanted to go where the action was, Foster went back to enlist. This time , it was a brand-new ball game. All tests were passed—no problem whatsoever. A walk-through, in his words.

Enlistees were viewed with considerably more tolerance—it not actual enthusiasm—than those still waiting to be drafted, trusting to luck their particular numbers would somehow be lost in the shuffle. The latter, understandably, just might have had a few other ideas about their own future careers.

Foster's father, Elemer, had been born in Budapest. To the day his father died, when Foster was still in the service, Elemer (pronounced "Elmeer" for reasons known only to Hungarians) had the most charming Hungarian accent I have ever heard. Elemer could only, for example, pronounce his son's name as "Fahsta"—although however he said it, it was more than enough for said son to jump up and ask "What is it, Pop?" But "Elmeer" was an absolute charmer. Compared to him, Zsa-Zsa sounds almost British.

Foster's mother Ella, on the other hand, was the exact opposite, although she certainly had her own brand of charm. Coming from New

England, and having been strictly raised in a fairly wealthy Old-Bostonian family, she was the gentlest, and politest, of persons. For Ella's generation, a "tour of the Continent" was almost mandatory. If a Bostonian family of any social standing were to send an "of-age" daughter anywhere, they sent her to Europe—and it was in Paris that Ella and Elemer met and, apparently, instantly fell in love.

The fact that they spoke two entirely different native languages at the time—his was Hungarian, hers was English—was no deterrent. Each could speak fairly fluent French, and the romance was carried on sans-souci en francais.

When Foster and I first started going together, no future bride could have had more of a private cheering section than I had in Ella. You would never have guessed I was just a future in-law, not her real daughter. Ella backed me to the hilt, every time, in whatever I did, and whatever I said. She was fond of telling me how pretty I was, how smart, and how lucky her son was. **And** what a good cook I was.

This last was a result of both families having just consumed an especially delicious dinner one night. It had been cooked as usual by my mother—the cook-of-all-time—who, before going into the kitchen, had absolutely insisted I pass it off as my own.

Although very relieved I didn't have to suddenly learn how to cook, I was a little apprehensive. What worried me was, Ella could very well come up with some embarrassing questions—and whatever they were, regarding how I had made this or that, I could hardly look over at my mother and say, "How did I do that, Mom?"

I would definitely be stuck for an answer. At that time, I did not have the remotest idea, nor did I really care, how Mom was putting meals together. Fortunately for all concerned, Ella asked no questions. To this day, I suspect she somehow knew very well what was going on.

Monday, the day after our Sunday "reunion," Foster started meeting my train at night and then dropping me off at the apartment. A few hours after that, we would be on the phone again. He was also at the apartment as much as possible.

That apartment house had four stories, and was a walk-up. Which was actually fortunate. An elevator in those days would have at least doubled the $40 rent. (What the rent would be today for that particular apartment, I couldn't even guess. I do know it remained at $40 until we eventually moved out—but somewhere along the way, our absentee landlord had mailed out notices to each individual tenant, requesting him or her to agree to an increase, and then to sign and return the enclosed permission slip. The increase asked for was TWO dollars per month. All tenants said NO, and the rent remained at $40.)

The entire four-story staircase—as well as whoever was down there, winding his way up—could be seen from each floor by anyone looking up or down. One evening, Foster having rung the bell downstairs, I had pushed the buzzer unlocking the door at the lobby, and he was on his way up. I had been watching him from our third-floor landing and, just as he was making the last turn, he looked up and saw me.

The building was absolutely silent, yet I could have sworn I heard a voice saying, This is Forever. It was such a strange experience I couldn't get it out of my mind—but it was a long time before I finally told Foster about it. He listened very intently, and then he told me something I never forgot. The instant our eyes had met across the room on that never-to-be-forgotten Sunday, he had heard the same Voice.

The day following our first picnic at the lake, Foster had no trouble convincing me of something. That the sooner I filed again for a divorce from Jimmy, the better. (This, of course, was long before we were being looked upon as just one more couple by both friends and family.) The attorney for whom I had worked a short time in the next town suggested an attorney friend of his. This man did agree to take the case, but it was only thanks to my former employer that he would even consider it. He made it abundantly clear from the start that he was averse to handling divorces at all. At that time, this was a more or less common attitude of the legal field. Divorces were not yet the run-of-the-mill cases they are today, and many lawyers had yet to take on their first.

As this new legal eagle phrased it, the "separation of families" was most distasteful to him, and he much preferred standard litigation cases. During most of our subsequent conversations, he did manage to conceal this better-than-thou attitude fairly well. Obviously, he was not above pocketing yet another fee. I was to find out in time, however, that in his practice, divorce hearings—being the least profitable—were usually the first to be postponed. After my Sarasota experience, this was all too familiar.

My new attorney's first name was Harry, commonly referred to in legal circles as "Sue-'em-till-they-drop" Harry—a nickname of which he was proudly aware. In divorce cases, this tendency to send his clients to the poorhouse could not be indulged, as a rule, except when trying to push through some particularly obnoxious property settlement.

Consequently, divorce clients were kept on the back burner as far as a firm hearing date was concerned, until there was nothing more profitable to take up this attorney's time in court.

In the meantime, what Foster persisted in referring to as his "courtship" (a term, as I told him, not heard since the days of King Arthur) continued. It was September, but addicted as we were to being outdoors every minute of every day on weekends, the Fall season was still picnic-time as far as we were concerned. But it did grow chillier and chillier, much as we tried to ignore it. Each time we packed up and took Rodney to one of the lakeside picnic areas, there were fewer and fewer people around. One Saturday in late October, it actually snowed. A real storm, not just a few flakes, and even we, the die-hards, were convinced summer was really over.

From then on, sleds and ice skates—plus more and more sweaters—were the way to go. Wherever we wound up for the day, Foster devoted a great deal of time and attention to Rodney. The three of us always had a good time, anyway, so whatever the weather decided to do really didn't make much difference. (A favorite saying of my grandmother Nannie who, after leaving England as a child, had lived all her life in New Jersey, always came back to me. It was "If you don't like the weather, wait ten minutes." Truer words were never spoken in the Garden State.)

Foster's older sister Josie was married to a college professor in upstate New York, and she was as anxious to see the two of us at the altar as we were to get there. Josie was becoming one of my best friends, although I had known her only briefly back in the days when her younger brother was one of my favorite playmates.

My own sister was equally in favor of our getting married, as soon as it was legally possible. I was more than a little upset, however, when I found she had told a friend that she would feel really strange attending what would be her younger sister's second wedding when she herself had yet to have her first. Fortunately, there were better days ahead for Bessie than anyone would have guessed at the time.

Finally, one day late in June, in a Newark courtroom, my divorce case was called. The courts there would be closing down for the summer as of July 1, so my own case was among the last to be heard. Even then, the decree would not be final until October. No thanks to my "sue-'em-till-they-drop" attorney, I just about got under the wire.

(My best friend Jeanne was my one and only witness. Jeanne had married while still in Panama, three days before I went through that same ceremony—though under far different circumstances—with Jimmy in New York. One more strange coincidence to add to the many she and I already had. After the war ended, Jeanne and her new husband Dick moved back to Dick's hometown in Ramsey, in northern New Jersey. She and I had kept in touch ever since.)

Details of that divorce hearing even at the time were somewhat of a blur to me. More likely, there was just nothing that happened that day in court that I really want to remember. I did get up and testify, as briefly as possible, although occasionally the Judge himself asked for more details. Jeanne followed me into the witness chair, answered all questions put to her—and suddenly it was all over. His Honor had only two words to say: "Divorce granted."

In a way, it was both a bad moment and a good. The bad part was, I couldn't help thinking of the long-ago Jimmy, even though for us a life together was never meant to be. Jimmy would always be Rodney's father, and I wished him well in whatever he did. The good part was, I was suddenly on the threshold of a brand-new life. Sometime that October, three short months away, Foster, the man I had grown to love with all my heart, would finally hear me say, "I do."

A few weeks before our wedding date, something rather belatedly occurred to me. No formal words of proposal had ever crossed the lips of the now happy groom-to-be. It was a Saturday night, and we were driving home from Jeanne and Dick's. Without stopping to realize this was hardly the ideal time for such an unromantic complaint, I said, "Foster, you know you never did actually propose to me."

Trying to conceal the biggest smile you ever saw, he very patiently explained that for him to get down on one knee, ask for my hand in marriage, and continue to drive at the same time could very well result in our crashing into the next building.

At this point, the ridiculousness of it all suddenly hit us both, and we started laughing. Foster pulled over into a park we were passing at the time and stopped—and by then we were almost hysterical. However, foregoing the kneeling position, Foster did formally propose, just to keep the record clear. And his future bride happy. And off his back. Needless to say, I had no objection. All in all, it had been a most interesting evening.

Only a few weeks before Foster came back into my life and turned it around (since I had no crystal ball at the time I had foreseen no such thing), Mom and Bessie and I had decided to take the "Big Plunge." To buy a house. We were all more than a little weary of the East Orange apartment we had shared since I was halfway through high school. In the nearby small town of Cedar Grove, a tract house then under construction was available, attractive and—most important—within our joint budget. Having contracted to move into the house sometime in August, we were all looking forward to what could only be a tremendous change in our way of life. So, the dye was already cast. Fortunately, Foster was as impressed with the new house as we were, along with the idea of living there after we were married. Two months before the wedding, the day finally arrived for Mom, Bessie and me to move out of the apartment. Foster took off from work that morning to help out, which was just as well. The rest of us were so excited we were continually in the way of the moving men, and things were almost at a standstill. Foster finally suggested we drive on over to the house and wait there for the van, leaving him to supervise in peace. Compared to the third-floor apartment we had just left, the house itself would be all OURS. No unknown neighbors literally inches away on the other side of the wall. The second floor was what was known as an "expansion attic," meaning the empty space up there could be eventually finished off as two separate rooms. One of the rooms had already been finished as my bedroom, which would also contain Rodney's crib. The other room-space was still empty, but would in time be made into a sitting room. Two windows had been installed in my room, as well as in the "future" room.

The original total price of the house, sans improvements, today would not even amount to a down payment. It was $9,900. Added to that was the cost of one room upstairs being finished, plus a one-car garage for Mom's car, as well as a small back porch—for a total price of $11,400. At that point in history, $11,400 was par for the course. These days, one would naturally assume—and be correct—that at least one "zero" had been inadvertently left out.

No matter how low the original cost, houses then were extremely well built. All materials used were top-grade, as was the workmanship.

And there was such a shortage of jobs in construction, they were almost fought over. Consequently, men lucky enough to be working at all made a point of being extremely good at whatever they did. Any house they put up could have been rated a "model"—and the day we moved in, this particular house was our idea of a palace.

Now that I had a "real" proposal under my belt, we were literally marking off days on the calendar. The wedding date of October 22nd (at that time known only to the two of us) was drawing closer and closer. Foster decided it was high time for him to officially advise my mother we were engaged. Everyone had assumed she was taking it for granted, but one never knew. At that time, Foster was still living with his widowed mother Ella in her Montclair apartment. Mom, Bessie, Rodney and I had moved into the new house, and Foster and I had gotten into the habit of taking my mother out to dinner somewhere every Friday night. One Friday, the three of us were in the midst of dinner at one of Mom's favorite restaurants. In collusion with my sister, who agreed with me that the fewer people present when Foster made this particular announcement the better, Bessie had taken Rodney over to a local amusement park as a special treat. Foster looked across the table at my mother and said, "Mom, Millie and I are getting married in October." My mother slowly put down her fork, her appetite having apparently just gone out the window. She looked over at us, and what she then said went into family history eventually as more or less of a joke, but it wasn't funny then. Her sole comment was, "I suppose you'll have a baby right away."

No congratulations, sincere or otherwise. Not so much as a hint of "I'm so happy for you, you've both waited so long for this," etc. Just a baby prediction.

With all my mother's solid-gold qualities in many areas, no one ever looked to her for anything resembling TACT. But that was Mom, and I don't think either Foster or I were all that surprised.

The morning of the wedding, which was set for 2 p.m. in an East Orange church, I was upstairs getting dressed. Or at least I thought I was. For some reason, concentrating on almost anything for the past couple of hours had been almost impossible.

My mother, who was justly famous for her sewing (knitting was still only for **other** people), had made a beautiful blue velvet, cocktail-length dress for me.

Frances, one of my friends at the T-Bureau where I was still working, had created a matching Juliet-style cap. (One week later, Frances officially opened her very own hat shop, having first practiced on me as the first live model. Frances, almost in a class with my Mom where sewing was concerned, had been dreaming for the past two years about opening a shop exclusively for hats.) So, as far as wedding apparel was concerned, I was all set—but I was still walking around in my underwear.

To me, it sounded like half the town was milling around in the living room. Complaints were getting louder and louder down there as to why it was taking the bride-to-be so long to dress—and I couldn't understand it, either.

Finally, my sister came up to see what was going on. According to her subsequent report to the waiting guests, I was still running around and had accomplished exactly nothing since the last time she came up. All the wedding finery was still draped over the bed. My suitcases were still open, waiting for the final items to be packed. Whenever Bessie spoke to me, and whatever she said, all she got back were a few more blank looks.

Confused though I apparently was, I still remember congratulating myself that I was really very calm, that everything was under control— yet wondering about all the commotion downstairs. Bessie took one look at me, and started to laugh. As she picked up my beautiful velvet dress and the little Juliet cap, still waiting there to be put on, she was still laughing.

When I was finally all put together, the best sister in the world gave me a big hug, wished me happiness—and pointed toward the stairs. My cousin Don then escorted me outside to the limousine he had rented for the occasion, and drove me, Rodney, Mom, and Bessie—and everybody else who could fit into the car—over to the church. It was a comparatively short distance, and there were only a few short minutes to think back on all that had happened during the past thirteen months.

All I could see was Foster, standing there in the doorway that long-ago Sunday morning, looking over at me with the happiest smile in the world. From that day to this, the day of our wedding, he had told me many, many times that particular moment was the **real** beginning of his own life. Here at the altar, hand in hand, Foster and I were promising to love and cherish each other—not just for now, but till the end of time.

As to the many reasons why the world-famous resort town of Atlantic City, New Jersey evolved almost overnight into the most popular honeymoon hideaway in the country, my brand-new husband Foster and I could have happily testified.

Our hotel was the Madison, which, besides being only a block away from the beach, had everything else going for it as well. For instance, their leave-'em alone policy was justly famous, and strict rules were followed by the staff when guests were known to be honeymooners. All housemaids who valued their jobs knew better than to knock on the door of the average bridal couple at what probably felt like the crack of dawn to them—no matter what time it was.

Only with the hotel itself burning to the ground would these most considerate maids consider using their master keys. One and all would literally check beforehand at the desk to see which rooms were now safe to enter. What more could one ask? It was no coincidence that maids consistently collected their best tips from honeymooners.

Hotel meals were another joy, not to mention the prices. Cocktails were 50 cents. Just reading the menu would make your mouth water—and when a full-course delicious dinner carried a tab of only $3.00, you knew you had made it to heaven's private dining room. In the unlikely event you were hungry again in a few hours, breakfast the next morning was 65 cents. Unless you chose to splurge on a **super**-breakfast, in which case same probably consisted of nine varieties of steak served on golden plates—for $1.50.

As for the beach at Atlantic City, the word "irresistible" puts it mildly—not only for honeymooners, but also those fleeing the overcast areas of the rest of New Jersey. While the Garden State has a great many elements in its favor, climate is not one of them. With the noted exception, that is, of Atlantic City. This world-famous resort town has a special dispensation where sunshine is concerned. No clouds held back the sun for very long, and when the sun did get through, it aimed right at the beach. We always had the impression we were gazing out at the Atlantic Ocean from the Florida coastline, not that of New Jersey.

Having originally been childhood playmates, Foster and I naturally thought we knew each other, yet, even after a year of going together, we still didn't. It took Atlantic City to do that. Foster was everything I could have asked for—and I was happier there with him than I had ever been in my life. A honeymoon is the getting-acquainted period of all time, and the very fact that on many subsequent anniversaries, we automatically went back to Atlantic City—**and** the Madison—was, in a way, a thank you for a wonderful honeymoon.

Back once more in Cedar Grove, the new house was now occupied by five—my mother, my sister, four-and-a-half-year-old Rodney, and the Bridal Couple of the year. Foster and I had the one upstairs bedroom. Eventually converting the rest of the space up there into a sitting room would depend on our future finances. In the meantime, Rodney had his own private room over there.

As far as the rest of the world was concerned, Foster and I were now just one more Mr. & Mrs. No longer the center of the universe, the way they made us feel on our wedding day, when everyone was cheering like mad and showering us with confetti. We were the stars of the show then, and loved every minute of it. But this was **now**—and sure enough, there we were back in the real world.

Although our friends and relatives sometimes acted as if we'd never been away, Rodney seemed very glad to have us both back. He now had a brand-new babysitter—thanks once again to my sister. Bessie had found a Mrs. Perelli for me on the very next street before we even moved into the Cedar Grove house.

Mrs. Perelli was a wonderful woman who, being Italian, naturally loved everybody's children. In return, all children instantly felt at home, and safe, with her. She gave Rodney a big hug every morning, and another, just as heartfelt, when I picked him up at night.

Before walking up the street every morning to wait for a bus, I would bring Rodney over to Mrs. Perelli for the day. That particular bus was only the first in a series of transfers involved in reaching downtown New York City, where I worked. You had to start out early to commute from New Jersey, in case you missed any of the connections. When you finally got to your job over there, half the day seemed to be gone.

From Cedar Grove, the bus brought one to the Montclair train station, where the train then headed for its Hudson River terminal. Next came the "tube" (under-the-river subway), which brought you into New York. At that point, I could either walk downtown to the office or take the subway.

Subways in that long-ago era were almost a pleasure. They were fast, they were frequent, and they were cheap (a **nickel** took you **anywhere**)—and even more significant, they were relatively safe. Women did hold onto their purses, and men did check their wallets from time to time, but you could read a newspaper in peace, or even doze off. The days of sitting there speculating on the odds of winding up on tomorrow's "Subway Killings of the Day" list were yet to come.

On those rare occasions when I made the right connections and could walk the rest of the way to the office, I usually spent it wondering if some miracle would ever happen so I could quit my job at the translation bureau—even though it was a job I really liked from my very first day there—to stay home with my little boy. Foster was well aware of how I felt, but for the time being we both knew it was out of the question.

Foster himself, from the day as a teenager he wound up with the first two jobs he applied for, had always held down two jobs at a time. My husband's philosophy always was, he could live one day at a time and let the next day take care of itself—OR, he could get out there and work toward something. In his opinion, only Plan 2 gave any hope of any kind of a future.

Foster's daytime job at the time was with the Public Service, a utility corporation in New Jersey. His second "job" was going to a Diesel school at night, the reason being a Government check for $120. which came in the mail each month as long as Foster showed up for four hours every evening, five days a week.

One hundred and twenty extra dollars in those days bought a LOT of groceries. When the very first $120 check showed up, being suddenly wealthy beyond our wildest dreams, we immediately threw an impromptu party for several friends, where a good time was had by one and all.

The next day was a sad awakening. We realized how many really necessary items some of that money could have gone for, and from then on, that particular check was all but sacred. Never again was any-thing as frivolous as a party even thought of—not if **that** check had to be dipped into.

However, with no signs of Diesel-related work coming his way in the near future, Foster had to find his next after-hours job elsewhere—this time at a local mercantile plant, ten minutes away from the house.

Unfortunately, one evening I had no choice but to call him there. We had an emergency. There was a mouse in the oven.

As soon as Foster's fellow workers heard about what to me was a major crisis (few women appreciate a mouse running around inside their oven), they almost laughed themselves sick. A few minutes later, they were shoving Foster out the door to rush home to the rescue. Their unanimous suggestion, given with the best of intentions, was "Just tell your wife to turn on the oven."

Having no desire whatsoever for baked mouse, as soon as Foster came in the front door, I went out the back. I therefore have no way of knowing how he dealt with the problem. Nor do I really want to know. When I finally came back in, propped up somewhat by the sympathy of my neighbors, Foster was out of there—and so was the mouse.

Two months after the wedding we celebrated our first Christmas together as Mr. & Mrs. With no fireplace in the living room, the traditional mantel for Christmas stockings was also absent. However, Rodney, being assured Santa could find anything anywhere, decided to hang his up by the staircase. His greatest worry was, whether Santa would remember to bring him all the toys he had asked for while sitting on Santa's lap. Young as he was, he had noticed the hordes of other children there, likewise reeling off lists to Santa.

We finally persuaded him that the sooner he got to bed and fell asleep, the sooner Santa could arrive. By morning, we'd ALL know what Santa had brought him. Not entirely convinced, Rodney reluctantly went to bed. His own bedroom was now on the first floor, across from the room my mother and sister shared. The one and only window in Rodney's room looked out into the back yard.

As soon as it was dark, "Santa" was out there—Santa being, of course, Foster. Complete with "Santa" costume to look like the real thing, he was right under Rodney's window, ringing an assortment of REALLY loud bells. The entire neighborhood must have heard them. Every small child already asleep no doubt jumped out of bed in a panic. All of them—including Rodney, the innocent cause of all this commotion—KNEW immediately it could only be Santa.

Not one neighbor phoned to find out what was going on. There was no way they couldn't have heard all this racket, yet not a soul ventured outside to investigate. Apparently, not only every child but every ADULT in the neighborhood still believed in Santa Claus

Christmas Day, the house was swarming with relatives, with Rodney's newest toys now wall-to-wall. Suddenly I didn't see him anywhere. He was only four-and-a-half, so I immediately panicked, thinking he might have quietly slipped out the door.

An all-points-bulletin had the family running in and out of every door, calling his name over and over. Rodney was nowhere outside.

He was upstairs, all by himself, perfectly safe and having a ball. In that still-unfinished spare room were stored several large empty boxes, but for once they were being put to good use. Rodney had stacked them all into piles, and was happily crawling in and out, obviously enjoying himself. And all it took was a bunch of big empty boxes. So much for brand-new, carefully-wrapped toys under the Christmas tree.

The first really big marital decision we made shortly after becoming husband and wife—and, presumably, future parents—was to wait a couple of years before bringing a baby into the world. We already had Rodney (a plus), but neither one of us was as yet making much money (obviously a minus), so it seemed like the practical way to go.

That wise decision lasted a about a month until we suddenly decided we really would like a little brother or sister for Rodney—whereupon common sense flew out the window. ("Never to return," my mother would have commented.) Mother Nature, however, had other ideas. Or possibly more common sense. Whatever the reason, here we had made the Big Decision—and nothing was happening. For many, many months, there were no signs of a Junior—or Junior Miss—on the way.

Three months before our first anniversary, Bessie apparently decided to "catch up" with her younger sister and also walk down the aisle. She and her new husband-to-be had met some time ago at the supper club where she worked part-time as hostess. (Bessie's full-time job was with a major insurance company in Newark.)

Our own wedding reception and dinner had been held at that same supper club. Partly, of course, because it was the most popular place around for that type of affair, but mostly because Bessie, as a part-time employee, could get substantial discounts. Where else would the charge per guest have been $5 for a complete dinner?

To add to the blissfulness of that occasion, champagne was lavishly supplied almost at cost. ("Cost" in those days almost translates to today's "freebie".) So, menu-wise and otherwise, guests were well taken care of.

Predictably, Mom was anything but pleased to see her only other daughter now at the altar—which had nothing to do with Bill, her new son-in-law, whom everybody already liked. Including Mom. What distressed her was the marriage itself, and my mother had made no attempt to disguise her objections to it. However, Bessie, for once in her life—a life devoted to putting everyone else's interests before her own—**finally** thought first of her own welfare. Up until then, she'd had very little of the kind of life she must have wanted all along.

To anyone in the family, my mother's long-cherished plans for coping with her eventual old age were no secret. Uppermost was the strong hope that neither Bessie nor I would ever marry, that we would both be content to remain with her forever—in which case, of course, she would never have to face the trauma of living alone in her so-called golden years.

Having seen the writing on the wall some time ago as far as I was concerned, Mom had written **me** off as a lifetime companion. She continued to take it for granted, however, that my sister would always be there for her.

Now, with Bessie's wedding day suddenly the focus of everyone's attention, my mother's fondest hopes and plans were null and void. She most definitely was not a happy woman. Unfortunately, aside from the fact the rest of us would always continue to care for her, there was nothing we could do.

Nine months later, almost to the day, Bessie and Bill's first baby, Amylou, was born. I think my sister must have been waiting all her life for that moment—never before had I seen her so happy. At forty years of age, said she, there was no time to waste.

After one year and five months, there were still no signs of our hoped-for heir or heiress joining the family. It was March of 1951. After many a discussion, we finally came to a decision. Budget or no budget—although we'd each had raises in the past year and a half—that baby just might never happen if I didn't quit my job then and there to stay home.

For some reason—possibly a trait of our particular generation—we both seemed to associate "staying home" with having babies. With only one salary to keep us going, we were well aware finances would be extremely tight—and yet it just didn't seem like all that much of a sacrifice.

Also, when and if we did have a baby, the two of us could certainly take care of him or her, along with Big Brother Rodney, without any outside help, or babysitters. And, once we'd shown the world we could do just that, we'd go ahead and have all the babies we wanted.

While we were no doubt living in a dream world back then, luck must have been on our side after all, since eventually, through the years, that was pretty much the way things worked out.

Our neighbors on both sides in Cedar Grove had so far been fairly friendly, although with everyone in our own house at work five days a week, we hadn't seen all that much of each other. **Except** for that one time when my mother, who was having a few days vacation, was home looking after Rodney. The neighboring couple—who had one small girl, Wendy, not yet in school—were also home. Rodney and Wendy—both under five—were out playing together somewhere in the neighborhood. After a while, neither was anywhere in sight—and no one my mother called had seen them.

One neighbor finally called back and told my mother not to worry. Both children had taken over a picnic table in her own back yard and were busily setting out paper plates, plastic knives and forks, and in general having a glorious time out there, pretending all kinds of social functions were going on.

Mom casually mentioned all this to the man next door. According to my mother, he immediately took off like a madman, leaping over every fence in sight, to get to where the children were innocently deciding who to invite to their "party."

The next thing that happened had my mother almost speechless. This so-concerned father was at our front door, all but foaming at the mouth—and he had Rodney by the hand.

"What is this child doing?" he roared, "playing with MY daughter in someone's back yard, all alone, nobody else around—WHAT is going on?"

Naturally, Mom thought he must have lost his mind, but she tried politely to calm him down—assuming, from what she'd already heard around the neighborhood, that he was just a very excitable type whom no one took really seriously, anyway. They just stayed away from him.

Everything Mom said to this man was falling on deaf ears, so at that point she took Rodney by the hand and was about to bring him inside. It was then that man made a big mistake. To MY mother—about HER grandson—he made a threat, i.e. "If I ever see this kid around my Wendy again, I won't be responsible for what happens!"

This man was well over six feet—my mother was five-four. Stepping over to where she was no more than three inches away from him, she glared up into his face and said "You lay ONE finger on this child and that will be the last thing YOU remember!"

Mom said afterwards it was like watching a balloon deflate before her eyes. The man actually gulped, and then backed away, never taking his eyes off her face. My mother might have been ten inches shorter, but he knew he'd met his match.

So much for neighborhood politics. The rest of the neighbors couldn't have been nicer. We just happened to live next door to the Neighborhood Nut.

Just before I actually did quit work to stay home, there was an idea I had been toying with for some time, and this one was a little less complicated. It involved going over to the local pound someday and looking for a puppy to adopt.

The more I had seen of several puppies in our neighborhood, the more I was convinced a puppy we should have. And I especially liked the idea of rescuing one from the pound. From all I'd heard, the expensive pedigreed dogs available at pet shops had nothing to worry about—they were certain to be adopted sooner or later, either by people with deep pockets or those who actually looked down their noses at strays. Either way, pedigreed pups could look forward to a life of doggie luxury. On the other hand, futures for "stray" or abandoned puppies at the pound were non-existent. So, the pound was where I wanted to go.

All votes were "Aye" in favor of a puppy—except Mom's, to whom any and all pets were just in the way. Rodney's "Aye" vote drowned out everybody else's, anyway.

So, one Saturday morning, my sister and I took a trip out to the pound, and the minute I saw how many forlorn little animals were looking out from all those cages, I of course wanted to take them ALL home. I should have known that visiting any place where animals were confined was, for me, not a wise move.

However, all it took for one especially adorable, VERY-mixed breed was one look at me. Recognizing a pushover when he saw one, he instantly elected himself my new puppy. No argument from me.

On the way home with the newest family member, Bessie suggested that we name the puppy "Bozo." She had suddenly remembered that Foster, as a child, had had a dog by that name. My husband still talked about Bozo and **only** Bozo whenever anybody brought up the subject of pets. When we walked in the door with the puppy, who was introduced all round as the new "Bozo," Foster's face lit up immediately. (Mom sighed a little, but made no comment.)

From that day forward, as far as Foster was concerned, Bozo could do no wrong. In the very beginning, Foster came up with the perfect solution to the puppy's nightly battle with insomnia. He wrapped up an old, loudly-ticking clock in a towel, put it next to Bozo's ear in the dog bed at night, and from then on, Bozo slept like a baby—as could everybody else in the house.

(Some time later, a little old lady down the street told Foster that a puppy, put next to a clock he couldn't see but could hear ticking away, would assume he was still next to Mama Dog. Whatever the reason, it worked.)

In August, 1951, my doctor at long last informed me I was really pregnant—and even Dr. Irwin, knowing we'd been hopeful one day and disappointed the next SO many times, was smiling. Now we could start counting the days. As soon as they heard the news, both Mom and Foster's mother came up with long lists of potential names for the baby. Unknown to them at the time, we had already selected our own. For a boy, it would be "Michael"—for a girl, "Michele."

As it happened, neither of the grandmas-to-be had included either of the winning names on her own list. So, no jealousy reared its ugly head—if anything, they consoled each other. They would both be "in-laws" now, anyway, not merely best friends.

A few months later, Dr. Irwin's prediction was for a boy, so we could assume "Michael" was on the way. He did, however, say "I **could** be wrong," a statement not often heard in public from the medical profession. With the magical days of ultra-sound yet to come, the Doctor was basing his prophecy on the baby's heartbeat. He advised me the heartbeat rate of boys was noticeably slower than that of girls, (the latter being, understandably, somewhat nervous and apprehensive about entering a male-oriented world). I told him I would be happy with either boy or girl—which he remarked was just as well, since the matter had been decided many months ago.

The baby was due on April 27, however, he/she had other ideas, and obviously babies have the last word. This particular infant decided to be a little early. On April 25, shortly before Foster arrived home from work, I had the distinct impression there was no time to waste. Not one minute. The message coming through to me was get-me-to-the-hospital FAST. The understatement of the year would have been, I was more than ready.

Foster finally walked in the door that evening, all set to collapse on the couch as usual. He never made it. Propelled by his loving but frantic wife, within seconds he found himself turned around and out the door again, headed for the car.

We set off for the hospital, which was about twenty minutes away in Montclair. Knowing Foster, I fully expected him, under the circumstances, to break all records for speed. To my amazement, he not only drove slowly, but also appeared to be very, very calm. (An absolute put-on, as I was to learn a few minutes later.)

Everything, he kept assuring me, was under control. We had plenty of time, there was nothing to worry about, don't worry, etc. etc. He was actually no calmer than I was, and probably had no idea what he was saying.

Once inside the lobby, I was immediately escorted to the elevator. Foster watched me out of sight, and then went to the desk to sign me in. The nurse waiting with the usual inescapable paperwork asked for his name. Foster had no trouble with that one. Then she asked him the really hard question. "And what is your wife's name?" she asked, naturally assuming that since he knew his, he would also know mine.

She was wrong. Foster just stood there looking at her—and said **nothing**. (As a later so-called explanation, he said the shock of finding himself in a hospital lobby only a few minutes after arriving home, then watching me disappear out of sight, **then** thinking his baby could be born any second—was too much. He literally could not think of my name.)

The nurse, trying to keep a straight face, but still waiting to find out if I had a name, suggested he go through his wallet—my name was probably in there somewhere.

Incredible as it still seems to me, taking out his wallet and thumbing through card after card after card was actually what Foster had to do to locate my name—and sure enough, there it was.

In family anecdotes, this was neither my husband's favorite nor mine. We both looked bad—I because in all the time we'd been married, I apparently hadn't made that much impression on him—and Foster because most husbands, if they can recall nothing else, are at least familiar with their wives' names.

(No reference to that particular episode was ever welcomed. Foster, if the subject was not changed immediately, would get up and leave the room—but eventually we realized that what had happened then was almost as funny as it was unbelievable.)

Michael John was born April 26—and, naturally, in the middle of the night—the time, for reasons known only to babies, which most babies prefer. Those endless nine months were finally over, and we could hardly believe that Michael had actually arrived.

In those days, babies were brought in to their mothers every four hours. No visitors were allowed in the room at such times. However, fathers and/or visitors could at least view the newborn from afar, by lining up at the nursery window and giving the attendant the name of the baby. Said infant would then be brought over to the window for all the oohs and aahs.

Nurses took turns carrying babies over to the window, and often said that was their favorite task. According to them, the most dignified and staid of individuals waiting on the other side of the glass seemed to lose all control on the spot—coming up with absolute contortions hoping the babies would at least open one eye. Unfortunately, their efforts were appreciated only by the nursing staff. Every baby slept throughout every performance.

An hour or so after Michael was born, Foster presented himself for a through-the-window glimpse of his new son and heir. Before he could even mention the name, the nurse inside took one look at **him** and said, "I know who YOU want to see." She then went over and picked up Michael, brought him to the window, and Foster saw his new son for the very first time.

Rodney was almost seven when Michael was born. He was, however, not allowed to visit. Hospitals at that time prohibited children under twelve from even entering the building—unless, of course, they were, unfortunately, patients themselves. Consequently, all visiting adults could be counted on to show up with the latest note from Rodney.

Those notes were absolute classics which should be in a museum of their own. Included in each note was Rodney's latest drawing of how he imagined his brand-new little brother to look. Fortunately for Michael, said sketches did not bear too close a resemblance to the original. All notes and drawings became a part of my family album collection.

When Michael was born, I was, in accordance with considerably updated rules, four days in the hospital. With Rodney, it had been ten. Today, in the so-called modern age, new mothers and infants are hustled out within a matter of hours. The birthing process—the reason mothers are there in the first place—appears to be less and less important. How much time mothers and babies are allowed there at all seems to be a matter of luck.

Until the very day Michael and I came home, I had often worried about what it would be like taking care of not only my husband but TWO children. Then, something my grandmother Nannie—one of the biggest influences of my early life—used to say, came back to me: If you think one child takes up all your time, how can two take any more?

Whenever Nannie came out with that particular quotation, I had to wonder what parents of newborn quintuplets might have to say—assuming of course that after taking care of FIVE babies, they could say anything at all.

Wondering if Nannie just might be all wrong for a change, I made out a list of "Things to Do" for the next day. It was just possible this "modern" generation **could** take care of any number of children, keep husbands happy (maybe even have a career on the side?), and still have time left over to just sit back and relax. (Careers-on-the-side being unthinkable in those days, I don't know how it even occurred to me.)

The first day of following the "List" was, predictably, also the last. I had rushed around like mad the entire day, really getting a lot of things done, and feeling prouder and prouder of myself, and at the end of the day, took out the List to check everything off.

With the exception of baby-feedings, preparations of formulas, sterilizing bottles, washing and hanging up diapers in the back yard, baby-baths and general clean-ups, there was not a single other item on the list I could cross out. Yet I couldn't remember sitting down once the entire day. I even crammed down my lunch while standing up, busily making out a List for Day Two. (Lists One and Two were discarded on the spot—and Nannie was right, as usual.)

A few weeks after Michael was born, and just about the time I thought I was getting back to what I liked to think of a half-way decent figure, nothing fit right any more. I decided to blame the washer and dryer. The washer was probably shrinking everything, and the dryer making it all worse. Everything seemed to be shrinking except my appetite, yet I was still faithfully adhering to a rather boring diet. It HAD to be those two uncaring machines in the basement who were making me look like Mrs. Fat.

Some expectant mothers, who show little or nothing in the first few months have no idea how lucky they are. Unfortunately, I was never one of **those**. I was, nevertheless, once again expecting.

Foster was congratulating himself constantly. I reminded him it does take two, but since my rapidly-changing figure was more and more of a give-away, it was not our secret for long. I think my mother was secretly looking forward to another grandchild, and yet Mom, being Mom, would of course never let on. Once in a while, however, she couldn't resist giving me The Look, which this time probably meant, "So SOON after the first?"

I couldn't have worried less, nor could Foster, about the fact that by the time this new baby arrived, only eleven months would have elapsed since Michael was born. Looking down at Michael in his crib, it was almost impossible to picture him as a Big Brother, anyway—although by this time Rodney could give him a few pointers.

Dr. Irwin, upon checking this baby's heartbeat, once again predicted a boy. On my side of the family, there had been only girls. (Foster had one sister, no brothers, so his side was a draw.) Boys only happened in **other** families. However, assuming the doctor was again correct, that tradition was now obsolete.

Foster's mother Ella was as delighted as we were about the new baby—but she was always on my side anyway. Definitely not your traditional mother-in-law. On occasion, she had even been known to defend me against my own mother, which, although they were still the best of friends, took a certain amount of nerve. At times like that, I would think to myself if I ever get to be a mother-in-law (unimaginable at the time), I'd like to be just like Ella. Probably the first genuine compliment in history ever paid to a mother-in-law.

The names ready and waiting for this baby were Stephen for a boy and Louise for a girl. Neither of the Grandmas was making a list of names this time around, since Dr. Irwin repeatedly said, "trust me, it's a boy."

Boy or girl, this baby was in no hurry whatsoever. Actually, as far as suspense is concerned, being ahead of time is a little easier on the mother—who has little say in the matter, anyway. The infants themselves get to call the shots.

The day Baby Stephen OR Louise was officially due, there were no pains whatsoever, no pushing the father-to-be out the door, no breathless dash to the hospital. The only activity was X'ing out the date on the calendar, also for the next day and the day after that. After six whole days of **nothing**, the doctor decided a little hurry-up medication was in order and within a few hours, Foster and I were en route to the hospital. This trip, we literally raced down, and for a few minutes, I thought the gas pedal would go through the floor. However, one good sign was, this time the nurse on duty, with only an eleven-month lapse, was familiar with my first name.

This same medication was well-nicknamed, "Hurry-Up." More effective than the doctor had bargained for, we couldn't even make it to the delivery room. "Stephen Roy" decided to be born in the labor room. Three sighs of relief were then heard round the world— Foster's, the doctor's, and mine.

Before Stevie was born, everybody I knew was telling me that having two babies that close together would be like having twins—but it wasn't. Michael and Stevie's personalities were, and are, totally different—yet to this day they are very close. (Maybe they ARE twins—eleven months apart.)

The Cedar Grove house was getting a little crowded. Bessie had moved out the day of her wedding, but the room she and my mother had shared was still Mom's. Rodney had his room to himself downstairs, while the other room upstairs, finally finished off, was now headquarters for the two babies. This room, while not particularly large to begin with, now had wall-to-wall cribs and baby furniture, and you almost had to walk sideways to get in the door.

Downstairs, there was less and less room. No longer were empty corners available for Bozo's naps, so every once in a while we would find him curled up, sound asleep, in some forbidden territory. Now guilty of yet another doggie-crime, Bozo always tried to look as innocent as possible. We usually left him where he was.

Since we had been putting away all the money we could for some time, Foster finally realized the perennial daydream of all mechanics—he opened his own service station. Also, he was beginning to do fairly well, so we decided it was about time to look around for a larger house.

Foster and I were totally different in many ways (i.e. the average couple), but we usually wound up agreeing on major items. Bigger and better rooms were something we had both wanted for a long time, and at this point really needed. A realtor drove us one day up to Caldwell, an older, well-established town west of Cedar Grove. In just a few hours, we had both fallen in love with a certain house—the one house we knew instantly we had to have—and told the realtor it was this or nothing. We had already been shown several others that day, without being particularly impressed by any of them. Our realtor, no novice at his profession, had saved this beauty for last.

The house had ten large rooms, three porches, a two-car garage, an attic and a basement, located in a nice quiet neighborhood and yet only a couple of blocks from the town center. It had been extremely well built half a century ago, and would doubtless stand there intact for the next millenium. The basement wall, for instance, in back of the furnace, was—for whatever reason—three feet thick. In the house itself, there was more than enough room for everybody and everything. The back yard was large and already fenced, just waiting for the boys and Bozo to play in. Compared to **this**, our present home looked like a cardboard model.

In the living room was the most beautiful fieldstone fireplace imaginable. Just taking your eyes off it was almost impossible. I immediately pictured three little Christmas stockings hanging from the mantel—which happy sight did come to pass many times. (There were, eventually, more than three.)

The asking price for this, the house of our dreams—all we could ever hope for—was $16,000, which even in those days was a steal. (A few years ago, that very same house was on the market for $400,000.)

Having agreed in a heartbeat on the $16,000 price, we returned to the realtor's office. There, an urgent message was waiting for Foster from his mother's doctor. Ella had just been rushed to the hospital with a heart attack, and was not expected to live. She was asking for her son. We left the realtor's office and raced down to the hospital. Foster stopped the car and ran in; I parked the car and followed.

While it took only a few minutes to locate Ella's room, Foster and I were already too late. One look at Foster's face, standing at his mother's bedside and holding her hand, and I knew she was gone. Ella had been a wonderful mother to Foster, and a fabulous mother-in-law to me. After several days, when Foster was finally able to sit down and talk about his mother, the first thing I thought of was the last time I had seen Ella at her apartment. I had taken the two babies down there for a visit with her, which now turned out to be the last time she ever saw them. Ella, for some reason, had always been a little shy with other people's babies, in spite of having had two children of her own—but this time was to be the exception.

Stevie, who as a rule allowed only his father and me to pick him up, actually sat on his grandmother's lap for the entire afternoon. He seemed to be perfectly content—and Ella was absolutely thrilled. **Nothing** like this had ever happened before with Stevie.

For some time before we left, Michael had been pushing Ella's carpet sweeper all over her apartment without the remotest idea of where he was going. I was terrified he might crash into something any minute— inevitably something of great value—but Ella just smiled and said, "Michael can do ANYthing he wants."

And she really meant it. Ella was so happy that day to have the babies there, she couldn't have cared less what they did. When she finally kissed Stevie goodbye, she had tears in her eyes. So did Foster and I. I only wish Ella could have had many more years to enjoy her little grandsons.

Before Ella passed away, she had been living on interest from a trust fund left by her father. Upon her death, this fund was divided between Foster and his sister Josie. Consequently, although our date for moving into the Caldwell house was still several weeks away, we could actually pay cash—a "first" in both Foster's family history and mine.

It was hard to believe, but there would be NO MORTGAGE. Other monthly bills would continue to rear their ugly heads until the end of time, but at least **this** house would be all ours. It was a great feeling.

Before even thinking of looking around at other houses, obviously our first step should have been putting the Cedar Grove house on the market. We had, as a matter of fact, decided upon the agent we wanted to use for selling it, but had not yet made an appointment. Suddenly having found the kind of house we really wanted, there was no time to lose. Fortunately, there was no real reason to anticipate any problem in selling our present house. It was not only attractive but well built, which would be evident to any experts looking it over. The neighborhood had a good reputation, and what few repairs had been necessary since the day Mom, Bessie, Rodney and I moved in had all been taken care of.

Considering the original price and the vast number of years houses of that era were known to last (ownership had been known to cover four generations), finding a buyer was just a matter of time. In this case the buyers were standing right there in front of us. Bessie and Bill were at the door, announcing THEY wanted to buy the house—and it wasn't even on the market yet.

Since Bessie had already lived in the house, she and Bill certainly knew what they would be getting for their money. And for them, it was a step up in the world. They had been living a block away in a veteran's housing project, and were fast becoming dissatisfied there.

They already had one daughter, Amylou, and a son, Billy, Jr., so they too were looking for more space. They weren't as crowded as we were, but our house would be a lot bigger for them, and they couldn't wait to move in.

Foster was equally delighted at the idea of the house being turned over to Bessie and Bill, and most details of the transaction could be settled over the phone. Another plus—no sales commission would be deducted by anyone. All realtors were left out in the cold.

Moving to Caldwell was now set for September 23, and for weeks ahead of time, we were hauling cartons up to Caldwell. On the 23rd we were officially installed. Rodney at that time was nine years old, Michael was two, and Stevie one. While this was a big event in their lives as well, only Rodney was old enough to remember any of it. I had been checking one room at a time to see if everything was in the right place—when I suddenly noticed "someone" was missing.

That "someone" was Bozo, and then it dawned on me that the poor dog must have been left behind. Out in the backyard, all alone, looking up at a silent, empty house. Instantly, we all felt guilty. As for alibis—I had assumed Bozo would be in Foster's truck with him and Rodney. Foster was under the impression the dog would be in our car with me and the two babies. (My mother drove her own car, and wouldn't have allowed Bozo in it, anyway.) Realizing mothers are expected to remember all things at all times, I naturally felt the guiltiest, so I volunteered to go back and get him.

Bozo was NOT sulking in a corner of the yard with his back to the world as I had feared. He was busily welcoming me with his usual running around in circles, stopping periodically to lap up some water, then running around again—apparently holding no grudge whatsoever. At the time, I couldn't help thinking it's just as well animals are incapable of human speech. Listening to what Bozo **really** thought might have been a little awkward.

One feature we had sadly lacked back in the Cedar Grove house was a dining room. Here, in addition to our new dining room with French doors, there was also a small room on the other side of the kitchen.

Eventually, we would use this smaller room when only a few of us were eating together, but in the beginning, that particular room was known as the Toy Room, and being so close to the kitchen, the Toy Room was ideal in many ways. I could keep an eye on the little ones playing in there with their toys without falling all over the toys themselves, which in the kitchen itself I could have been doing every time I turned around. From the very first time they saw it, the Toy Room was the favorite room of all three boys.

A few weeks before Stevie's second birthday, I was changing him one morning on the bathinette in the Toy Room—when I discovered to my horror that he had what turned out to be a hernia. As a rule, I don't panic in a split second, but I did then—and I didn't even know what I had been looking at. I raced to the phone and called the doctor. Dr. Irwin's house, where he also maintained his practice, was only two doors away. (Very convenient for emergencies, but for anything routine we were always last on his calling list.) He told me to bring Stevie over immediately.

The diagnosis was a hernia, which should be operated upon the very next day. I immediately asked if that was a dangerous operation—and then I was afraid to hear the answer. He replied, "No, but it's necessary," so I started breathing again. Happily for all—the patient, the two parents going crazy, and the doctor—the operation was a complete success, except that our littlest son was not at all impressed with the hospital. Stevie made it clear to one and all he wanted to be HOME.

The first time I was allowed to see him, shortly after the operation, Stevie was not only awake but actually standing up in the crib. As I walked over to him, he actually backed away. I could only assume Stevie was afraid I was about to take him to yet another strange room, to be again surrounded by people he had never seen before. To see my own child literally backing away from me—from ME, his own mother—was too much. I reached over and grabbed him, and then I held him until we both calmed down. A nurse standing by said, "They all do that at first," so then I felt a little better. Not much, but a little.

That same nurse, Sheila, had already made Stevie her favorite patient, and Stevie would eat **anything** for her, whatever she put in front of him. At home I had to go through one contortion after another coaxing him to just **try** something. One of my approaches was pretending the spoon, containing the latest baby food, was really a noisy airplane coming in to land—Stevie's mouth being the airport. This worked until Stevie caught on. The "airplane" was that awful food again, so it was time to think of something new.

Once Stevie was home again, Sheila and her husband joined our whole family for many a picnic at the lake, and there, once again, Sheila never took her eyes off Stevie. (A Don Juan, at the age of two?)

Unbelievably, two months later, Stevie had **another** hernia. This time, it was on the other side—and once again, an operation was necessary. But this time at least we all knew what to expect, and managed to get through it again , hoping it would be the last. After Operation #2, the doctor remarked, "If he had to have **two** hernias, it's too bad they couldn't both have come at the same time." I also couldn't help wishing neither one had happened at all. Even Sheila had lost her professional calm when she saw Stevie being brought in for the second time.

About two years later, Michael, who was then five years old, apparently decided it was his turn to be star-of-the-show at the hospital. Once again, it was a hernia—you'd almost think they were contagious—but luckily for us all, it was the one and only one for him. At least Michael was old enough to be told the night before, in terms that hopefully made sense to a five-year-old, what would be going on the next day at the hospital. All went well with the operation, and since Sheila was still working at the same hospital as head nurse, Michael had a friend-at-court, so to speak. She even tried to smuggle Stevie in one day to visit Michael, but Sheila's influence stopped at the door. Stevie never got past the guard.

As soon as they gave us the go-ahead, we brought Michael home—and he seemed to recover from **his** ordeal as fast as Stevie had. I don't know that the two of them ever ran around the neighborhood proudly showing off their scars to all their friends, but these almost-twins now had one more thing in common—their operations.

As for their loving parents—Foster and I began to toy with the idea of having a nervous breakdown or two. It was OUR turn. We just never found the time.

Michael's first day at school that September was coming up in a few days. Rodney, having been delegated to escort his little brother there, seemed to be looking forward to it as much as Michael.

The day finally came. Aiming my ever-present camera, I watched the two of them from the front door. As soon as they reached the sidewalk, they both turned—as per repeated directions—and waved to the camera. They then proceeded to the corner, turned and waved again, and stood there waiting to cross the street. I could see Rodney once again instructing Michael as to all the proper precautions.

Michael must have listened well that first day, because a few days later, when Rodney was at home with a cold, Michael was on his own for the very first time. He approached the corner very cautiously, looked up and down the street what seemed like several hundred times, and finally crossed over. All by himself.

Back in 1954, two months after we had moved up to Caldwell, about 3 o'clock one morning I had a miscarriage. It was a shattering, almost unbelievable experience, and by the time it was all over, I could not imagine ever feeling happy again.

Dr. Irwin stayed for a few hours after that, talking to Foster down in the kitchen. He wanted to make sure there was only **one** baby, for it was possible a twin was still waiting. Doctors did do things like that in those days—but he was not just our doctor. He was a wonderful friend.

Later that morning, Foster brought Michael and Stevie into the bedroom for a few minutes. Rodney had just left for school, and Foster was going to be both father and mother for the day. He was hoping to give us both a chance to recover, and to act as if nothing had happened. No one but Foster and I had known about this pregnancy.

Had nothing gone wrong—and to this day, I don't know what did—that baby would have been born the following April 18th. Many years later, a certain wonderful judge I worked for, who was actually many years younger than I, happened to have that same birthdate. He was always amazed that I was one of the few people he knew who never forgot that particular date.

There was no way I could ever forget April 18th, the birthday that never happened, and the baby I never got to hold.

Foster, after some two years' experience in running his own service station, was finally more or less forced to take out a small mortgage on our (until then) debt-free house. Too many customers had reneged on too many bills—and eventually Foster was unable to pay his own. Saying "No" to any salesman, no matter what the product or service, had never been easy for Foster, and equally difficult was turning down neighbors and/or friends just looking for credit—which credit he always gave.

Unfortunately, no firms mailing periodic statements to us were willing to wait until we found it convenient to pay. We had a choice to make: either declare bankruptcy or take out a mortgage. The latter course would at least keep the service station in business, so that seemed to be the way to go.

With the proceeds of the loan, we were able to pay off enough bills to keep our credit intact—but mortgage-free days were once again history. It was an expensive lesson.

A few months later, things began to look up. Foster had come across a smaller garage in town, but one which happened to have a much more visible location. Transferring his lease to an old mechanic friend who was looking to start up for himself, Foster then brought the bulk of his own business over to the new location. One memorable morning that winter, if I had just remained at home for the day with the boys, we would all have been better off. Instead, Michael and Stevie and I decided to stop by Foster's new station.

It was unusually cold and damp that day, and the building had been closed up tight to hold onto what little heat there is in any service station in the winter. Both boys had been running around inside—and suddenly there was only Michael. I asked where Stevie was, and Michael said, "over there." He was pointing to a far corner. Stevie, who was then three years old, seemed to be walking around in circles over there, almost tipping over as if for some reason he couldn't keep his balance.

Foster and I and one of the mechanics all rushed over to see what was going on. When no one could figure out what was wrong, we decided to take him to the nearest medical center. Outside in the fresh air again, Stevie in a matter of seconds was himself again, and began to act perfectly normal. By this time, another mechanic, who had followed us all outside, accidentally discovered the unbelievable cause of what had been going on with our three-year-old. Some person or persons unknown had for some reason stuffed a rag into one of the outlets from the garage—this outlet being for the purpose of expelling any odors from chemicals being used inside—but with the rag being jammed inside the outlet itself, these chemical odors could only back up inside again.

Stevie, who had been playing in the corner nearest the outlet, was the first—and only—one to be affected. If we hadn't noticed him starting to keel over, sooner or later we might all have been knocked out. The vent-stoppage was remedied on the spot, with the two mechanics almost fighting to be the one to whisk out the rag. It was a pretty scary experience—anything but the best of omens for a brand-new business.

It was also time to call it a day and take the boys home. No longer was I in the mood for shopping, not after what almost happened at the garage.

For me, the best way to get over a miscarriage would have been to be carrying another baby as soon as possible, but Mother Nature, never one to be pushed around, was again not in that much of a hurry. Not until the Spring of 1956 did I see my doctor, with a big smile, hold his fingers up in the air with a V-for-Victory sign, saying, "Shall we assume it's another boy?"

The next several months, as far as moods were concerned, were like being on a roller coaster. Foster and I were both delighted that a baby was finally on the way, but we were also very much aware that a series of miscarriages was very often the norm. When you've had one "mis" you practically walk on eggs until you actually see that next baby. The further I got past the first trimester, reputedly the most crucial, the easier it was to breathe. Not until the eighth month, however, did I begin to relax. An eight-month baby—which Foster himself had been—at least had a fighting chance.

At the conclusion of a full nine months, close to the stroke of midnight on January 12, 1957, Gary Evan was born. Intact, healthy, and well worth waiting for. That was one happy day.

A few months before Gary was born, Dr. Irwin (with the best of intentions), had come up with what HE apparently thought was a great idea. In case I was running out of names, said he, I could always name at least one baby after **him**, if I planned on having one a year (which I didn't) since he, the doctor, would always be there, year after year, to assist. I advised him that was one idea I was not about to present to my husband, as I could guarantee he would take a very dim view of same. Some time later, when I could no longer resist relaying this conversation to Foster, he did indeed react as predicted. In spades.

In the daytime, we kept Gary's crib downstairs in the dining room, next to the radiator. The dining room was probably the warmest in the house. (The original coal furnace called for countless trips to the basement to shovel in more coal, and it had been a relief to finally switch over to oil heat.)

As per the doctor's advice, Gary as a baby always slept on his back. My choice would have been to put him on his stomach, because he always turned his head to the right and I was afraid the back of his head might become flattened on that one side. I needn't have worried. My arguments with the doctor were soon resolved by the infant himself. That little head remained as round as an apple—and when Gary had had enough of lying on his back, he simply rolled over onto his stomach.

Michael and Stevie were fascinated to see someone in the house smaller than they were. And especially whenever Gary was in the playpen. There, he was the center of attraction for his MUCH older brothers, who took turns holding him on their laps every day. (A stopwatch might have come in handy, just to prove there was no favoritism being shown.) Being constantly switched back and forth didn't seem to bother Gary, anyway. He was very easy-going almost from Day One. And like most babies, as long as he was being held by **someone,** he was happy.

Shortly before Christmas of 1958, I bravely took all three to visit Santa Claus at a Newark department store—and wound up with a photo of Michael, Stevie and Gary all sitting on Santa's lap at the same time. Santa was no doubt giving silent thanks that trios didn't come around that often, and how he ever managed to hold this triple lapful without anyone sliding off, no one knows.

But the trials of Kris Kringle were not yet over. When Gary was about four, with both Michael and Stevie being in Cub Scouts (guess who was the den mother?), Foster had been persuaded it was his duty to be that year's Santa Claus at the Cubs' pre-Christmas party. Once again, Gary was sitting on Santa's lap, busily telling Santa Claus what he wanted for Christmas. He had not the faintest idea THIS Santa was actually his father—who was certainly in a much better position to deliver the right toys than his department-store counterpart. Oddly enough, both Michael and Stevie refrained from clueing Gary in on

Santa's real identity that evening. I always suspected they'd been heavily bribed (if not actually threatened) by a certain jolly old gent whose initials were S. C.

Late in 1961, Foster decided to try his luck at a different service station on the highway north of town. While a fairly new area, prospects of bigger and better business out there were reportedly very good. We named the new station Chevron City, thinking it sounded good—and did offer many more items for sale than the usual gas and oil. Foster crossed his fingers, opened the doors to the public, and hoped for the best.

The (now three) boys and I drove out there every few days to cheer him on, and I eventually managed to pump gas each time for a few patient customers. A first for me, but much admired (and at that time envied) by my sons.

After several months, however, the number of customers per day was nowhere near enough to keep up with the bills. Financially, the place was rapidly becoming a disaster. Even back at the last station, Foster had finally stopped giving credit to anyone, whether friend or foe, and salesmen now knew better than to stop by too often.

Unfortunately, those precautions came a little too late. One day, Foster called me at the house and asked me to drive out to the station. Alone. He simply said there was something I'd better see, and then hung up. I left the boys with my sister, and drove out. More bills than I had ever seen at one time were strewn all over Foster's desk. Each and every one unpaid. The top of the desk was literally hidden from sight. I was then updated on the following: The mortgage on the house, small though the payments were, was three months overdue. We were threatened with foreclosure. The telephone was about to be disconnected. No more heating-oil deliveries would be made. (The oil company's new policy was, if you can't pay at the door, don't ask for oil. They also were no longer giving credit to anyone.) The rest of the bills covering the desk represented supplies for the garage—already delivered, not paid for.

Up until that very day, Foster had handled all finances, with no input from me. Back when I quit the translation bureau, we had agreed that since he would be the only one working and bringing in the money to live on, he and he alone would keep track of where the funds went.

At that awful moment, neither of us had the remotest idea how to simultaneously pay all the bills, stall off the foreclosure, exist without a phone, and heat the house—but we at least came to terms on one thing.

From that day on, all budgeting, bill paying and money worrying would be my department—and while I had certainly inherited a headache, at least there would be no more surprises.

My own plans for that day, whatever they may have been, went right out of my head. Foster was standing some distance on the other side of the desk, almost with his back to the wall (somewhat symbolic, as I thought later) just looking at me.

My heart ached for him. This had to be the worst day of his life. He was not only the man I loved, but the hardest worker I had ever known, yet in **his** mind he was absolutely convinced that in spite of everything he'd tried to do, he was letting us down. And, losing the service station as well.

I hugged him and tried to assure him everything would work out. We just had to hang in there. After all we'd gone through together, this was no time to give up. I could get a job for a few months, or for as long as it took until we were back on our feet again. No problem.

Foster patiently reminded me I was once again expecting. I told him I could hardly forget that, but I certainly could work long enough to make a difference. Somehow we'd get all those bills paid and pick up our lives again.

From my mother, who was then on the verge of retiring, we were able to borrow enough money to satisfy our many creditors—this loan we repaid in full before I quit work a few months later. With, I might add, interest. My mother had never once mentioned the word "interest," but with a non-working future ahead of her, the least we could do was **not** take advantage of her generosity.

By presumably sheer coincidence, by the time I got home that day, the phone was already shut off. Also, a bill was in the mail from the oil company. All I needed was a truck at the door waiting to haul the house away. It had certainly been one interesting day.

At that time, Bessie was working as a supervisor for the County mental hospital, which was located only a few miles away in Caldwell. Upon hearing I was unexpectedly in the market for a job, she suggested I put in an application at the hospital for whatever might be available.

Which I did, the very next day. Fortunately for me, Bessie apparently had enough clout with whoever ruled the roost there to convince them I was just what they needed. I told my sister I really owed her one this time.

Only Bessie—not my mother as yet—was aware that Number Five was on the way, and we had good reason to fear the hospital might not even accept me as an employee. Pregnant women were not the most desired of employees in those days, and employers shied away in horror from the mere idea. This widespread attitude was not only taken for granted by the general populous, but as a rule not even questioned. If preggies wanted to work at all—or for as long as they could get away with pretending there were no Little Ones on the way—they would have to answer "No" to "Are you pregnant at this time?"

Consequently, I "forgot" to mention this pregnancy when filling out the application. Then, since I managed to pass even their physical tests (which obviously did not include any for pregnancy), they were still in the dark. As an additional precaution, I was wearing a very loose-fitting dress the day of my interview. Then, when I subsequently reported for work, I managed to put back the uniform which had been handed to me, quickly substituting one which was far too long. This larger one wouldn't have been too roomy for too long, but it worked for as long as I needed it.

Having no particular nursing skills, every odd job that came along was automatically mine. Whatever task everyone else avoided like the plague was immediately assigned to me. I was gradually turning into a female jack-of-all-trades.

Working in the vicinity of literally hundreds of mental patients was a really unique experience, and one I certainly never expected to have. For instance, all hospital employees had master keys to all doors, and all doors, of whatever description, were kept locked. From the Inside. If you wanted to enter a patient's room, or a ward, you could walk right in. Nobody walked out unless they had a key.

At the point of leaving a room, and with the all-important key in your possession, you had to be very much aware of whoever happened to be in the immediate vicinity and just how anxious they might be to accompany you out the door. One of the female inmates, with whom over a period of time I had become fairly friendly, was telling me one day she still couldn't understand why her very own father had had her committed. According to her, all she had done was to toss several pieces of furniture out of her second-floor bedroom into the back yard. As if justifying a perfectly innocent action, she then carefully explained that, after all, it was HER furniture.

At the time, this struck me as so funny—**truly** insane—it was all I could do to keep a straight face. I immediately thought up some urgent reason to leave, and escaped from her room as soon as possible. I had been specifically instructed by the authorities not to let any of the inmates get the idea you were laughing at them. This could be very easily—and rapidly—misunderstood.

Most of the mental patients I met seemed somewhat on the defensive just for being in the institution in the first place (Assuming, of course, that they realized **where** they were.) They were very easily provoked, and on such occasions were fully capable of coming at you—not only without any warning whatsoever, but with fantastic strength.

My own sister, some time ago, had been suddenly hit in the face one day by an inmate. (This was a woman to whom Bessie, as was her custom, had been especially kind, having even taken this very person home with her occasionally for a weekend visit.) And all because Bessie happened to be smiling at something she herself was reading. This inmate decided SHE was the one being laughed at, and hauled off and struck her.

My sister was home for a week, totally out of commission—and not just physically. She felt totally betrayed by this woman. A week later, Bessie was back on the job again. Understandably, she'd had second thoughts about returning to the hospital at all, and yet she never once blamed this particular inmate. Knowing what inmates were prone to do, she realized she should have had eyes in the back of her head, so to speak. She did not, however, invite the woman to her home again.

In that most unusual of hospitals, sometimes the weaker a patient appeared to be at first, either mentally or emotionally, the stronger he or she often turned out to be physically. One day, I had been helping an extremely frail, 80-year-old woman into her bed. She had, tragically, been committed since the age of seventeen by a family who assumed they were doing the right thing, but never attempted to find any alternate course of treatment; nor had anyone in that family, not once in all those years, come to visit her.

She was most grateful, smiled up at me, and very gently took my hand, as if to thank me. Unfortunately for me, this poor woman was totally unaware she had a grip of steel. She had no animosity toward me whatsoever, but she did not know enough to release me—and I literally could not free myself. A handcuff couldn't have done a better job.

If one of my associates, sensing something was wrong, hadn't finally run over with some cookies to distract her, how much longer that weak, pathetic little old lady would have kept me captive was strictly up to her.

My mother's last day with the Veterans Administration in Newark was set for the end of January, 1962—as was her retirement party. Since 1933, two years after my father died, she had been working for various branches of the Government, and this was a day she had been looking forward to for many years. Mom had asked me to come down for the party.

My hours at the County Hospital were the infamous graveyard shift, 11 p.m. to 7 a.m., but I assured Mom that one way or another I would definitely make it down to Newark that afternoon for her big day. What I did not mention was, I also planned on bringing the four boys along. Rodney, Michael and Stevie were normally in school all day, but it was a safe bet they'd welcome a few hours' reprieve to go down and celebrate with their Grandma. Gary, at five, and several months away from kindergarten, was still at home with me.

Mom had apparently been watching the door from her desk. When I finally walked in with the four boys—all enjoying their unexpected holiday and knowing they had their grandmother to thank for it—my mother's face lit up like a Christmas tree. It was pretty obvious **that** moment was the highlight of her day.

With an eye to avoiding the notorious five o'clock Newark rush hour, I could only keep the boys there for a couple of hours. Meanwhile, I finally met all the office personalities I'd been hearing about from Mom for ages. While they all seemed really sorry to see Mom go, the feeling was not exactly mutual. After 29 long years of working for Uncle Sam, my mother was, understandably, ecstatic to be walking out the door for good.

Several times during our visit, Mom had asked first one co-worker and then another, "What do you think of my FOUR grandsons?" My mother was enormously proud of her grandchildren. In her mind, they could do no wrong, whereas my sister and I, growing up, seldom did anything right.

Considering the fact I was expecting our next baby in July, had Mom only known, she had FIVE grandsons there at the time celebrating her retirement, including the one she couldn't see and as yet didn't know about.

The day I began working at the hospital, Foster had started closing down his third and last service station. At the same time, he was looking into any and all job possibilities, never having been one to sit and wait for a job to find him. (I should have known better than to even mention unemployment compensation, but when I did, there was no answer, anyway. He looked at me as if I were a complete stranger.)

In a very short time, however, we were both thoroughly convinced that giving up the service-station way of life must have been preordained. Two days after turning the key in the office door and walking away, Foster received an urgent phone call. One of his many applications had been to a major insurance company for a job as claims adjuster, and they had been checking him out ever since. The job was his.

Congratulations came from all sides—not only from family members but from everybody else keeping tabs on us. There were several reasons. The salary offered (unspecified at the time of the original interview), turned out to be more than he dared to hope for. Also, that job was an absolute natural for Foster. He knew cars, and he definitely had a way with people. (His Hungarian father, Elemer, may have passed on years ago, but that famous charisma was still very much alive.)

Several fringe benefits also came with the job. To us, the one that immediately made the biggest impression was, "Pop" would now have the use of a company car.

Two days later, sitting proudly at the wheel of a brand-new company car (which to all of us looked like a limousine from heaven), Foster pulled up to the side door. Everyone had been waiting for this big moment and were at the curb almost as soon as the car stopped. We all piled into the car, and took off—it was OUR car. The fact that it was registered in the company name meant nothing. It was OUR car.

"Pop" now had a really good job, and everything was coming up roses—what more could one ask? That crazy hilarious ride all over town in OUR new car, up and down streets we'd been on hundreds of times before, made up for a lot of bad moments.

In April, the hospital authorities, who had always been very friendly to me, could no longer pretend to ignore the fact that I was pregnant. And six months along, at that. My purposely ill-fitting uniforms had done the job longer than expected, and I was well aware the top brass had been looking the other way for a long time. They were now telling me, however, that it was too much of a risk for them to keep me on. Just in case I fell down on the job, literally.

For me, this was a re-run of the time in East Orange when I was pregnant with Rodney and the attorney I was working for had to "let me go" (face-saving term at that time for firing someone). That had been almost seventeen years ago, and the practice was still unquestioned by the public—or even the now-former employee.

In any case it would be a huge relief not to have to keep working at the hospital. Leaving the house in the middle of the night to go to work was not my idea of a 9-to-5 job, and while the work at the hospital was certainly interesting, to say the least, that check-in time of 11 p.m. seemed to arrive sooner every evening.

There had also been another problem from the very first day, which I shared with most other employees. I had always been afraid of not being able to stay awake all night. As a rule, one crisis after another in the various wards kept us going, and by the time everyone had calmed down from the first uproar and might have dozed off, the next emergency was usually on the way. It was anything but a dull job, so there wasn't much chance for sleep, anyway. All things considered, it was a miracle a few employees didn't wind up as patients.

It had long been the custom for each ward to tip off the next, via phone, whenever a supervisor was on the way for a "surprise" inspection. Consequently, when he or she did burst through the door, hoping to catch at least one or two exhausted employees dozing off, everyone in sight was very busy doing **something**.

Long before April, my mother had been informed that she had yet one more grandchild on the way. This time, she seemed to be either looking forward to—or was finally resigned to—having what appeared to be oncoming hordes of grandchildren,—but Mom was still not into the proverbial knitting-of-tiny—garments. A sewing machine was all she ever needed, and Mom was definitely a fantastic seamstress. In no time at all, she had produced all of her newest grandbaby's wardrobe.

July 15th was the date given me by the doctor for the baby's arrival. As per family tradition, this day naturally came and went as just one more day. As did the next day, and the next. Recalling the eleven days I had waited for Rodney, none of us were particularly surprised. To complicate matters, Dr. Irwin had been very generously postponing his annual vacation down at the Jersey shore on my account. He finally sent his family on ahead, confident that any moment now, Baby #5 would say, "I'm Ready,"—following which he could dash down to the shore and belatedly join his family.

In that historic era, doctors actually did things like that for expectant mothers—with no charge being added to the bill. At most, they would politely suggest your NEXT baby be timed to arrive at a more convenient period of the year.

On July 20th, having seen five vacation days disappear down the drain, Dr. Irwin arranged for another doctor to take over for him. He then left for the shore, hoping to make up for lost time. Not only were his children watching out the window for him every day, but his wife was decidedly irate.

At that time, a trip by car from Caldwell down to the Jersey shore took an unbelievable four hours. Superhighways did not exist. Driving through a maze of narrow, occasionally unpaved streets, the small towns all seemed to be meshed together, and it was hard to tell which one you were actually in at the moment. You also had to stop almost every block at equally narrow cross-streets, which seemed to have the right-of-way forever.

If only Dr. Irwin could have looked into a crystal ball, he would never have left home. He was probably no more than ten minutes away from his shore cottage when Baby #5, four hours to the North, came to a decision. The time was NOW.

Foster phoned the stand-by doctor, who advised us to get to the hospital ASAP. This doctor also, unknown to us at the time, then left a message for Dr. Irwin at the shore, bringing him up to date on the latest development. Unfortunately, Dr. Irwin, upon eventually receiving the message, **mis**interpreted it to mean he should return immediately. Within minutes, he was on his way back. (Understandably, his wife, for months thereafter, did not speak to me.)

I couldn't have cared less which doctor was going to be there. What was driving me up the wall was totally unexpected. At this, the eleventh hour, late as the baby already was, the labor pains had completely stopped.

Much later that evening, feeling a complete and utter failure, I was still sitting on the side of the hospital bed. Dr. Irwin suddenly appeared, sent the other doctor on his way, and handed me a dose of the latest miracle medicine—this one for persuading unborn babies, who apparently couldn't make up their minds, to get moving. I managed to swallow whatever it was, and it worked fast indeed—and at least this time we did make it all the way to the delivery room.

John Robert—thereafter known as Jackie (at least to his mother)—was born on July 21st. Only six days late.

There had been no alternate girl's name waiting for Jackie. Nor had there been for Gary, when he was born. Each time, the doctor had come up with the now-familiar prediction—It's a Boy—and since by then it was obvious Dr. Irwin knew what he was talking about, lining up names for girls would only insult the doctor's intelligence.

The day Baby Jackie and I were to leave for home, I knew ahead of time Foster would be unable to get to the hospital that particular day, so we had made other arrangements. Rodney, who was then 17, was slated to come down and drive us home, and that morning one of the nurses came in with a rather unexpected message from the desk downstairs. It was "Your husband is down here, waiting for you and the baby."

I knew very well it had to be Rodney, not Foster, but for some reason, I could NOT get up enough nerve to explain: That's not my husband, it's my 17-year-old son. (She would immediately think, this must be some kind of **Methuselah** having a baby—and at 41, I was close.) As we later passed by the desk, I can only assume that nurse fainted on the spot.

Rodney drove us home, as per schedule, and left us at the house. Inside, Jackie found he had a few more brothers to meet. Michael, Stevie and Gary were waiting for him—and finally even Gary had a little brother.

My mother was standing by, all smiles. She had the bathinette in the Toy Room ready and waiting for the baby, so the first thing I did was to place Jackie on it. Suddenly, all three big brothers rushed out of the Toy Room and into the kitchen. Voluntarily, under no compulsion whatsoever, of their own free will, they were racing en masse to the sink to wash their hands. Repeat: Wash Their Hands.

When my mother was finally able to stop laughing, she explained what was going on. Somewhere, the boys had heard that the hands of newborn babies, for the first few days only, have a very strong grip. They were determined to test this theory by taking turns holding Jackie's hand—and were thus performing this sacrificial act of washing their own hands in the **middle** of the day.

All three boys then lined up alongside the bathinette, no doubt in order of seniority. One by one, they very reverently held one of Baby Jackie's hands. (In later years, Jackie naturally never let his brothers forget this touching scene. According to him, they should have paid him, and paid him well, for the privilege.) Unfortunately for either album or blackmail purposes, there was no film in the camera at the time, so this truly historic moment went unrecorded.

By the time Jackie was a few months old, Mom, who was still with us in Caldwell, began to think about making other living arrangements. The reason: some friends of ours in Miami had been trying to talk us into selling the house and moving down to Miami—and we were seriously thinking about doing just that. Growing increasingly weary of New Jersey' eccentric weather pattern, Florida—and Miami in particular—sounded more and more attractive.

We never got around to even putting the house on the market—it had all been more or less idle talk with us, but Mom was convinced a move to Florida was just a question of time. While she herself had never been to Florida, she KNEW she wouldn't like it there, and had no real desire to leave New Jersey, the state she'd lived in most of her life. As a result, Mom discussed the matter from time to time with my sister and her husband. Bessie and Bill were then in the process of moving to a house in the next town, closer to where Bill was then working, and they had a suggestion for Mom—whether sincere or not, no one ever knew—i.e., that Mom move out of our house in Caldwell, where she then had two rooms to herself, and move in with Bessie and Bill and their two children.

That era being somewhat of a holdover from more ancient times, families automatically expected to take care of their own. If a wife suddenly found herself a widow, all other family members would meet to decide—with said widow's approval—with which branch of the family she would reside from then on. Not which retirement village to check out, or the most convenient senior nursing home, but with which **family** member she would live.

And it was still the same with Mom. She felt she needed all of us, so the family had always managed to find a way to keep her feeling secure. And happy—or, at the very least, not unhappy. It's probably just as well

Mom never lived to see the staggering turn-around in today's so-called "family values."

The day before Thanksgiving, my mother, knowing I would soon be taking over the cooking, stood at the sink demonstrating everything one was supposed to do with a turkey prior to conveying it to the oven in all its glory—cleaned, stuffed, sewn up, etc. Cooking, about which I still knew less than nothing, had always been her domain.

The more I watched (actually only pretending to, since the process seemed somewhat gory), the more I thought, I don't want to do anything like THAT. But the dye was cast. My mother, chef-of-all-time since the day I was born, would be living elsewhere in another week. From then on, all the poor souls left behind would have to somehow survive on MY cooking. It was an awesome thought.

After Mom moved over to Bessie's, once again we rearranged the upstairs rooms. Foster and I again had the master bedroom, with the fireplace that hadn't been used since the day we moved in. It was still unlit. (Who had time for a fireplace in the bedroom? In the daytime, kids were running all over the house. At night, on those rare occasions when there was time to sit back and gaze into a crackling fire, there was always that beautiful fieldstone fireplace in the living room.)

Rodney had a room to himself, as befits Number One son. Gary and Jackie shared the room next to ours, while Michael and Stevie moved into the so-called "Play Room."

The Play Room upstairs, over the front porch, was 25 feet wide and 9 feet deep. On three sides, no less than fifteen windows required almost constant attention—fifteen storm windows in winter, fifteen screens in summer. By the time you finished hauling out fifteen storm windows and finally getting them installed, it was almost time to take them all down again and start on the fifteen screens. No one ever stood in line for the privilege of helping "Pop" with that job. At "window time" everyone was strangely absent—and the first son and heir to eventually show up knew what he'd be doing from that moment on.

One day, as Foster was walking through the Play Room, he tripped more than once over the wall-to-wall toys. Not being in the best of moods at the time, he immediately issued an ultimatum, namely: the next time he saw the Play Room, he did not want to see ONE toy. (Meaning, on the FLOOR.)

A rash statement, since the boys took him literally. Foster was no sooner out of the house when Michael and Stevie—having been given the green light—immediately opened up all fifteen windows. (This being wintertime, all our expensive heat was gone for the day.) They then picked up every single toy, and THREW OUT every single toy through the nearest open window and into the front yard.

A barrage of unknown objects was flying out of every window. Comments made by motorists passing by are better left unreported. When all the fun was over, the two boys did eventually have to lug everything back indoors and upstairs. (The next time Foster walked through the room, however, very few toys were on view. He obviously never looked under the beds.)

In June, 1963, while eleven-month-old Baby Jackie remained at home entertaining a babysitter, the rest of the family looked on and applauded as Rodney graduated from high school. The entire day had been for once cloudless—a rare state of affairs in the Garden State—so ceremonies could be conducted out in the football field. That field itself, and the fact they were actually in it, was probably more impressive to Michael, Stevie and Gary than the sight of their big brother accepting what to them was just another piece of paper.

Rodney already knew about one of the presents he would be getting for graduation. Since the day he was born, my mother had saved whatever she could salvage out of each and every paycheck towards the college education she dreamed of for Rodney. The eventual total she managed to accumulate only paid for his first year, but it fulfilled a dream for Mom. However, once in college, Rodney decided that for him, his first year should also be his last. In his opinion, he could do better career-wise out there on his own for the next three years than waiting the same length of time to emerge with a diploma—and no job.

While this way-to-go might not have worked for everybody, it did for Rodney. He called the shots right that time, as later events in his life were to prove. He was, and is, a born wheeler-dealer, and run-of-the-mill education was just not for him.

One of Stevie's more memorable school projects was the brainchild of a teacher brought up on a farm, whose innocent intention was only to show off what she herself had learned as a child. Namely, hatching chickens.

Each and every student, a farmer-to-be in the eyes of this teacher, was instructed to purchase eight Rhode Island Red fertilized eggs, to be kept at home in an incubator. Instructions for making the incubator itself were handed out to the class. That evening, when Foster walked in the front door and saw what was waiting for him, he just **might** have wanted to walk right out again.

Instruction sheets were prominently displayed on the kitchen table. Every tool we owned was either on top of the table or waiting underneath. The crew, consisting of the future-farmer and Michael, stood at attention, waiting for orders. Incubator-construction was under way within the hour.

Once the eggs were installed in their new home, they were to be turned over every few hours. In the daytime, this turning-over detail was no problem, as the boys were all but standing in line for the privilege. The night shift was something else again. Once all the boys were asleep, Foster and I took turns at the periodic egg-roll.

These school projects invariably wound up involving the whole family—and if that had been the idea in the first place, it worked every time. Of the original eight eggs, only two chicks eventually broke through their shells on the predicted date—and a date right on the dot, certainly more accurate than my doctor's had ever been. It was fascinating to watch the shells slowly crack a little at a time. We were all practically holding our breath, and as first one chick, then another, finally pushed all the way through, everybody cheered. A worker at the egg farm cautioned us that if any or all of the chicks appeared to be having difficulty pushing through the shell, not to help them. In other words, if they weren't strong enough to break through by themselves, they weren't going to last long once they were out, anyway. It was still hard to hold off and not give the chicks a little shove.

Of the two chicks who did survive their shell break-out, one did not appear to be quite as hale and hearty as the other—not that anyone present knew the first thing about poultry in its pre-dinner-table phase, anyway. The weaker chick only lasted two days, even though the boys and I had actually taken it up to the vet's office. There, we were regretfully advised by said vet that he himself knew little or nothing about baby chicks. So, we took "Chickadee" (its name for as long as it lasted) back home again.

We were all sitting around the kitchen table, just talking, when I looked down at the chick in the palm of my hand. It had stopped moving, and was dead. Tiny though it was, everyone felt sad. Chickadee was then given a proper, almost elaborate, burial in the back yard by Stevie and the attendant mourners.

The one surviving chick made up for all the rest, not only in strength but longevity. He grew up to be Chirper, the most ferocious Rhode Island Red rooster in captivity. And maybe captivity was the problem. While Chirper had the run of the back yard, for him that wasn't enough. He wanted to be on the OTHER side of the fence, and did his best to get there.

Chirper's favorite pastime was chasing me all over the back yard until I could finally run up the steps to the back porch. He was one mean critter, but—giving him the benefit of the doubt—was probably just missing the companionship of his seven brothers and/or sisters, who never got that far.

A year after Mom moved in with Bessie and Bill, news from that particular homestead was not good. Bessie and Bill, the most accommodating of people, had set up the entire house with Mom's comfort in mind, but the present arrangement there did not appear to be working out at all. Once again, Mom had two rooms to herself; same having been originally designed as a master bedroom and second bedroom. The two children, Amylou and Billy, shared what was actually the attic. Bessie and Bill's own bedroom was located in the very lowest level of the house, under both the living room and my mother's two rooms. Mom, with more space than the rest of them put together, was more or less satisfied with where she found herself, but she and Bessie were not now seeing eye-to-eye on anything. Mom's opinion of not only how Bessie lived her life, but how she **should** was freely given. In Mom's view, almost nothing Bessie did was right—yet she was living in Bessie's home. Bessie, on the other hand, was famous for getting along with everybody she knew. She was anything but critical, and probably for that very reason had a host of friends. But even Bessie, with the patience of a saint, finally grew weary of hearing, day after day, that everything she did left much to be desired—even the way she handled her own paychecks. My long-suffering sister, normally a happy, easy-going person, was miserable. After discussing the situation time after time between themselves, Bessie and Bill came up with what they desperately hoped would be an amicable solution. They would tell Mom they were extremely dissatisfied with the neighborhood (not true), and were putting the house up for sale. Once the house was sold, they could then (so went the theory) buy some place—any place—elsewhere. There, they could live by themselves in peace, with their two children. What they were hoping was that Mom would say she was not going to go along with them. There was no other way for them to ask Mom, politely or otherwise, to just move out.

Still lacking the courage to bring up the subject with Mom herself, Bessie phoned our cousin Alice and her husband Don, in East

Brunswick, in southern New Jersey. Alice and Don, on separate phones, both listened at some length to all details of the latest family crisis, and then told Bessie they would talk it over and call her back.

Not ten minutes later, Alice phoned with the best news my sister had heard in a long time. She and Don were going to invite Mom to live with them. (Alice's mother, Belle, had been my mother's only sister.)

Fortunately for me, I was nowhere in the vicinity when Bessie finally got up the nerve to discuss the situation with Mom. As calmly as she could, under the circumstances, Bessie informed her that she and Bill, for all the above-fabricated reasons, planned on selling the house. Only the fact that Bessie at that very moment could hastily add that, #1, Alice and Don were hoping Mom would move in with them; #2, they were then in the process of fixing up the upstairs of their own house for Mom (two rooms, as usual), and #3, that Mom could move in whenever she was ready, kept the occasion from escalating into the civil war it would doubtless otherwise have been.

Unfortunately for their family finances, when Bessie and Bill did put their house on the market most "lookers" kept on going, or at most made offers which were far too low. Ant yet it was a really nice, well-built house and had been well taken care of. Eventually, they did manage to sell it—but only for the amount they had originally paid. No loss, no gain. But, they could at least live their own lives again. Shortly after the buyers' offer had been accepted, Mom moved out—apparently looking forward to being with Alice, but still in a huff.

In the Spring of 1965, my mother had been living with Alice and Don in East Brunswick for over a year. While experience should have taught all of us by then to take nothing for granted, the whole family assumed—without ever having heard anything to the contrary—that all was well down there. Until the phone rang.

It was Alice. Somehow, I'd always known that one of these days she would be calling me. She was. And that it would be about Mom. Of course. Cousin Alice was extremely upset, saying she had just given my mother what could only be described as an ultimatum. There was no particular hurry, Mom could take all the time she needed, the family was not to worry, etc. etc. But my mother was going to have to find some place else to stay.

When I asked what had been going on, Alice said she hardly knew where to start. She and Don had given up trying to get along with Mom, who was apparently still trying to manipulate other people's lives, and they'd had all they could take. In other words, said Alice, enough was enough. Although she never did actually use the phrase, "How about your mother coming back to **your** place?" the thought was there. (She may not have said it, but I heard it.)

The odd thing was, as far as manipulation was concerned, the only tactic Mom had occasionally used on me was her famous "Look". She had never tried to foist any of her ideas upon either me or Foster—and especially not Foster. In the way he catered to her needs, he was practically a saint, and even Mom always knew she could go just so far.

When the phone rang again that evening, I knew it had to be Mom— and oddly enough, she herself didn't seem all that upset It was basically, "Well, I knew it wouldn't work out here, anyway." She then added, "I'd really like to come back with you and Foster and the boys." Later, when Foster and I talked about it, as far as he was concerned Mom could move back in tomorrow.

It wasn't exactly the very next day, but the time did come when Mom reappeared with her well-traveled suitcases. For both her **and** the suitcases, it had been a full circle. From our house to Bessie and Bill's, from there to Alice and Don's, and now back to us. She looked to be no worse for the wear, and as a matter of fact, seemed happy to be back at the starting gate.

In July of that year, I had an even more interesting phone call. It was Rodney's girlfriend Carol—whom I had not yet met—and she had an announcement. She and Rodney were engaged, and had decided upon July 29 for their wedding date.

What could be more interesting to plan for than a wedding?—Weddings were work for the bride's family, of course, but fun for the groom's. Which is why I had five boys.

Immediately, I thought it would be nice for both families—as yet total strangers to each other—to get together as soon as possible before the ceremony. The next day I dressed three-year-old Jackie in what we considered his "Sunday suit," and drove up to call on Rodney's future in-laws.

Carol's parents lived in Fairfield, a small, almost rural town a few miles away. (Fairfield was the place my parents moved us when I was two years old.) Helen and Arno turned out to be a most hospitable couple, both retired, who saw to it that both Jackie and I felt at home. They were also delighted over the news they'd only just heard themselves.

Not until Jackie and I were on the way home again did something suddenly occur to me. I would soon be a **mother-in-law**. At that point, of course, I couldn't help but remember Ella, the very special one I'd had. I only hoped I could be half as good.

Since the wedding was only three weeks away, there was no time to waste. Foster and I hastily put together a welcome-to-the-family dinner for Carol's parents, as well as the future newlyweds, and everyone seemed to enjoy themselves. Our family was getting bigger by the minute, and it was a nice feeling.

Michael, Stevie and Gary seemed somewhat awed by Rodney's future status as a Husband, being, and actually a little upset, possibly fearing it meant he would no longer also be a Brother. (All three boys were totally in the dark as to what constituted a "husband.")

As for Jackie, he was getting to stay up much later that evening, which doubtless made a far bigger impression on him than the upcoming nuptials.

The wedding was held in a fairly ancient Presbyterian church in town, and as a special concession all four of Rodney's younger brothers were among those present at the ceremony itself. Their names were not

included, however, in the guest list for the reception and dinner to follow—which was probably a wise move.

Following the dinner, amid the customary uproar as they took leave
of all their guests, Rodney and Carol were off on their honeymoon.

For the rest of us, it was déjà vu time, with Mom now back in the
house and Rodney having just vacated his room. Mom wound up with
what had been the master bedroom. She seemed to appreciate the huge
walk-in closet, saying it was almost as good as another room (a not-too-
subtle hint that she was accustomed to having two rooms).

Michael graduated to Rodney's room, where he suddenly looked very
small there in Rodney's bed. Stevie now had his and Michael's former
room to himself—and his first official act was to throw all of Michael's
belongings out in the hall. Gary and Jackie had to share the room next
to Stevie, but with them, togetherness was not a problem. Foster and I
then moved into our new "quarters"—the former Play Room, now definitely toy-less. So, everybody was all taken care of—again.

For the coming summer of 1968, we had been planning the longest
vacation trip ever—this time to **Arizona**. Larry, a former insurance pal
of Foster's, had moved to Tucson the year before. From the day he
arrived, Larry deluged us with letters ecstatic about the state itself—the
wonderful climate, the friendly people, and, of course, the fantastic
scenery. Everything was absolutely super, the place was incomparable—
and he was SO lucky to be there. Each letter invariably ended with,
"WHEN are you guys all coming out"—and each time we had to give
the idea a little more serious thought.

To Foster and me, not only Arizona but the entire West might as well
have been on the other side of the world. But, why NOT Arizona? As a
teenager, I had never been farther west than Pennsylvania—and even
then, only a few feet inside the boundary line, just to be able to say "I've
been there."

Eventually we decided Foster's July vacation would be the ideal time
to at least head for Arizona and see what happened—or how far we got.

Once they were in on the plans, the boys were almost beside themselves. From then on, the first one up in the morning raced to the calendar, and one more day between them and Arizona was crossed off. Mom started making other plans for herself, as she detested long car rides to **any-where**, and Arizona, as far as she was concerned, was located on some other planet. The rest of us were more than ready, and when those two precious weeks finally arrived, we piled into the car and took off.

Most of the driving was necessarily via highways, but even so, just knowing we were actually going through one new state after another made every day seem like the first day out. On previous trips, the boys had always dozed off now and then—but not this time. Not only stay-ing wide awake, they were trying to see ahead down the road as far as possible

According to Larry (who was sometimes inclined to exaggerate), he would have us traveling around the entire state, twenty-four hours a day—however, anxious though we were to see all Arizona had to offer, none of us had any desire to be peering at landmarks in the middle of the night.

Unfortunately, Arizona, destination of all our dreams, was not to be. (Well, not **that** year.) Just before pulling into Terre Haute, Indiana, Foster very reluctantly gave us the bad news.

There was no way we were going to make it up and over the Rockies. Unknown to the boys or to me, Foster had been having increasingly more problems with the car, and none of the rest of us had been paying that much attention.

My own knowledge of mechanics was known to be non-existent (as long as the car kept going, how could there be a problem?) The boys, being their father's sons, were fast acquiring an interest in the world of cars and **anything** mechanical, but they were a little too young as yet to either notice what was going on with the car, or to be of any real help.

Foster turned the car around in Terre Haute and headed back. He helpfully (he thought) suggested we instead make a tour of the

Southeastern states, so the trip wouldn't be a total loss. At least we'd get to see SOME part of the country, said he.

For hours, not a voice was heard in that car. Nobody had a word to say to anybody else—least of all to that **mean** husband and father. I was every bit as disappointed as the boys, but I could at least see the logic of having to turn back. The boys, however, were still heartbroken.

From time to time, Foster would pull over to a rest stop, or a park, so the boys could run around and work off a little excess energy. He was obviously hoping, and doing his best, to somehow get them in a better mood. But wherever he stopped, at least one of the boys, while getting out of the car, would whisper in my ear, "Mom, make Pop turn around."

Each time they returned to the car, they found it still pointed in the direction of Washington, D.C., and they finally got the message: Forget about Arizona.

By the end of the day, finally resigned to the situation, their usual high spirits took over. The Far West was obviously not going to happen, at least not right now—but we promised them we would try again. And, the rest of **this** trip could still be fun.

Which it was. The boys got to see more historic buildings and famous cities than they ever expected. Michael and Stevie were keeping elaborate lists for future display to their buddies back home of where we went and what happened. Predictably, their all-time favorites were bat-tle-grounds. Big or small, it didn't matter. They just had to be labeled "Battlegrounds." Needless to say, countless rolls of film were used up in no time.

But not one of us for one moment had given up on eventually reaching the Grand Canyon State. It was still farther and farther away, yet it had been so near. And we'd ALMOST made it.

Each and every one of us had to be thinking: NEXT year, ARIZONA!

In July, 1969, **this** time we made it all the way. Almost twelve months to the day after the first foiled attempt, and in the very same car whose engine had thrown in the towel, mechanically speaking, back in Terre

Haute. Seeing us coming, the Rockies backed off, presumably welcoming us to the Golden West. We were over the top in no time—and Arizona was waiting.

And was Larry ever **right** about Arizona—the Grand Canyon State was the exact opposite of all things back East, and we couldn't wait to see it all. Hopefully not at night. From the day we crossed over the state line, Foster and I were comparing everything we saw to what we'd left behind, and almost every time New Jersey came in second.

Larry met us in Phoenix—so excited he was running back and forth, giving us each a big hug. An expert on all things Phoenician, he had made reservations for us at the Western Village, so that's where we were headed, but before we even checked in at the motel, he was showing us around.

The famous Chamber-of-Commerce weather made an instant hit. Sunshine all day and every day was a most welcome change from all the clouds back East, to which we were all too accustomed. As for Phoenix itself, only when we noticed how comparatively new the buildings were, did we realize that the **only** modern buildings back home were new houses here and there. Age-old offices and apartment complexes, until they crumbled to the ground or went up in smoke, stood forever.

Also, the uncrowded streets were a revelation. At that point in history in Phoenix, you could go straight to wherever you were going without aging half an hour at each red light. Or, what seemed like half an hour. Unfortunately, this was a status quo too good to go on forever, but it was great while it lasted.

Wherever we went, Larry stood by, absolutely beaming. He also seemed to be watching us very intently, which we assumed at the time was merely to note our reactions. Much later, he told us he had been hoping against hope we would be so impressed with everything we saw, and everywhere we went, that we would decide to move in on the spot. Being the main reason we were all there in the first place, however, Larry was determined to show us everything, and the sooner the better. He was, in a way, very proudly offering us the keys to HIS city and HIS state.

Larry in less than a week had escorted us all over Phoenix and its many suburbs—winding up with the justly-famous Phoenix zoo. There, we spent most of one day, and it of course turned out to be the boys' favorite. Left to them, we would have spent the entire week just exploring the zoo.

Tucson being where Larry himself had lived for the past year, we then followed him down there to make a Grand Tour of **that** city (though we still liked Phoenix better). Only then did we learn Larry had taken a whole week off from a brand-new job, one he'd started only a month before we arrived, just to show us HIS state. Naturally, we all had our fingers crossed from then on, hoping he hadn't lost the job on our account, and that it would still be there for him after we left. (Which it was, Larry's boss, fearing Larry had left for good, was only too happy to get him back.)

When the day finally came to leave for home, we had news for Larry—news which at first he was overjoyed to hear. Later, he said rather sadly that it would probably be foolish for him, considering his past experience with first-time visitors who changed their minds overnight, to really count on anything like **this** happening. What we told him was, we had decided to sell the house in Caldwell and move out to Phoenix. A classic case, if ever there was one, of throwing all caution to the winds—but it was what we both really wanted to do. As for the boys, they were actually trying NOT to get too excited right away. This brand-new idea of moving permanently to the Wild Wild West had their imaginations running equally wild—however, they were afraid if they counted on it, "something" might happen. Or, Mom and Dad might just change their minds. Or, it was all just idle talk. They were keeping their fingers crossed.

At first, Larry's face lit up, and then he seemed a little dejected. He tried to explain he had heard that very promise from SO many first-time visitors that he was afraid to really rely on this one. That if he did count on our moving back, and then nothing happened, it would be too much of a disappointment.

Larry, who was divorced some time before moving from the East, had always called us his second family—and, more than anything, he wanted us back permanently in his favorite state.

Driving back home, there was naturally only one topic of conversation. To begin a brand new life on the other side of the country was a pretty intoxicating idea, and no one in the car could talk of anything else.

We were taking the southern route home by way of variety, but by the time we reached Oklahoma City, Michael and Stevie were becoming more and more frustrated with just sitting in back and looking out the window. In desperation, they finally managed to convince their unsuspecting parents they had come up with a really good plan—and while at first it sounded like something out of the nut farm, after a while it began to make some sense.

The boys' proposal was, the two of them could be put on a plane then and there in Oklahoma City and head for Newark. There, they could be met by, for instance, Rodney (so far unaware, of course, of this devious plot).

Once Rodney had dropped his brothers off at the house (so went the plan), these two conspirators would then work night and day fixing the whole place up for sale before the rest of us even got home, thereby, of course, making it possible for us to put the house on the market even sooner.

Among the chores they assured us would be history by the time we were all reunited were vacuuming, sweeping, dusting and general cleanups. (With none of these activities were they even remotely familiar.) However, with no crystal ball at his disposal, Foster and I naively went along with this well-meant but **crazy** idea and proceeded directly to the airport.

Fate being on the boys' side at the moment, said airport, strangely enough, was less than ten minutes away. Once there, we were able to get tickets for them on the very next flight to Newark—and since this would be Michael and Stevie's very first flight to **anywhere**, I took my camera along to the starting gate.

These flying novices were trying their best to appear the most seasoned of travelers—with this, of course, just one more routine flight. Unfortunately for them, there stood Mom with her trusty 35mm camera in full view of everyone in the airport, recording the occasion for all the world to see.

The boys did their best to pretend they'd never seen me before and I must be aiming at somebody **else**, but at that moment if looks could have killed, there would be no Me.

Nevertheless, this historic "First Flight" went well, and Rodney met the plane in Newark as per schedule—still finding it hard to believe we were actually thinking of moving to Arizona. He finally decided the boys were just putting him on, in a big way. Once Rodney had dropped them off at the Caldwell house, transforming it into the Buy-of-the-Year would be up to Michael and Stevie.

By the time Foster, Gary, Jackie and I returned to the old home town, how much had actually been accomplished is a moot question. From outward appearances, nothing looked any different—or improved. Nor did the interior appear to be changed at all—or improved. As for cleaner—well, let's be real.

But the whole episode was far from a total loss. The boys got to enjoy their first plane trip (once the obnoxious photographer was out of the way), and the flight was safe. And while the house was NOT miraculously improved overnight, at least it didn't look any worse.

Three weeks later, this house we had all loved for the past fifteen years was officially on the market. Some of our friends—and ALL of our neighbors—were still astounded at the very idea of our moving away from Caldwell, a town we all knew like the backs of our hands, to a state we'd only briefly visited.

In the beginning, everyone's unspoken comment was, you must be out of your minds to take such a chance. Yet in time, first one neighbor and then another admitted they themselves had occasionally toyed with equally radical ideas—and they all seemed a little envious, in a way.

In that particular neighborhood, houses similar to ours had become harder to sell lately. They were mostly very large, for one thing, and anything but new. We had originally been told ours was built 50 years ago, but it would have taken a lot more than that to discourage us, once we'd seen it. Everyone we spoke to cautioned us to expect a long wait.

Nevertheless, almost overnight we were firmly convinced this proposed move of ours must have been ordained from above. That house appealed, and in a big way, to the very first "lookers" brought in by the very first agent.

They were a fairly young couple. The husband was one of the many vice-presidents of a New York bank, and they had a year-old baby. Not exactly the ones you expect to find looking for a house of that size. As he and his wife came through the front door, the husband was loudly insisting the house was in every way a veritable incarnation of his childhood home. He literally ran from room to room, upstairs and down, saying over and over again, "I never thought I'd see it again. This is wonderful."

Meanwhile, his wife was equally taken with one room after another, continually pulling out list after list, checking off certain items—and smiling. Foster and I could see ourselves in those two people—back in 1954, we had reacted the very same way when we saw that house for the first time.

From the moment these people walked in the door to start looking around, something told us they just **might** be the ones—and when the agent, after a brief consultation with his clients, announced, "We'd like to sit down and talk," (real estate jargon for "make a deal"), we knew we had it made. Unbelievably, the house was sold the **first** day to the **first** lookers.

Fifteen years ago, we had paid $16,000 for it. We were now agreeing to accept $32,000, a fairly impressive profit in the economy of that time. "The Road to Arizona" had opened up in a hurry, and we were on our way.

Well, maybe it wasn't all that simple. Once everyone concerned eventually signed in all the right places, Foster and I remembered something. While selling the house had to come first, we hadn't made enough practical plans for the move itself. Having just returned from his annual vacation, and with his employers now agreeing to an eventual transfer to Phoenix, we were now advised they were not about to consent to any more time off for him in the meantime—at least not at their expense.

Prior to hearing that decision, we had assumed that one of us— preferably Foster—would fly out as soon as possible to Phoenix and **rent** a house somewhere. Once moved in, we could take our time looking around for a house to **buy**, but when the Company, in no uncertain terms, rendered its no-more-time-off decision, suddenly I was the obvious one to make the trip. For me, this was bad news. I was a most reluctant candidate, to say the least. And stalling for time didn't work for me. Within days, my ticket to the Golden West was staring me in the face, and it was time to pack. Then, it was time for the goodbye scene at the house.

The very idea of leaving New Jersey, the state in which from Day One I had been surrounded by family, friends and acquaintances, and flying **alone** to the other side of the country (there to encounter whoknows-what) was making me more nervous by the minute. Nothing in the preceding twenty years of being a stay-at-home wife (which I had loved being, apologies, of course, to all liberals), had not in any way prepared me for this giant-sized step toward an independence I hadn't even been looking for.

What was almost the very last straw came in the form of a chorus of pleadings from the boys, to wit: "Mom, get a house with a POOL." My heart almost sank at **that** request. (In New Jersey, who knows about pools?) But since no one except Foster had the remotest idea how I felt at the time, I decided to pretend a pool should be no problem.

Foster drove me down to Newark Airport, and I finally took off to meet whatever Fate had in mind for me out there in the Great Southwest.

The closer the plane got to Phoenix, the more I longed to be somewhere else. ANYwhere else. Then, shortly before landing, an announcement came over the P.A. system regarding the arrival time at Ontario.

Ontario??? Ontario was in CANADA. How in the world had I managed to get myself on the wrong plane? All those people who had been checking my reservation, sending on my baggage, and waving me on— what city had THEY seen as my destination?

My until-then silent seatmate noticed my distress—he could hardly miss, I was climbing over him frantically to get to the flight attendant (in those days, politically-incorrectly known as stewardess)—and very kindly reassured me that no, we were not really in Canada. Ontario in this case was in California, and would be the next stop AFTER Phoenix—a fact apparently known to each and every passenger on the plane except me.

At Sky Harbor in Phoenix, I somewhat shakily got off the plane. With my courage evaporating by the minute, I rented a car and managed to locate the Western Village motel, site of our first visit to Phoenix. At least **that** looked familiar, and when the room clerk even recognized the last name, I began to feel a little more at home.

Looking ahead to the next morning's sure-to- be ordeal already had me literally pacing the floor, so that evening I decided that doing something would at least pass the time. Taking the bull by the horns, i.e., calling the nearest real estate agent, I was lucky enough to reach one still at his office who was actually walking out the door when the phone rang. (No real estate agent ignores an incoming call, whatever the hour.)

Together, we discussed over the phone whatever rentals might be available. He assured me he had listings galore, and we arranged to get together the next morning.

With that first crucial step behind me—and feeling for the first time I just **might** be able to accomplish what I came out for—I felt a little more relaxed. The motel carpet was now safe from being walked on back and forth that night.

My new-found realtor was not one to lose any time. Early the next morning, his phone call woke me from what had turned out to be a surprisingly sound sleep. He already had several prospective rentals lined up for me to see, and within the hour we were meeting in the motel lobby to check out his list.

As a New Jersey native, I had taken it for granted autumn temperatures were as chilly in all other states as they were back home, consequently, I had packed the usual sweaters and jacket. Even an umbrella, just in case. (Umbrellas in the Grand Canyon State tend to gather dust.)

As my agent was driving us to house #1, he observed the sweater I had brought along, and politely concealing a smile, inquired what temperature I would guess it to be at the moment. I said, about 70 degrees, since to a Jerseyite it felt like a Spring day. He then advised me it was actually 90. (My first brush with Arizona's famous lack of humidity, and of course I thought the man had to be kidding. He wasn't, and now I had one more reason to be addicted to Arizona.)

Disastrous is the only word for the very first house he showed me. And that was just from the outside. On the sidewalk, we climbed all over trash bags, presumably waiting to be moved out to the curb. Inside, it was even worse. The ceiling in the dining room had stains from one side of the room to the other, indicating leaks from the roof were not exactly unknown. One appliance after another in the kitchen was "temporarily" just not working.

Worst of all, throughout the whole inspection, the owners stood by very expectantly. How they had the nerve to put a place like that on the market, let alone stand there waiting for me to snap it up, I couldn't even imagine. (My agent was literally speechless—usually a "No-No" in his profession.)

Oddly enough, it was almost funny. We left as soon as we could, but I often wondered if that house was **ever** sold.

The second house was a little more inviting from the outside. It was also at least semi-clean indoors. However, it didn't have much of anything else going for it, so we headed for house #3. And then #4. By this time I was less and less hopeful, and trying to resign myself to looking at probably ten or twelve houses a day, each one worse than the last, then finally calling home to announce, "There's nothing here. Nothing."

For some reason, the number 5 has always been lucky for me. (Shining example: 5 sons.) So maybe I could have been more prepared for **this** #5.

Reason: House #5 was finally IT. All the features I was to look for, everything we had talked about—even the location. The perfect house, just sitting there waiting for us to move in. Compared to this house, everything we had seen that day had been a sheer waste of everybody's time. This was by far the most attractive, located in a really nice section of the city, yet not that far away in distance from all the miserable houses we had been going through. To expect anything in the same class to ever come up again was impossible. My agent, needless to say, was equally delighted.

Also, besides being nicely landscaped, it had a pool. Repeat: a POOL—as per the boys' request. The owners were out of the state, and the house was empty.

The two of us took our time checking out every room. Every closet. All the utilities. Also (what is probably, in Arizona, the top item on everyone's list) the refrigeration system. Going through the house itself, as well as the grounds outside, without any owners standing by, waiting for an offer, was a lot easier. I finally reached for my checkbook. There was no way I was going to let what looked like the answer to a prayer get away from me. Or us.

After handing the agent a check for $600, which was the two-month deposit required on the rent, I checked out the house a second time, admiring all its features even more now that I could picture all of us actually living in it.

Eventually something dawned on me. Not only was this the best house for me to rent, it was the ideal house for **us** to buy. To me, this was a perfectly logical decision—I'd never been so sure of anything in my life—and I so informed the agent, who had been patiently standing by.

He was still clutching the check originally handed him as a deposit on the **rent**. This same check now magically represented an "earnest money" deposit on a **sale**. He looked first at me, then down at the check, then back at me, in utter amazement. I couldn't blame him. Things were moving a little fast for me as well. (Something told me this agent couldn't wait to get home and say, "You'll never BELIEVE what happened today!")

This interesting turn of events seemed to be a first for him, and although delighted, he seemed to be a little dazed. Phoenix houses in that era were not being snapped up that often, or that fast—even at the current bargain prices—but I've never had occasion to regret, nor has anyone in my family, the way things went that day. (From the day we moved in, each of us loved that house—and the location itself, for many reasons, turned out to be right for all of us. Schools were nearby. Foster's future office was located over on the freeway, which was practically the center of town. Shopping malls were all over the place. With all that going for us, plus a climate from heaven, what MORE could one ask?)

That afternoon, back at the Western Village, a few second thoughts began to set in. Not about the house itself—I had no doubts there—but what kind of reaction I'd get from Foster and the boys. I was to call them later that evening, and they would be expecting to hear only about a **rental** house, the reason I was out here in the first place.

At the prearranged time, I called home. No more than two seconds had gone by when Foster answered. (He said later he'd actually been sitting there with his hand on the phone.) My immediate impression was, at that very moment he was surrounded by all the boys (which he was), and that everyone in the room was waiting with bated breath (which they were) for news of their future (**rental**) house in far-away Phoenix.

Realizing there was no tactful way to break the kind of news no one was expecting—least of all the loving husband who had entrusted his loving wife with this Mission Impossible—I simply asked, "Are you sitting down?"

There was a brief pause. He somewhat nervously replied, "Yes."

My announcement, "Well, we just bought a house," met with total silence. Even the boys were quiet in the background. They naturally had no idea what I had just said, and probably thought I was still talking. As for me, I decided either we had just been disconnected—OR, their father had just keeled over.

He hadn't. In fact, when he finally found his voice again, he was really sweet (well, the damage was already done, right?), and from then on, everybody in the room was talking at once. Including me, on the other end of the phone. Then we all calmed down a little. That lasted about a minute—until the boys got the word about their new POOL, at which point there was an uproar that probably had the entire neighborhood dialing 911.

Back in July, with the six of us all back in New Jersey again, my mother finally accepted the fact that we were indeed going to wind up in Arizona. She also knew she was more than welcome to remain with us forever—and wherever—we happened to be. But for some reason, though she herself had never been anywhere out West, she KNEW she would not want to try living out there. (Judging from prior events, my mother would sooner or later have a change of heart and decide to join us in Phoenix. In the meantime, Foster and I went along with whatever she decided for herself.)

Shortly thereafter, Mom arranged to share an apartment with two women she had worked with at one time, who lived in the very next town. (It happened to be the same town Bessie and Bill had lived in, until they and Mom were no longer able to get along—and then came the famous parting of the ways.)

Considering my mother's track record, just how long **this** would work out for her, was anyone's guess. Foster eventually got her moved in with her new hosts, and we wished them all the best of luck.

Before our own moving day arrived, non-stop packing went on every day and occasionally half the night—even so, those few weeks went by faster than we expected. We were still trying to believe we were actually moving to Arizona, and could still talk of nothing else.

All four boys had to be officially checked out of school, more or less in mid-term. Their records from kindergarten on would be forwarded to an elementary school for Gary and Jackie, and to a high school for Michael and Stevie. Both schools were within walking distance from our new house.

Up until the very day we left, almost everyone we talked to (most of whom were more and more downcast as they watched us getting ready to go), assured us that they themselves also had secret plans to one of these days escape to some place like far-away Arizona. (There IS no place like Arizona.) To my knowledge, however, to this day each and every one of them still resides in the Garden State.

The two cats we had at that time, who would eventually follow us to Phoenix, were Pokey and Lightning—both very aptly named. Pokey, as a tiny black-and-white kitten, had been left shivering in an equally tiny **Tupperware** dish on our front porch one winter's night by person or persons unknown. (Whoever they were, they picked the right house. Pokey had a home for life with us—almost 18 years.)

A few days later, our local veterinarian advised us that Pokey, though physically in very good shape, was probably lonesome. Later that day, Foster and I stopped by the pound and immediately fell for a red, super-energetic kitten. We instinctively named him Lightning, and brought him home to Pokey.

Lightning, whenever the spirit moved him, was fully capable of streaking across the room, jumping on Pokey, and waking him out of a sound sleep—the latter being Pokey's favorite occupation. Lightning himself, who had the energy of 10 cats, slept less than any I've ever known. To him, sleep was a sheer waste of valuable time.

Moving day itself was a real winner, but it came dangerously close to making us real losers. That afternoon, after the van left, Fate once again took over. The moving men themselves were out of there. They had arrived at 8 a.m., made what seemed to be hundred of trips from the house to their over-sized van (which had done an excellent job of blocking traffic out there) and finally left.

Their truck was literally just turning the corner, and this being a rather significant day in all our lives, I was standing at the window watching it. Then the phone rang.

Foster answered, in the next room. It was our realtor—who, as far as we knew, had already handled all details of the closing to be held the following morning. He had the kind of news you never want to hear. He began by saying he was really sorry to be the one to tell us, BUT some unforeseen technicality had reared its ugly head at what must have been the very last second. Therefore, the signing of all the final papers could

NOT take place tomorrow as scheduled, but would **probably** have to be postponed for a week. Or ten days. Or possibly even longer.

I will never forget standing by the window in the living room (the boys were all at my sister's for the day), listening to Foster's side of the conversation, and deducing from his explosive replies what apparently, unbelievably, was going on. I actually wondered at that moment if the day would ever come when we could look back to this day and think all this was funny. It was a long time coming, but that day did arrive. Back then, it was anything **but** something to laugh at.

At the time, Foster, never one to sit calmly wondering what to do, had already charged out of the house. It was a safe bet that **some**where **some**body's head was about to roll for allowing this to happen. All Foster had to do was find the right strings to pull—and the right **some**body.

Which he did. What steps he actually took he never did say, but when he walked back in the door, he strongly resembled the cat that swallowed the canary. The crisis was over, and the closing again set for the following day, as per schedule.

Unfortunately for family togetherness, a temporary split-up lay ahead before we could all wind up in Arizona. Out in Phoenix, yet **another** set of closing papers, for our future house in that city, was waiting to be signed, and it was now Foster's turn to fly out there alone. As soon as the boys and I had dropped him off at Newark Airport, we would set our own sights for Phoenix and drive out, trusting to encounter no more false alarms en route.

Fortunately for everyone's nerves, there were none. We were taking the northern route as far west as Flagstaff, then turning south in the direction of Phoenix, and this time the trip all the way out was really fun. Of course, we'd made the same trip going home via the southern route only a few months before, but to all of us it still felt like an adventure into the unknown.

To me, the biggest help in driving across the country with four boys was that Michael, at seventeen, now the proud possessor of a driver's license, could take over from time to time—otherwise, we might not be here yet.

Stevie was then sixteen. Both Foster and I strongly suspected the biggest attraction for Stevie in moving to Arizona was that he was already more than old enough there for a learner's permit, the requirement being only fifteen-and-a-half, as opposed to New Jersey's seventeen.

It wasn't a sea of roses, however. I did have to keep one eye open whenever Michael was at the wheel. Each time it was his turn, the car would gradually and mysteriously pick up speed it probably didn't know it had until then. I would then call the above to Michael's attention. A typical teenager—a term to be construed as both compliment and insult—he was then absolutely amazed to look down and discover whatever RPM the car had sneaked up to. At this point, of course, we slowed down for a while.

Exactly four days after leaving New Jersey on a cloudy, rainy, overcast day (i.e. the norm), Michael, Stevie, Gary, Jackie and I were gleefully reading aloud the "Welcome to Arizona" sign at the new Mexico border.

We were really, really there. The newest citizens of Arizona—that beautiful state for which all of us had turned our lives upside down. At that particular moment, crossing over into the state, what probably impressed us most of all was the sunshine that we'd seen nary a trace of on the way out, but which was to be a most-appreciated part of our lives from then on.

Between us and Phoenix there were now only a few short hours, and at long last we'd see "Pop" again, waiting for us at the Western Village (which was almost home-like by this time.) Oddly enough, all the way down, from Flagstaff to Phoenix, the radio played almost non-stop the two most appropriate (for us) hit-of-the-year recordings

One was my current favorite, Glenn Campbell's "By the Time I Get to Phoenix" (talk about **timing!**)—and the other was just as appropriate— "Arizona". If that wasn't a sign this trip was **meant** to be, I don't know why else those two colossal hits followed us all the way down to Phoenix. No one ever convinced any of us that it was sheer coincidence.

South of Flagstaff, the scenery reversed itself almost by the minute, from snow-covered mountains down into the beautiful desert. Temperatures, of course, grew gradually warmer, so even without a map you had to know you were changing climates.

Flagstaff itself, in the northern part of the state at a fairly high altitude, had been surprisingly chilly—even to Easterners, who unfortunately expect nothing else at that time of year. Snow all over the mountainsides proved that winter is a fact of life in Northern Arizona almost immediately after summer.

Finally in Phoenix, first on the agenda was finding "Pop" as soon as possible. Having called him the evening before, we caught up with the family's "missing link" at the Western Village that afternoon. Foster had spent the last few hours pacing up and down in his room (which brought back a few memories) trying to decide how soon he should start getting upset in case we were late. We actually arrived a little early (with Michael at the wheel), so he never got a chance to worry.

The long-awaited family reunion was finally under way, which should have been high time for all of us to relax a little. However, as usual, everybody was trying to outtalk everybody else—until we finally agreed upon making a certain trip a few blocks away.

The new house had to be inspected—for the boys' sake, at least. They had talked of nothing else for ages, and waited long enough. We couldn't expect them to wait much longer.

Foster had been advised that very day that the moving van had not yet even arrived in the state, let alone in Phoenix. We would be motel prisoners for a while, but we could at least start getting acquainted with our future residence. At first, just seeing the house from the curb, the boys politely but rather hurriedly admired it. Then we all went inside. Foster and I naively assumed our sons would first carefully examine each and every room—but having been parents for some time, we should have known better. First of all, an ear-shattering stampede, from the front door to the rear patio, was under way. We moved aside ASAP. Not one of those **kids** (and I use the term advisedly—you wouldn't have guessed even one of them was over seven) glanced to either right or left as they tore through the living room. Fortunately there was no furniture in the way. Once out on the patio, all four raced en masse over to what else?—the POOL (sole object of the entire trip, as far as they were concerned). Peace and quiet in the neighborhood from then on was history. Two days later, the movers called. They were about to emerge from desert, and would be at the house sometime the next morning. It seemed like ages since we had seen our own furniture, but it was from then on we began feeling really at home. We even enjoyed seeing the movers again. Theirs were the first familiar faces we'd seen since leaving New Jersey, which now seemed like the other side of the world.

When the movers were finally all done with the job, we were really sorry to see them go—but then they had an announcement, which to our ears sounded strangely familiar. Two of the three movers, who happened to be New Jerseyites, had become more and more enamored with Arizona—and especially Phoenix. All three decided to remain in the city for a "day or so," and take a look around—just in case.

From all we had been told back East, Foster had been **officially** transferred by his employers to their branch office in Phoenix. Normally a fairly routine procedure, this should have been nothing to worry about. We soon discovered there might be a great deal to worry about.

Now that we were here, everything connected in any way with the transfer seemed to be slowly but surely falling through the cracks. As yet, not one official transfer paper had come through. Because Foster was technically on "unpaid personal leave," we were of course not looking for checks. In lieu thereof, we did receive constant double-talk, day after day, from an assortment of company officials supposedly in charge. As if that weren't bad enough, what funds we had brought with us seemed to be shrinking by the minute.

Foster, highly resentful as he was about the company's apparent negligence in this case, was predictably too restless to just wait around and do nothing. Every morning, he was out looking for some kind of interim job, to cover the bills that never stopped coming. Overnight, the whole situation appeared to be almost out of control. Yet, from Day One, everything had fallen into place as it if were meant to happen. And now this. Saying times were tough was the understatement of the year. It was getting **scary**.

Late one evening, I had a suggestion. From past experience, I assumed Foster would again object strenuously, but I thought he would at least appreciate the offer. I very casually remarked it might be a good idea for me to go back to work. (This after eighteen years of "non-work", meaning the wife/mother/housekeeper bit, which, being uncompensated, was obviously not "work.")

As I all but froze in my chair (not easy in Arizona), Foster's totally unexpected reply was, "Well, maybe that's not such a bad idea." **Surely** he was just being funny.

He wasn't. Nothing like having your bluff called—and this time in spades. There I had made the grand gesture of all time and it was coming right back at me. (How could I now say "I was just kidding?")

Ready or not, the time for me to get out there and jump into the cruel, cruel "World of Jobs" was, as a certain younger generation would so eloquently put it, like NOW. The next step being in MY ballpark, I started checking out all the classified ads for stenos. Ads far less interesting than any of the sales pitches from the various malls, which I normally turned to right after scanning the news. I'd almost forgotten how to shop anyway, thanks to our current budget crisis.

Hoping my shorthand speed of yore could at this late date somehow be retrieved, I started to practice at all hours of the day, taking down dialogue from soap operas or news bulletins on the radio—meanwhile hoping that people in real life were not **dictating** that fast.

Since I still typed letters occasionally, that particular skill was probably up to par. I took out the typewriter anyway to practice, pretending I was part of a real live office crew again.

The Great Computer Era was then far in the future. While computers had probably been in existence for some time, I had never heard of them, nor had most people I knew. Only geniuses in far-away places were into computer technology, and so far they were sharing it with no one. Consequently, I was at least spared an expensive dash to the nearest computer academy—which was non-existent, anyway.

Whatever shorthand and typing skills I would need were apparently there for me a week or so later. I applied for—and got—a job with the County. The gentleman looking over the results of the various tests I had taken seemed rather pleased, and said "Congratulations. We've got the **ideal** job for you—Court Clerk." It **was** an absolutely fascinating job, once I knew what I was doing, but it did take a while, memorizing a minimum of at least 50,000 details—and in the first few weeks of my employment, the term "ideal" never would have occurred to me.

Even the term "Court Clerk" was new to me, but my asking, "What is that?" drew an interesting explanation. The job basically called for the Clerk being in court during all kinds of proceedings at a desk alongside the Judge's so-called "bench." Not only do trials and/or hearings obviously require the presence of a Judge, they can't even get off the ground without a Court Clerk.

Reason: One of said Clerk's myriad duties is pressing the button that summons His Honor to appear at precisely the right moment—meanwhile keeping track of all proceedings by way of written "minutes." These minutes—along with the court reporter's transcripts—constitute the official court records of who was there and what happened—all of which sounded very simple at the time, and proved to be anything but. Courtroom clerks are expected to be fully acquainted with rules of procedure in every imaginable type of case—criminal, civil, domestic, probate, you-name-it.

These particular rules surely date back to the Stone Age. However, should any be overlooked, this is a crime in itself, and the gallows are waiting right outside the courtroom.

(Well, not really, but they might as well be. All courtroom clerks of my acquaintance will now rise and solemnly swear to the truth of the above. Or at it, whichever comes first.)

As with most jobs, the hiring procedure itself sometimes turns into such a long-drawn-out ordeal that, once it's over, you feel it's O.K. now to relax, your troubles are all behind you. In my case, being hired was only the beginning. It is still a mystery to me how, after 18 years of being completely detached from the business world, I apparently took it for granted I could walk right back into it and pick up where I left off—certainly a case of "ignorance is bliss" on my part. Even so, I was becoming more and more apprehensive about showing up for work the following Monday.

Fortunately, that first day with the County, about which I had been so nervous, was fairly encouraging. Everyone I met there, and later got to know, did their very best to be helpful. What more could one ask?

What did come as a surprise was finding myself so regimented as to time. In all my previous jobs, I basically just kept track of what I did, and when. In the County, half the day was consumed with signing in and out. Even for coffee breaks. And there was always the chance that while you were waiting in line to sign out, the cafeteria might be putting up a certain notice, dreaded by all. For any office staff, there is no crisis even remotely comparable to seeing the sign OUT OF COFFEE.

This was a whole new way of life for me. At home, as far as time was concerned, clocks were little more than decorations on the wall, not something controlling your every minute.

A few days after I turned into a Court Clerk by day, the long-awaited papers sanctifying Foster's formal transfer (and resumption of salary) arrived by Special Delivery—a postal extravagance certainly called for under the circumstances.

All parties back East responsible for the long delay were SO regretful and, of course, individually blameless. (The official cop-out was, "Well, it was just one of those things.") At that point, Foster and I and the boys were so happy we couldn't have cared less whose fault it was. The time had come to celebrate—and only now, **finally,** were we REALLY bonafide residents of ARIZONA!!

Part II

The Newest Residents

The newest residents of Phoenix, Arizona, at long last arrived after much turmoil from the Garden State, had expected to immediately feel like natives; however, Foster, the four boys (Michael—17, Stevie—16, Gary—12, and Jackie—7), and I soon found this could hardly be accomplished overnight.

Rodney, our first-born son, had already called from New Jersey to say he would be putting Pokey and Lightning, the two cats we had temporarily left behind, on the next plane for Arizona. Both cats had doubtless been pacing the floor ever since, wondering what kitty-crime they could have committed to suddenly find themselves apparently abandoned forever.

There was no reason to suspect these two feline certified-members-of-the family were not well cared for en route—but they were **not** taken off at Sky Harbor in Phoenix. I had been patiently waiting there in the cargo office for some time, but when the plane had taken off again and NO CATS had been brought in, I was on the verge of hysteria. I was soon advised Pokey and Lightning had been mistakenly carried on to Los Angeles.

What Pokey and Lightning thought of LAX International, we'll never know. (Hopefully, they will one day include it in their memoirs.) Fortunately for us, some kind soul out there finally noticed our cats were destined elsewhere and hastily transferred them to the next plane for Phoenix.

By that time, those two cats had probably given up all hope of ever doing anything more interesting than flying in a kitty-crate over a country they couldn't even see. In my opinion—which I made known to all those within hearing distance—they were more than entitled to a couple of nervous breakdowns. As was I, still waiting in Phoenix at the airport, first imagining all kinds of horrors—and later toying with the idea of a lawsuit.

However, our wandering kitties did make it back late that same night. The family was at least a complete unit again, and cats and humans alike began to recover.

Most unhappily, one week later, Lightning, by far the more active and hyper of the two, disappeared, never to be seen again. Since both he and Pokey had always been "outdoor cats," and Phoenix being unknown territory to them, I had kept them indoors for over a week, hoping to get them used to the place and to consider it home. Apparently, that wasn't quite long enough for Lightning, although Pokey always stayed close to the house. With no success, I scoured the entire neighborhood for weeks looking for Lightning, and every third day, checked out all the cats being held at the Humane Society (where, if only I could have figured out how, I would have opened each and every cage in an instant).

The reason for going every third day was that I had been informed the animals were put to sleep on their fourth day there. It was such a traumatic experience to go through the place at all that every third day was more than enough. I never found Lightning anywhere, and can only hope some fellow cat-lover somewhere picked him up and took care of him for me.

The years seemed to pass very quickly in Phoenix, almost competing with the rate at which our family was now growing smaller and smaller. In the late 80s, the boys were all out of high school, but somewhat scattered about the city and no longer living with us. Michael and Stevie were both married, Gary was still a carefree bachelor, while Jackie was now enrolled at Northern Arizona University in Flagstaff.

Back in 1973—four years after we moved to Phoenix—quite a few changes had affected many members of the family. My mother, as predicted, had moved out to Arizona that year to be with us, and apparently adapted, with no problems whatsoever, to the very climate she had **known** ahead of time she wouldn't like. The only sad note that same year was the sudden, unexpected death of my one and only older sister, Bessie; the one person who had always been there for me from the day I was born. I wished I could have been with her, and held her in my arms, before she passed away.

A very happy event that year, however, was the birth of our first grandchild Mark, son of a very thrilled Stevie and Cheryl. I myself had just had my 52nd birthday—and Stevie had already made me a **Grandma**. For a while there, I felt like Methuselah.

Another family occasion to celebrate came in August when Michael and Barbara were married back East in Barbara's home town, in New Jersey. While Foster and I were unfortunately unable to attend the ceremony, we were later supplied with many photos of the wedding itself. Not only that, but the newlyweds would be returning to Phoenix after their honeymoon, whereupon our extended family would be even larger.

All in all, 1973 was a momentous year for all concerned—my mother coming out to join us, the very sad death of my sister, Bessie, the joyous birth of our first grandson Mark, and the happy marriage of our son Michael. It was a year certain to go down in family history.

A few years later, we had also lost Pokey, due mainly to his fairly advanced cat-age of almost eighteen years. For me, the one sad thing about owning pets is trying to accept the fact they won't live forever. From time to time, for instance, when an emergency arises—you have to remind yourself that one of these days this cat, or that dog, won't be here. Your very next thought is—but not **NOW**. You're never ready, and it's never the right time.

But we were glad we'd had Pokey as long as we did—he was truly one of a kind. Once God had donated Pokey to the world, the mold was probably destroyed. That cat took no guff from anybody, anywhere, any time. Particularly from dogs, who literally backed up when Pokey showed any sign of heading in their direction. As sweet and affectionate as Pokey was with humans, that arrogant "Super-Cat" never hesitated to smack any **DOG**, of whatever size. And usually for nothing—the poor dog just happened to be in the way.

There is no doubt in my mind the day Pokey checked into Cat Heaven, every cat in the vicinity jumped up and saluted.

One Sunday in 1977, Foster and I were just casually driving around, still getting acquainted with the rest of the state, when we accidentally "discovered" New River, an out-of-the-way unincorporated, very rural community located about thirty miles north of Phoenix.

Compared to Phoenix, New River was like another world. It was smog-free, fairly mountainous—the views were spectacular—and at that time very sparsely settled. Every once in a while we would notice a For Sale sign sitting on totally empty land, and very often the sign would be covered with dust, or almost overgrown by desert vegetation, certainly implying that particular area was seldom visited—least of all by prospective buyers.

One particular sign caught our eye, and we were actually able to decipher the local agent's name. The sign was set out in front of a six-and-a-half acre parcel, most of which sat on top of a hill, in a beautifully scenic area, as is most of New River. We decided to stop and just take a look around.

After climbing up the hill, pushing our way through every imaginable type of desert growth—saguaros, junipers, Joshuas, and every kind of cactus known to man—we finally made it up to the top. And that's what did it. We were both hooked in a matter of minutes, right on the spot, and for all time. It was hard even then, when land parcels were plentiful, to believe such a beautiful property hadn't been sold long ago, and at any price. Chances were, it had probably never even been shown, and in any case, not too many people would have wanted to climb that hill.

There were mountains on all four sides. Not one house in sight (not at that time, anyway)—and the views were gorgeous. Oddly enough, until that very moment, neither of us had ever given a thought to living anywhere in the state besides Phoenix. The asking price for the six-and-a-half acre property was $10,000. Irresistible then—and unbelievable now. We managed to track down the agent, and returned with him to the property. A sales pitch of any kind at that point would have been superfluous. We wouldn't have even heard it—the property had sold itself.

With a bona fide sale in the agent's pocket, so to speak, we returned to our cars for the usual paperwork. It being the end of the month, the balance sitting in our checking account was negligible—$50, but that was the amount we gave him (also, the amount he accepted). It was, after all, legal tender—and he'd probably forgotten the last time he made a sale in that area.

We subsequently became very friendly with that particular agent, who, in time, confided that the owner of the property had been outraged, complaining that if we were to back out of the deal, $50 was all he could recover. He had been looking for at least $1,000 down. But the deal was done—and we had a binding contract: $10,000 for six-and-a-half, ultra-scenic acres is a deal you don't run across too often.

All the way back to Phoenix, we were congratulating ourselves, and a week later, we had sent the owner an additional $4,950. In 1977, a $5,000 deposit was a fairly impressive sum. The asking price today for raw land of those dimensions in that particular area is probably escalating as we speak—and the 10% deposit thereon would NOT be $50.

Those five big ones were the extent of our resources, but it eventually dawned on us that each month's payment on the $5,000 balance was no more than a drop in the bucket. Fading far into the future was our dream of one day owning the New River land, selling our Phoenix house (naturally at some astronomical figure), and then building our own home on top of that hill; there to be surrounded by all that breathing room and gaze out upon scenic views galore. In Phoenix, our lot size was a third of an acre, which was fairly average in the city.

One day in the spring of 1978, our guardian angels apparently decided to come to the rescue—and real estate-wise, our fortunes changed almost overnight. Reason: our son Rodney and his wife Carol were flying out for a visit from New Jersey (unknown to us, Rodney had been in contact for some time with Michael about our New River venture). He had asked Michael to find out the amount then due on our note, which at that time was about $3600, sent a check for that amount to the title company, and had the recorded deed sent to Michael. (Foster and I still knew nothing of what had been going on.) As per their arrangement, Michael held onto the deed until the day after Rodney and Carol had left for home.

That afternoon, Michael and Barbara very casually stopped by. Foster and I were out in the front yard at the time, and suddenly Michael was handing me a large, official-looking envelope. With an ear-to-ear grin, he said, "This is from Rodney. You'll never guess what it is."

Michael had **that** right. Not in a million years would I have had a clue. Being suddenly presented with an official deed to property you expected to be paying on forever is not, to put it mildly, a run-of-the-mill occurrence. To say that Foster and I were forever grateful to Rodney for his generosity, and concern, is probably the understatement of all time. We called as soon as possible to thank him and Carol, but still couldn't say enough.

Early the next morning, a certain realtor in Phoenix had probably just walked in the door when his phone rang. Now that we were the official owners of the New River property, Foster and I wanted to have our Phoenix house listed for sale as soon as possible—and this was the very same realtor who had originally shown me around Phoenix and then sold us that very house. The prospect of pocketing yet another commission had this very happy realtor ringing the doorbell within the hour.

Although we mistakenly assumed the house would be sold to the first "looker" as fast as I had fallen for it several years ago, Foster, nevertheless, decided to limit the time period with the realtor for selling the house to thirty days (which turned out to be a very good idea).

In 1969, the price we had paid for the house was $26,450. Eight years later, with Phoenix rapidly becoming the city to which the rest of the country would be moving, real estate prices were fast going out of sight, and the realtor advised us to ask for $65,000.

At the end of the thirty days, there was still no buyer. Various agents had showed the house several times during the day when both of us were at work, but not one offer had been made. And yet this was the one house we sincerely believed to be among the most attractive in that particular area.

As time went on, there was good reason for hoping the house would be sold as soon as possible. We had already approved plans for what we wanted built in New River, and work had already been started up there. Payment for same would be expected as the work went along, but a lot more progress was being made on the New River site than in Phoenix, as far as finding a buyer was concerned.

As we lost more and more sleep worrying about it all, it was becoming very obvious that if the date eventually set for moving to New River

preceded the day the Phoenix house was sold, we could find ourselves knee deep in lawsuits. This was a very real possibility staring us in the face, and the 30-day contract with the realtor having expired, it was high time to take a few brave steps.

With no longer any commission to consider, we reduced the price to a firm $58,000 and put our own sign reading "For Sale By Owner" out in the front yard. (The term "lawn" is seldom heard here. The area normally devoted to grass in the rest of the country is usually well-filled in by desert plants—plants which have their own built-in advantage, i.e., no lawn mowers needed.)

For our immediate future, "Fate" had other plans. The F-S-B-O sign had been out in front for less than a week, and one Saturday morning when Foster was working at the office—the doorbell rang.

The three people standing there—a man and his wife and their teenage son—were already smiling and apparently anxious to come in. They had read the sign, liked the looks of the outside of the house, and asked to be shown the inside. Starting with the living room, I happily showed them all around, pointing out certain features here and there. (Having picked up a few pointers in the showing of houses to prospective buyers, I tried to act like a realtor showing off his prize property.)

It wasn't very long before both husband and wife made it very clear they were more and more impressed with all I'd shown them so far. (Not surprisingly, their son was spending most of his time out by the pool.) I decided now was the time for the **coup de grace**.

The original asking price of $65,000 had been reduced, I told them, to a firm $58,000 and since a realtor's commission was no longer a factor, it was understandable that we came down on the price.

The faces of both man and wife lit up immediately. Their son, who was still outside but apparently with one ear tuned in on what we were saying, came back in—**fast**. From then on, all four of us were taking a second tour of every square inch of the house, the grounds, and the pool—but considerably slower this time, much as I had done after putting down first a deposit and subsequently, "earnest money." A short time later, my "lookers" had turned into buyers.

What had finally clinched the sale for them was something in the back yard which they hadn't expected to see. We had some time ago converted what was originally a large empty shed into a totally separate room for Gary, hoping to keep him with us as long as possible after high school. These people happened to be running a consulting agency from their own apartment, which business they soon decided could be easily transferred to our house, while the unexpected extra room out in back was ideal for an office, something they had long wished for at their present address.

The teenager, taking in every word, soon realized this was a done deal and that he was now standing in **his** future home. He immediately ran back to check out the pool again—doubtless envisioning (as our own sons had, not too many years before) weekend parties galore out there, with himself as host.

By the time Foster arrived home that day, I had finally figured out a really neat way to break the news that the house was actually sold. The only reason I hadn't phoned him at the office was that I wanted to see the expression on his face when he heard the latest. At first, I had rejected, "Guess what happened HERE today!" as a little too coy. Next, I decided against merely calling out, as he came up the walk, "We've SOLD the house!" Then I had an idea. Admittedly a little crazy, but I couldn't resist it. The "For Sale By Owner" sign being directly in front of the house and highly visible to anyone driving by, I dug out an old white pillowcase, painted "SOLD" on it, in huge letters—and pulled it down over the sign. (Neighbors paying any attention would have few doubts about my sanity—but I did it, anyway.)

This up-dated sign hadn't been out there ten minutes when Foster ran in the front door, carrying not only the pillow case but the sign itself, spilling dirt all over the place, and yelling, "We DID it! We DID it!" I restrained myself from asking where HE was at the time of this particular sale—but he wouldn't have heard me, anyway, he was that excited.

That was certainly a day to remember. Not until a few weeks later, with reams of paperwork behind us and the house officially sold, did we even begin to realize all that **could** have happened if it HADN'T sold. Our guardian angels must have put in a lot of overtime.

In the meantime, we had the go-ahead from the contractor building our new house, the first house ever built for us alone. It was ready and waiting. While New River was actually 32 miles north of Phoenix, it was now just around the corner as far as we were concerned—and no longer just a dream. It was time to start packing.

Aside from the usual furniture, appliances and miscellaneous items to be taken along were the two current feline residents. Rulers of the house, as any cat-aficionado would confirm. They were named Mickey Mouse and Tiger. We no longer, of course, had either Pokey or Lightning. A few years before we ever heard of New River, however, we had acquired first Tiger and then Mickey Mouse.

The name "Tiger" almost came with him. He was well supplied with stripes so it **had** to be Tiger, but there the resemblance ended. His disposition was very sweet, anything but tigerish. Tiger was very formally presented to me by Jackie the afternoon of the day Pokey died. Jackie and his father had gone to the pound to try to replace Pokey, and saw Tiger climbing the walls of his cage. He was meowing like mad, and pleading—according to Jackie—"Take ME, take ME." Obediently following these instructions, Jackie and his father adopted Tiger on the spot.

As for Mickey Mouse, as a mere kitten he had been given to us by a friend of Foster's. (Any animal in the market for a home knew enough to head for our house.) Mickey Mouse arrived without a name, but all it took was one glance to know what he should be called. Though he was still very small, and at the time quite frail, his ears in comparison were enormous and stuck way out. The rest of him eventually grew in size to match those ears, but by then he was stuck for all time with "Mickey Mouse." But as with all cats, as long as he was fed on time, he couldn't have cared less what we called him. Tiger and Mickey Mouse were eventually as close as Pokey and Lightning had ever been—and it was Tiger and Mickey Mouse who moved with us up to New River.

Once again, a never-to-be-forgotten moving day. Mom sat in front with me in the car, while the two cats were in "Pet-Taxis" on the back seat. Some sort of contest was going on back there as to who could howl the loudest, so I finally asked my mother if she would please turn around and console them. Mom, not in the habit of consoling cats or even noticing their very presence if she could help it, did not exactly welcome this request, but she did turn around and speak her piece. Because of all the traffic noise on the freeway, I couldn't hear what she said. It may have been some kind of a threat, for all I know—but it made sense to Tiger and Mickey Mouse. They shut up immediately, never to complain again. Not around Mom, they didn't.

As usual, being moved from one house to another was traumatic for everybody, but it turned out to be an interesting day. Nerve-wracking, but interesting. First of all, once we all reached New River, the movers discovered that just getting the van up the hill to the house was a real challenge—one they'd never encountered before, according to them. (The moving-in process itself later on, however, was a breeze in comparison.)

As soon as the driver of the van located the address and pulled over, everything came to a halt. At first sight, to them the hill resembled Mount Everest. The second shock came when they finally spied the house way up there on top—with only a dirt driveway curving every-which-way leading up to it.

The driver and his helpers huddled there in the truck, presumably debating whether to turn around and go back where they came from—or try their luck with "Driveway Impossible." Whoever won the argument (which would have been interesting to overhear) apparently opted for the driveway. The truck started up, **VERY** slowly.

Foster, my mother and I, having arrived some time earlier in the day, were all watching from above, literally holding our breath. The suspense was awful. If that van had ever given up, turned around and headed back to the city, we would probably have all rushed screaming down the hill—with the exception, of course, of my mother. It was like looking for a miracle to expect that huge unwieldy truck to make it to the top at all, but it slowly managed to conquer first one curve and then the next, pausing at each to recover from the last. We could only imagine the comments being made inside the cab each time they stopped.

My main concern, once the van appeared to be making it after all, was our beautiful china closet with its curved-glass doors—pride and joy of the entire family from the day we bought it. That truck never missed one bump in the road, and my heart sank a little lower with every thud. I was trying not to picture what might be happening to the china closet itself, let alone the glass doors.

By the time the van actually reached the top, the men on board still looked cheerful but somewhat glassy-eyed, which was certainly understandable. Everybody congratulated everybody else, and sighs of relief were heard on all sides. At first, as the men started unloading, I tried not to watch—then after a while, I didn't want to miss anything. All the heavier items, at the very rear of the truck, were coming out first, but as far as I was concerned, all hope was gone for the rest. Anything even slightly fragile, let alone our most-prized piece of furniture, **had** to be in pieces.

To the eternal credit of those movers (who at least eventually fell heir to a big fat tip), not only our sacred china closet came through unscathed, but even the cartons packed with crystal, china and glasses arrived intact. Not one was broken. It was just unbelievable. (But I silently vowed to never move again.)

The next morning, bona fide residents of New River at long last, it was nevertheless time to make a brief trip back to Phoenix, partly to reassure ourselves we had left nothing behind (as, years ago, we left poor little Bozo alone in the back yard in Cedar Grove), but also to make sure we had left the house as presentable as possible. The new owners were expected to move in the following day.

Even that first night in New River, we couldn't fail to notice how isolated we were—our nearest neighbor was several hundred feet away. Now, back once more for the last time in the Phoenix house, what unexpectedly amazed me was how very close we had been to the houses on either side. Our former lot, the same size as everyone else's there, suddenly looked so tiny. We left as soon as we could for our beautiful wide-open spaces.

As of the day we all moved up to New River, we still owned only the two cats, Tiger and Mickey Mouse. **NO** dogs. Unknown to us, the local underground canine/feline network had apparently been sending out bulletins statewide to all homeless, hungry four-footers. The message: "Check out the new residents."

Fortunately for us at that time in history, no cougars or mountain lions (which occasionally **could** be seen from afar) were roaming around out there looking for new quarters. Or, if they were out there, they were respectfully avoiding our territory, its boundaries being "marked" daily in true cat-tradition by the residents Mickey Mouse and Tiger, who were definitely not looking for new cats of any description to move in, least of all **wild** cats.

Dog #1 to arrive—except that he never officially moved in, was a large, friendly dog of (let's be very tactful here) **extremely** varied ancestry, whom we nicknamed "Loner." Loner checked in on us several days a week, visited briefly, ate whatever came his way, and took off for parts unknown.

In a matter of months, Loner—who evidently had not spent too many evenings alone—showed up with a little puppy in tow. Not displaying a great deal of imagination, we from then on just referred to the little one as "The Pup." A short time after we saw what turned out to be the last of Loner, "Pup" moved in with us permanently. Whatever happened to Loner, no one knew. However, in view of Loner's notorious propensity for invading neighborhood chicken yards in the middle of the night, I decided not to question any of the local farmers. They would have been all too willing to fill me in on any and all details of whatever happened, but I didn't ask, figuring I was probably better off not knowing.

So the newest four-footed member of the family—also self-invited— was Pup. A few months later, Pup who appeared to despise all cats, no longer had to yearn for some canine company. She suddenly had her very own live-in companion—although unfortunately for Pup's moral and physical well being, the new puppy was also female. "Jet" was a greyhound-type puppy—actually a whippet, as we were later informed by the local vet. This thin, almost emaciated-looking animal was standing forlornly by the side of the road one Saturday afternoon as Foster and I, with our grandson Mark, were returning from lunch in Rock Springs, a small town a few miles north of New River.

I happened to be the driver at the time, and when we all spotted this pathetic-looking puppy, shivering almost uncontrollably—and yet the day was warm—looking very hopefully in our direction, my foot automatically hit the brake pedal. The car stopped, the puppy shot across the road (traffic on New River roads fortunately was negligible most of the time), and jumped in. Jet had found her new family.

The name "Jet"—short for jet-speed—was a natural. According to our vet, whippets have been clocked at 40 miles an hour, and at that time Jet could have easily broken the record. Foster catered to that puppy from the moment she jumped on his lap. Jet could do no wrong. When she was full-grown—about as big as she would ever get—he built her a fancy doghouse close to the garage, later adding a small light over the opening. My comment at the time was, "Do you think she's going to read?" The only answer I got was a look plainly saying, "You just don't understand dogs." So, for all I know, Jet sat up all night reading.

After our first week in New River, we were both used to commuting to Phoenix via the one and only freeway (alternate highways being in short supply), and driving was almost peaceful compared to the stop-and-go traffic in the city. Having totally different work hours, we each had our own car, and although I would have preferred having Foster with me, I eventually noticed that the solitary drive each morning did give me the chance to concentrate on whatever was the problem of the day, and I usually managed to come up with some sort of solution so it never seemed to be a totally wasted period of time.

Driving back home was something else again. At the end of a day in court, with one "procedure" crisis after another, I was as exhausted as anyone else. Also, less inclined to start problem solving as a means of passing the time. All I really cared about at that point was how soon I'd be home.

A certain criminal trial which I, as court clerk, was really privileged to sit in on, was fascinating from the very beginning. Unforgettable, to say the least. Worldwide publicity had preceded it for several months, guaranteeing that the courtroom would be packed. It was the trial to end all trials, involving a man indicted for bigamy—i.e., marrying two (or more) women with no time out along the way for divorce proceedings. This Lothario turned out to have been a husband-in-name-only of not merely two, but **One Hundred and Four** women.

He was not a "kill-and-run" sort of guy. All these 104 so-called wives were at least still alive on whatever day he chose to vanish forever from their lives. Somehow, he always managed to disappear within hours after each "honeymoon"—along with whatever money, property and/or valuables the current "wife" had been trusting enough to turn over to him.

Eventually, two of the wives, in an understandable rage, tracked Romeo down. They each filed a complaint, and one of them very cleverly managed to have him arrested. And only two wives—not the entire 104—were all it took.

With both of these women scheduled to testify sooner or later, reports of the 104 marital victims AND the upcoming trial spread literally throughout the entire (and, in some cases, admiring) world, all of which naturally proceeded to zero in on Phoenix, Arizona—and our courtroom.

The courtroom itself had limited space for reporters, but more and more of them were crowding in daily, not only from all parts of the United States but foreign countries as well. From the time the Judge's secretary walked in the door, she was besieged by phone calls from literally all over the world—several were even from Japan—all requesting the latest details.

In time, our entire staff, caught in the middle of all this craziness, gave up fighting their way through the crowds on our floor. In self-defense, we all took elevators to the floor above, by-passing our own floor, then walked back down the stairs. The Judge himself, since he was usually in his chambers long before his staff, anyway, was able to arrive in comparative peace, undoubtedly praying he would not be recognized en route as THE Judge.

Jury impaneling in this unfortunately notorious case was no problem whatsoever. Normally, every conceivable excuse not to serve is offered every day of the week. To be chosen to serve in this trial, however, prospective jurors would have sold the family jewels in a heartbeat.

Once the trial was finally under way, one day during the State's case, just prior to the noon recess, the defendant was requested by the State's attorney to write down the names of all 104 "wives." He complied immediately. No hesitation whatsoever, not the slightest trace of embarrassment. That (presumably) envy-of-all-men rose, walked over to a blackboard visible to all, and within minutes was writing down the name of each and every bride, the date of each and every wedding ceremony, as well as the city or town in which each ceremony had taken place.

It was an incredible performance. Had we been anywhere but in a courtroom, everyone in the place would have stood up and applauded. Not for the 104 marriages—that was just the man's way of life—but for his phenomenal instant and total recall of 104 names, 104 dates, 104 wedding locations—and probably 104 unsavory details.

As for the testimony of the two wives responsible for the actual tracking down and capture of this unrepentant scoundrel—a man who simply "forgot" 103 times that he had been married before—what they each had to say seemed to affect the jury in entirely different ways.

The first wife, the one who had caused the defendant's actual arrest, came across as being very calm and collected. Very matter-of-fact, not in the least emotional as one might well have expected. She listened to counsel's questions, deliberated about each one before answering, and related her story almost dead-pan. As a result, it was probably really difficult for the Jury to sympathize with her, despite how horrendous her own experience of having been loved and left behind (also penniless) must have been. While juries as a rule make every effort to at least **appear** non-committal, somehow with this particular victim and her robot-like tale of woe, one had the impression this jury didn't quite believe her—or possibly couldn't have cared less.

Wife #2 was something else again, a complete opposite in every way to the first, and, toward the end of her testimony, had the jury literally on the edge of their seats. When she first took the stand, she seemed to find it difficult to even answer questions and for some time was very obviously choking back tears, but according to her eventual testimony, she had absolutely fallen for this charmer—and he made every minute count.

In record time, he had her convinced that he had huge sums of money stashed away in some foreign (probably non-existent) country, that he had waited all his life for someone exactly like her, and that he truly desired to marry her. The one trifling condition was that prior to marriage she was to turn over every piece of property and every last dime.

Most of these romantic declarations—presumably excluding the money-grabbing clause—she said she had waited all her life to hear. She did, somewhat reluctantly, admit to having hesitated—although not long enough—before actually signing the money/property transfer. Unfortunately, she was so completely under the spell of this truly hypnotic person that she wound up signing on the dotted line whenever he pointed to it.

The happy pair exchanged vows in Mesa, Arizona where she lived and where her (now former) property was located. They then flew to Los Angeles for the honeymoon. She told the Jury she felt like Cinderella, that she had never been happier.

The one and only concession her new Prince Charming had made was that she could take her little dog along. For some reason, there was no one she felt safe in leaving the dog with for the next few days. The newlyweds checked into a high-rise motel—on the very top floor, as it happened. Within minutes, the groom had informed his adoring new bride he had to see some important C.E.O. downtown on equally important business—but would, of course, hurry back to her as soon as possible.

Four hours later, he had neither returned nor called, and she was frantic. In a city totally strange to her, knowing not a soul there and having no idea where her new "husband" might have been headed, in desperation she finally thought of calling the police.

Just as she reached out to the phone, it rang. Prince Charming was calling—but not with any message of love. Very briefly, he said—verbatim—"I'm outta here. You'll have to take care of yourself. I'm gone."

His brand-new bride, having the distinct impression he was about to hang up (she still had no idea where he was calling from), screamed into the phone "Where are you? Where are you? I thought you loved me, how can you DO this to me?"

His reply, in a somewhat amused tone of voice, was simply, "Baby, it was a piece of cake." And he hung up.

Several hours later, she was still standing at the hi-rise window, looking down at the street far below. As far as she was concerned, this was the absolute end of her entire life. She could not go back home and face the certain ridicule, even if disguised, from everyone she knew. They were all aware of how desperately she had fallen for the man she'd thought of as an absolute prince, and to whom she had given everything. Literally. And now she had nothing.

Nothing but a sudden plan. She would run as fast as she could to the door leading to the balcony, then rush over to the railing, trying to not even think. With one hand actually on the doorknob, from the corner of her eye she noticed her little dog, curled up asleep in the center of the bed. What rooted her to the spot was the sudden thought, "Who will take care of him?"

As of that split-second, all thoughts of self-destruction were totally erased. She burst into tears, picked up the little dog and held him close. At that moment, he was all she had.

The Jury, hanging on every word, had long since given up any pretense of being totally impartial. Kleenex boxes were being passed all around the jury box, while not a dry eye was to be seen in the courtroom.

The day for which the media had been holding its collective breath—the day on which the defendant himself would testify—finally arrived. The crowds of people outside the courtroom door waiting to rush in were almost out of control. No one was giving an inch—and no one was looking for any. However, since the number of seats for spectators in the back of the courtroom was limited, it was just a matter of time until the last few lucky persons slipped through and the doors were shut.

(I remarked at the time it might be a good idea to lock them, but one of the legal eagles, overhearing this, reminded me that locking courtroom doors is illegal. Guarding them, he said, is one thing—turning a key in the lock is a no-no.)

The proverbial pin dropping on a carpet could have been heard as this world-famous defendant, about to testify in his own defense (if any) approached me at my desk for the swearing-in routine.

By this time I must have sworn in literally hundreds of people vowing to tell the truth, the whole truth, and nothing but the truth, etc. The actual oath is quite long, but prospective witnesses, all preoccupied with what they're going to say on the witness stand, don't hear it anyway. Consequently, glassy-eyed, non-comprehending stares looking up at me were pretty much the order of the day. The erstwhile Prince Charming (consort of, alas, too many Cinderellas), stood there, raising his right hand. He was looking at me—only **ME**—and I almost lost it. My composure, that is.

(What had been puzzling me from the very beginning about this individual was how, with his fairly ordinary looks—average height, dark hair, rather swarthy complexion—104 women had reputedly lost all control, forgotten all they'd ever learned, and fallen all over themselves to give him whatever he wanted in the way of money or property—and usually both.)

Now, I had the answer. The one and only feature this man had going for him—which apparently had been all he ever needed—were his **eyes**. The word "hypnotic" wouldn't begin to describe them. When those almost-black, impenetrable eyes looked not only at you but THROUGH you, your knees would turn to so much jelly. At long last, I understood why those 104 victims never had a prayer.

Not wishing to embarrass the Judge and the entire staff by actually forgetting the oath in front of a courtroom full of people—yet determined not to look directly into **those eyes** again—I got through it all by simply not looking at him. While swearing him in, the ceiling had my undivided attention.

It worked. He answered "I do" (the 105th time for him) and proceeded to the witness chair.

Our world-famous defendant was the last-scheduled witness—and how much more of this trial we could have all survived is a moot question. Once on the witness stand, of course, he indignantly proclaimed his utter innocence of all charges—which, considering the staggering memory he had displayed while listing all the names, dates and location of all his "marriages," took real nerve. It was also an unforgivable insult to the Jury's intelligence.

The Jury listened to every word, never once taking their eyes off him. Oddly enough, they also seemed somewhat fascinated. (Fortunately for the sake of justice—which is **supposed** to win out in the end—the Jury was far enough away from the defendant's eyes to entertain any second thoughts about the verdict.) After hearing closing arguments by both sides, the Jury retired to the jury room to deliberate.

The verdict rendered in this, one of the world's most notorious trials, was returned in less than 45 minutes. Barely enough time for jurors to sit down, count heads, and cast votes. It was, predictably, GUILTY. It didn't do much for the 104 "wives," but at least a potential #105 was safe.

Meanwhile, back in New River, courtroom proceedings—even the infamous "trial-of-the-year" in Phoenix—were not exactly back-fence gossip. Partly because of the distance from the state's capital city, but mostly due to their way of life; New River residents felt somewhat detached from whatever might be going on down there.

Our life in New River, however, had been anything but run-of-the-mill lately—and a few dull moments here and there might have been appreciated. Thanks to a totally unexpected turn of events, Foster and I had almost overnight become the proud new owners of two burros.

Prior to our moving to New River, I don't think either of us could have identified a "burro." As children, we probably thought we knew all there was to know about domestic animals—meaning cats, dogs, birds in cages, etc. But what in the world was a burro? It was just a question of time before we were enlightened by the first person we asked in this farming community. Answer: a burro was a smaller-than-average donkey, a little sturdier—and a LOT of fun.

The first burro to join us at what we now happily called "the ranch" was Buttercup—and how many people would have selected that name for a burro? Shortly thereafter, even more unexpectedly, Buttercup was joined by Jennie.

Buttercup, who was not yet fully-grown (but in my opinion, very cute), was adopted by us because, according to the local grapevine (the most reliable source of information out in the boondocks), her owner was on the verge of turning Buttercup out into the so-called wild. This small burro was already somewhat domesticated, and consequently without a clue as to any survival techniques. The reason given for her proposed eviction was, the owner would be moving out of the state and considered the burro to be excess baggage.

Foster, hearing this sad tale, knowing nothing whatsoever about burro-care—and without even seeing the animal—arranged through a few helpful neighbors to "adopt" Buttercup before the owner could open the corral gate and just walk away. What Foster and I knew at that point about burro-caretaking was non-existent, but compared to the empty blue skies she would otherwise be looking at, Buttercup would at least have a roof over her head. Once we figured out how to get one there, that is.

Foster's first call for a roof-solution was to Jackie, at N.A.U. Our youngest son being immersed at the time in studies of political science, his experience with corral-building was on a par with ours, but he was more than willing to come down and see what he could do. The following weekend, Jackie was back in New River, measuring everything in sight.

Over the next few weekends, Son #5, unassisted, managed to put together a pretty good-looking corral, one that, to our eyes at least, looked very professional. Any and all homeless burros would have gladly moved in.

Once the corral was on display, however, with Buttercup officially installed, there was a new challenge. Hay, the traditional food for burros, is normally kept inside a shed. We had no shed—and while rain is not a frequent visitor to Arizona, not even burros appreciate rain-soaked hay. Once again, Jackie put his new-found talents to work. In a relatively short time, not only could he show off his new corral, but an honest-to-Pete shed had appeared. This sudden farmland activity was definitely a complete turn-around for Jackie career-wise, his major at N.A.U. being political science, not yet considered a one-way ticket to corral building.

When Buttercup moved into both corral AND shed, we naturally assumed she would be our one and only burro. Which she was, for about a day. Then, a neighbor we had never met before stopped by to introduce himself. In a very short time, "New Neighbor" was wondering aloud if we would be interested in also—but temporarily, of course—sheltering **his** burro, at whatever might be the going rate for burro-care. He would be going back to Minnesota for the summer, and needed some safe place to leave "Jenny."

Neither Foster nor I saw anything wrong with that idea—and it would be company for Buttercup—so we told him, "fine, bring Jenny over."

Which he did. This neighbor—not your typical "Good Neighbor," as we were to learn—then handed us a small check and promised to send another the following month. He then took off—presumably for Minnesota. Since we never saw or heard from him again, his present whereabouts are anybody's guess—if anybody cares.

From old-time residents of New River, we were continually told that there must be a sign down by our gate reading, "This Is The Place, Guys.

MOVE IN." If true, said sign was visible and legible only to four-footed animals, which is probably just as well. But at least Buttercup was no longer in solitary confinement and Jenny was every bit as welcome as Buttercup, with or without subsidy check.

Throughout the fourteen years New River was home to us, an amazing number of cats and dogs found their way up the driveway. Happily, not one coyote, bobcat or mountain lion—all of which were occasionally present in the area—ever ventured that close. For reasons known only to them, all of the latter preferred to remain at a respectful distance.

One by one, all our "strays" joined the menagerie, and when from time to time we lost first one and then another, while it may have been inevitable, it was never a good day. We loved them one and all, and they knew it. An enormous amount of pleasure, affection and fun in both our lives came from just having them around—and as far as the animals themselves were concerned, the feeling appeared to be mutual.

Back in the work world—unfortunately for all concerned—things can happen. One day in 1985, Foster had an accident at work, and from then on, life was never the same again—certainly not for Foster and, to almost the same extent, not for me.

As a claims adjuster, Foster had been in and out of the office all day long. Indoors, there would be one interview after another with clients concerning claims they wished to file, followed by the usual paperwork. Outside, he was in and out of—and frequently **under**—various cars to assess the actual amount of damage to whatever vehicle. This particular day, he had once again, for the thousandth time, slid under a car on a so-called dolly. After only a few minutes, upon sliding out from under it again, one of his legs for no apparent reason suddenly failed him—and he couldn't get up.

When I first heard about it, I was in the courtroom, next to the Judge, who was trying a case. Suddenly the bailiff—a substitute for the day totally unfamiliar with courtroom etiquette—burst in the side door only a few feet away from me and handed me a note.

(This particular door happened to be a private entrance for the sole use of the Judge—a door no one else was to use at anytime as it led directly to his chambers—and seeing our new bailiff suddenly coming through it as if it were any ordinary door **should** have given me at least a clue that something was wrong.)

The note said: "Your husband has been in an accident. You are wanted at the hospital as soon as possible." As soon as I read it, I handed it to the Judge, who immediately declared a recess.

From the courthouse, I drove directly to the hospital—but as I was about to go in one door, Foster was already on his way out the other. Fortunately, the two co-workers who had originally brought him to the hospital noticed me in time and ran over. I was then brought up to date on what had happened back at the claims office.

Oddly enough, the doctors, in what apparently had been a very cursory examination, were unable to find any visible damage at that time. They advised him to merely go home and rest.

There being considerable constant pain, rest unfortunately was not the answer, although if ever a man was anxious to return to his job, it was my husband. To Foster, not to be in control of whatever was happening to him was maddening—and for a long time, no one really seemed to know what was wrong. He was constantly under the care of first one specialist and then another.

The injury which had occurred at work to Foster's right leg was very real, despite what the doctors had **not** found, and a series of what were apparently experimental treatments did little or nothing to lessen the pain. They did, however, prevent his return to work, at least for the time being.

A few months later, **still** at home, angioplasty (due to a chronic heart condition) was performed on that very same leg. As far as we knew, this particular surgery turned out well. The leg was no longer painful, and Foster was advised he was recovering "as well as could be expected," whatever that means in medical mumbo jumbo. Then Mother Nature, apparently not quite finished with my husband, threw in one more ailment. This time the diagnosis was diabetes.

While all these catastrophes came crashing down on Foster, one after the other, I cannot recall hearing one single complaint out of that man. We had been together for many years, starting out as playmates when we were just a couple of innocent kids, and more times than I can remember, Foster could make other men look like so many wimps. He was still not looking for sympathy, but it made my heart ache not to be able to comfort him.

His doctors were very much impressed with this considerable stoicism—especially where pain was concerned, presumably not having seen that much of it before with other patients. It was then I recalled that even when we were children, Foster was already known for not being a whiner.

There was one good thing that eventually, and most unexpectedly, emerged from all these trials and tribulations. Literally overnight, Foster gave up smoking. This was a habit he had acquired at the age of twelve back in the days when smoking by minors was perhaps an annoyance to their parents but definitely not yet recognized as a potential health hazard. Shortly after his diagnosis of diabetes, Foster had awakened in the middle of the night with chest pains. He also seemed to be having considerable difficulty breathing, so we rushed out to the car and I drove him to the nearest hospital.

There, several attendants took over immediately, and the doctor who was on duty at the time started a rather lengthy cardiac examination. Meanwhile, I had been waiting in the next room. Suddenly, the doctor was at my side, saying, "I'd like you to step into the office with me." Foster was lying down in there with a somewhat shocked expression on his face—and a few minutes later, I could understand why.

After showing me several chest X-rays, the doctor led me over to the ultra-sound machine. As he explained it, what I was looking at there were Foster's lungs. At the very bottom level was a considerable amount of water, which to me almost seemed to be making waves. The doctor then turned to Foster and said, loudly, clearly and most emphatically, "If you don't quit smoking, you will die." As of that instant, after 54 years of smoking, Foster had had his last cigarette.

The examination having been concluded, we went on back home. It was almost morning. While I was getting ready to leave for work, Foster, who had been unusually silent, had a question. He wanted to know what I would think of his smoking only two cigarettes a day. While I could only imagine—not being a smoker myself—what he must be going through at the very thought of **NO** cigarettes at all, to me this just did not sound like a very good idea. Reason: those two cigarettes could very well become the highlight of each and every day, that he would be watching the clock until it was cigarette-time, and the rest of the day would be, for him, absolutely empty. Until, of course, the next morning, when he could start watching the clock again.

So, I told him what I thought. Foster sighed the deepest sigh I think I've ever heard—but all he said was "Okay." Nevertheless, when I left for work, I took along every pack of cigarettes in the house. Even half-smoked butts from the ashtrays. Not until I got to the office, did I discard the whole mess.

As it turned out, I could have left everything where it was. Foster never picked up another cigarette—and in time would become highly annoyed at the smell of smoke from **other** people's cigarettes.

After several more weeks at home, Foster had convinced himself that official retirement was no longer an option. It was the only way to go. To begin with, he was still saddled with a bad leg. Not as painful as it once had been, but definitely enough to preclude any of the physical checking-out of cars he had done for many years.

There was also a chronic heart condition, to be monitored by weekly visits to the doctor. Plus, what was for some reason to Foster the most aggravating of all, the recent diagnosis of diabetes.

He finally took a deep breath, picked up the phone and called the office, telling them they should not look for him to return to work, that in fairness to his employers and to himself he was going to officially retire. The next week, the entire office threw an enormous going-away party for him. Foster had always been very popular with everyone he worked with, and the party did help his spirits for a while.

Eventually he seemed to have finally resigned himself to being retired—for some reason one of the most traumatic experiences a man, seemingly much more so than a woman, can have.

Back in 1982, my mother's health had begun to go downhill. She insisted this had nothing to do with the passage of time, that there were simply too many "minor' ailments catching up with her. Considering the fact that she herself had retired a few months before Jackie was born—which had been twenty years ago—Mom had been in remarkable shape for a good many years. One of her ailments, however, was **not** minor. It was diabetes.

Mom was in her late 80s by then and much more frail than any of us had realized. Eventually, her doctor recommended she enter a nursing home in Phoenix. Knowing Foster and I both worked in Phoenix during the day, he said he had to warn us against leaving Mom alone in the house in New River by herself any longer. She finally agreed to the nursing home.

Once she was officially settled in there, we noticed that a majority of the other elderly patients also seemed to have a slight degree of mental problems, along with whatever physical disabilities they already had— and after visiting several times, we were still concerned as to just how well Mom could fit in, but according to the nursing staff, my mother was one of the few patients with whom the nurses felt free to converse intelligibly at any time, on any subject. And Mom could still do more than just talk. Up until three weeks before she died, she continued to work every day on her favorite hobby—crossword puzzles.

One Saturday morning, after visiting Mom at the nursing home, I drove a few blocks away to check out a different facility in town. We had been advised Mom's insurance would cover only a few more weeks, unless she transferred to some place less expensive. The one I was heading for would cost considerably less, but had still been highly recommended.

Unfortunately, there was no comparison whatsoever to the nursing home I had just left. Although this one looked fairly clean, and the personnel apparently very efficient (they liked to replace patients ASAP after losing one, which they had that very morning), it seemed to be rather crowded.

Overcrowded, I soon decided. Most of the residents were in bed, either staring up at the ceiling or apparently asleep. There was no casual walking around by the patients, and each bed was remarkably close to the next. There were no private or even semi-private rooms, only wards, and the nurses went about their business in almost complete silence. From what I could observe, they spent a minimum of time at each bed and rarely said anything to the person in it.

I happened to notice one elderly patient holding out her hand as the nurse hurried by, as if trying to stop her to ask her something. The nurse ignored her—or very possibly didn't see her at all—and kept going. At the risk of being thrown out of the place, or at least reprimanded, I felt so sorry for this woman that I went over to see if there was anything I could do.

Fortunately, there was. All this poor soul had wanted was a glass of water just beyond her reach. If the nurse racing by had given her so much as a glance, there would have been no problem. Thinking this could be MY mother lying there trying to get a little attention, I was very glad I was there for that particular patient at that moment.

For Mom, this new place would be a whole new way of life. The room where I had left her a few minutes before was an extra-large private room. Nurses and attendants were constantly in and out, attending to her every need. Without exception, they were all very friendly, going out of their way to be sociable not only with Mom but with whoever was visiting at the time. Here, in **this** nursing home, private rooms were non-existent, and shortly before I left, I was shown the now-empty bed, vacated that very morning, in the center of a five-bed ward. This one would be my mother's. Since I had no choice but to make some temporary arrangements right away or risk losing even this alternative, I signed her in on the spot, but with a heavy heart.

All the way home, I couldn't stop wondering why, if my mother **had** to die, it couldn't happen in that beautiful nursing home where she was now, surrounded every minute of the day by loving care. **NOT** in a cold, impersonal shelter such as the one I had just left. There, she could only feel forgotten, if not abandoned entirely.

Later that same day, after returning home, I was outside working in the yard when the phone rang. The instant I heard it, I knew it was bad news.

Foster came out on the porch and called me. He didn't have to say a word. One look at his face, and I knew my mother was gone.

Mom was almost ninety years old when she passed away—and she had been a wonderful mother. A few days later, in accordance with Mom's express wishes, her body was cremated. I took her ashes back to the New Jersey cemetery where my father had been buried when I was ten years old—and Mom's ashes were now, at long last, as close as they could be to those of the husband she had lost so many years ago.

By 1985, the year Foster retired, I had been with the court system over sixteen years. Looking back at my very first day there, I had to laugh when I remembered how afraid I had been to even show up for the job—and yet going back to work at **that** time was the best thing I could have done. Had I instead remained at home all day, with Foster working and the boys at school, I would have been climbing the walls in no time.

The furthest thing from my mind now was retirement for me. I had no desire whatsoever to leave, and couldn't even imagine what it would be like. Right now the most fascinating job in the world was mine. The staff I had worked with for so long were like family, and sooner or later everybody in the universe seemed to wind up in our courtroom. No two days in court were ever alike, which is not something that can be said about the average job—and of those run-of-the-mill jobs I'd already had my share. There were times every one of us working there was convinced we must have seen and heard it ALL in that courtroom, and yet I still didn't want to miss whatever might be coming up the next day.

Nevertheless, in December 1986 I finally talked myself into calling it quits. It was just before the Christmas holidays, when the Judge and his staff always took one week of their annual vacation time. Knowing we were all leaving at the same time—a few days for them, **forever** for me—helped a little. But not much. **They** would all be coming back.

Foster, knowing exactly how I felt about the "courthouse world" and about the people I'd worked with for so long, and about my job, had never once directly asked me to quit. But I also knew how HE felt. He just wanted me home with him. Any two people who have been together for as long as Foster and I had (it had been 37 years ago that we said "I do"), are each pretty much tuned into how the other feels, with or without conversation.

The day I walked out of that courthouse for the last time is not my fondest memory. I was trying not to think about what I was actually doing—leaving the job I loved—but rather about all the good things I could look forward to, being home again. I did feel I owed more to Foster than I did to anyone else—so, the courthouse would have to struggle on without me.

From what I hear, however, they're still doing business down there as efficiently as ever, and **without** me.

Six years later, I had reason to be very thankful I left when I did. For Foster and I, those six years together, just the two of us—along with the ever-changing assortment of animals—were, for many reasons, among the very best.

Not all our time was spent at the ranch, however. We exchanged visits with other retired couples all over the state—everyone forever trying to impress everyone else with how important and how crucial to the company, his or her own job had once been. No one really believed all of these stories, of course, but they were always fun to listen to, and the more exaggerated the better.

Also, we drove out almost every day to have lunch somewhere—usually in either Carefree or Cave Creek, the two nearest towns—but now and then in Phoenix. Wherever we went, lunchtime became the highlight of the day. We could take our time, no one was telling us where we should have gone—or when we should get back—and we enjoyed every minute of it.

One lunchtime I will never forget was at a fast-food restaurant in Phoenix, a place we'd been to several times. We were seated at a small table, facing each other, when two couples sat down at the table next to us. (The tables were separated by a glass partition about 18 inches high.)

Those four people were no sooner settled in their seats when Foster, inspired by who-knows-what, looked across the table at me and said, "You look beautiful today."

Had we been entirely alone at that moment, I would have loved it. However, we were anything BUT alone, and Foster's voice had a habit of carrying to the far corners of almost any room. The people next to us were obviously not deaf—out of the corner of my eye, I could see each and every head instantly swivel to look over at us.

At that point, I had no idea what to do. If I were to look over at my husband and give my normal (assuming no one else could hear) answer, our audience would have heard that, too. They would immediately giggle, and I would feel like an idiot. On the other hand, after such a beautiful compliment, I couldn't very well sit there like a stone and say nothing.

In desperation—not really wanting to—I finally turned and looked over at them, fully expecting to see four snickering faces, with eight hands politely trying to cover up the sneers. After all, this was the Twentieth Century, when guys no longer look at their gals and say so much as "Hey, kid, you look pretty good"—let alone something as hopelessly romantic as "You look beautiful today."

Not one sneer, not one snicker. Instead, and I could hardly believe what I was seeing, each and every one of those people was absolutely beaming at us. You would have thought they were looking up at their favorite movie, with everything coming up roses at the finale. And that wasn't all. As if rehearsed, both of the two male escorts then raised their water glasses high in the air, as if for a champagne toast, and WINKED at us.

On November 22, 1992, Foster woke up to his 72nd birthday. The usual morning insulin injection was the first order of the day. He had started on this procedure only recently, which was followed by taking his blood pressure, then a glucose reading, jotting down results and comparing all with those of the day before. Not exactly a thrilling morning routine, but happily this time each and every test turned out to be the very best in some time.

As he came out to breakfast, his eyes were shining. He felt really good about the tests, ready to take on the world for a change, and it WAS his birthday. I had stacked his presents by his plate and, actually ignoring his coffee for a moment, he started to open them. I went over and gave him a hug, kissed him, wished him a happy birthday, and said, "I'll bet your best present is how those tests came out." We both agreed on that.

After breakfast, Foster went back to bed. He said he'd gotten up too early, what with worrying about all the tests, and thought he'd lie down for a while. He then said, "Don't worry, I feel great."

About twenty minutes later, thinking to find out where the Birthday Boy wanted to go for lunch on his special day, I walked out of the kitchen and into the bedroom.

Foster was lying on his back and his eyes were closed. When I spoke to him, there was no answer, and as he was normally a very light sleeper, this was unusual for him. I said something else—I don't remember what—and still there was no response. No movement. I went over a little closer.

My beloved husband was gone from me forever. He lay there as though sleeping, and on his face was the most peaceful expression I have ever seen.

At least he hadn't suffered. He **couldn't** have suffered, not looking like that. That was all I could keep telling myself at that awful moment—but it didn't help. The chance for me to tell Foster just one more time how much I loved him would never come again.

For the next several months, I had no way of knowing I was still in shock. The world around me just seemed so unreal. The loss of the man I loved, the man who had been my husband for forty-three years—and who died on his **birthday**—was impossible to accept.

He was no longer here—**why** did I have to be? If only the two of us could have somehow, at the same instant, vanished from the earth together, neither would have known the other was gone. It would have been a million times easier and would have made a lot more sense.

As far as I knew then, I was adjusting as well as anyone around me might expect. I assumed I was giving perfectly logical answers to whatever they asked, and only much later did I realize everyone had just been waiting patiently for me to be myself again—whatever that was going to be.

Eventually, as I started coming back down to earth, so to speak, I did become aware of something very new to me, something very peculiar—and for a while it was scary.

My sense of direction while driving was completely turned around. I almost had to **guess** what street I was on, or where to turn. I had never before had any such problem, and was afraid to mention it to anyone for fear they'd insist that I turn in my driver's license—meaning, before something happened and they took it away. So, I told no one—yet I kept thinking of my mother, who all her life could almost get lost just going around the corner.

The first time I noticed something was wrong, it was such a weird feeling I actually toyed with the idea of giving up driving altogether. I had been driving to Mesa one day to pick up my grandson Mark for lunch, something I'd done many times, and over the same identical streets. Suddenly, I was on a totally unfamiliar street, and without realizing it, headed East. Nothing I saw looked the least bit familiar—which was understandable as I was supposed to be heading West.

I came as close to panicking that day as I ever have in my life, trying to figure out what was going on with me, why I apparently had so little control over what I was doing—or at least where I was going. It was like being on another planet. I kept driving straight ahead regardless, when I finally remembered to check the street signs—and then I had a clue.

It wasn't the city of Mesa that was turned all around, it was yours truly. I did have sense enough to change directions—but at first that was no help either. I had already come so far East it seemed to take forever to finally see a familiar building.

Eventually, I arrived at Mark's apartment in one piece. Physically, that is. Mentally, I was a wreck. It was a long time after that before I felt like doing much driving at all—but when I did, everything was fine. (My **newest** guardian angel up there was now keeping his eye on me.)

Every one of my five sons, from the moment they learned of their father's death, had been of enormous comfort to me. Losing their father so unexpectedly had been very hard for each of them, yet I somehow felt they were now forming some kind of invisible protective shield around me. When I needed them the most, they were all there for me, and for that I will be forever grateful.

In practical matters, each son in his own way was also very helpful. Rodney, who had moved to Carefree several years ago from New Jersey, was at that time—fortunately for my peace of mind—only about a half-hour away.

Number One son, realizing I was now virtually isolated on top of a hill with only pets for company, came over to install outdoor lights all over the place which could be operated by remote control from inside the house when I was at home. They could also be turned on from the car whenever I drove up the hill after dark—and the indoor lights could be turned on at the same time.

This sudden lighting-up of the entire landscape, not only outdoors but inside the house, must have been something to observe from a plane, and I often wished I could have seen it from up there. Fortunately for all concerned, no airplane pilots passing overhead ever mistook this awesome display for runway lights.

Michael, the second oldest, then and now rapidly scaling the corporate ladder in a major insurance company, was naturally the one I had called when, in the Spring of 1993, a totally unexpected crisis hit New River. What happened that day was one of the most frightening experiences of my life, and I later had reason to be very grateful for Michael's insurance expertise.

That morning after breakfast, I was standing as usual at the sink, finishing up with the dishes. All was calm and peaceful—that is, until I casually glanced out the window into the back yard. In a split-second, what I saw out there almost paralyzed me.

A solid wall of flames, at least **eight feet high**—no more than twenty feet away from the kitchen window—was moving slowly but steadily towards the back of the house. When I first saw the fire, it had just about reached—and apparently stopped at—the wire fence surrounding the back yard. This yard had years ago been thoroughly cleared out so one of our dogs could run around in there, and fortunately, inside the fence, there was not so much as a blade of grass, or even a weed, waiting to be consumed.

(The fire itself had been caused, I was later informed, by a spark— ONE SPARK being all it takes in the desert—coming up from an electric company's transmitter down at the bottom of our back hill. And, since fire reputedly can think of nowhere to go but UP, it was soon on its way. UP to my house.)

My first thought was to grab the phone and dial 9-1-1. For some reason, once I had explained the emergency, the girl answering the phone gave me some kind of truly inane reply—which made me even more frantic. At that point, I, perhaps understandably, screamed at her, "GET the Fire Department! MY BACK YARD IS ON FIRE!"

Someone else then hurriedly took over the phone and quickly assured me they had my address. The Fire Department had actually seen the fire from two or three miles down the road and the engines were on the way over at that very moment.

I then hung up the phone, planning to push or carry all the animals out the front door. Not one of them wanted to move. THEY had seen no fire—what was the problem? Each animal apparently had other plans for the day, none of which included rushing out into the Arizona desert.

It was all I could do to shove the cats out the door, one by one. (The dogs were only too glad to leave, having just smelled the smoke.) The cats, who normally were "house cats," still wanted no part of the Great Outdoors and once on the front porch, where they of course couldn't see what was going on in the back yard, they kept clawing at the front door to get back in.

By that time, what looked like every fire truck in the county was zooming up the driveway or already out in back, tackling the fire. Rural Metro was the official name of these particular heroes—and I was never so glad to see anyone in my life.

Although all the firemen were very professional, very well organized (and, considering the circumstances, fairly calm), from that moment on it was sheer bedlam as far as I was concerned. My three dogs had long ago taken off, wanting no part of this scene, which I could well understand, but the cats were still as close to the front door as they could get.

Strangely enough, the fire—even before the firefighters arrived—never came any nearer to the house than the rear fence. From there, it actually went **around** both sides of the house and **around** the garage, touching neither. Then, as it reached the front yard where the ground leveled off, it stopped altogether.

Some days later, the daughter of a friend of mine, surveying the damage, had an interesting theory. According to her, only God could have so inexplicably diverted that fire at exactly the right time, and in exactly the right places.

Once the fire was totally out, and the firefighters gone, all I felt like doing was crashing onto the nearest couch. But before that could happen, I had to call Michael at his office.

The fire itself being out and this latest crisis in my life now a part of history, there was no need for him to rush over immediately, but if **anyone** was thoroughly acquainted with all the ins and outs of filing insurance claims, it had to be Michael. He not only filed all the necessary papers but, from then on, followed up on all the details. (My favorite insurance man.)

My third son, Stevie (a nickname he reportedly responds to from no one but his mother), is the Certified Public Accountant of the family. Any family counting a CPA among its members considers itself lucky indeed. When confronting the esteemed I.R.S., the best thing we taxpayers can have between us and Uncle Sam is a CPA. (Everyone likes to be on the best of terms with Stevie when Tax Time rolls around.)

As for my own tax returns, I had always done ours for Foster and I as a couple, and I was still doing my own. It is, to put it politely, a real challenge, but once they're done, at least I know enough to run them by

Stevie before mailing them in. Like any proud mother watching her son accept his medical school diploma, and thereafter inserting "My son, the **Doctor**" into any and all conversations, somehow the phrase "My son, the **Certified Public Accountant**" comes to mind automatically with the first lull in any discussion whatsoever.

Gary, Stevie's younger brother by four years, is an architectural draftsman, who lives in Payson, Arizona. The Payson area being in the midst of an unprecedented building boom, Gary's face is probably one of the most familiar and well-liked in town. If he ever decides to run for Mayor, he should be a shoo-in (slight maternal prejudice secretly hidden here).

One day, totally out of the blue, Gary suggested that I consider selling the house in New River and moving to Payson. While there were still a few months to go before that horrendous fire would come charging up the back hill, I was already a little uneasy at living alone in New River—especially at night.

Back in November, in the midst of making funeral arrangements for my husband, I had been given some rather unexpected advice by the funeral director. He cautioned me to think twice about putting any notice at all in the obituary column.

The reason he gave—which did nothing whatsoever for my nerves at the time—was, certain people are very interested in the addresses of those who have passed on. If situated in a particularly isolated area, the person or persons still living there are looked upon as sitting ducks—and I was beginning to feel like one.

The gate down by the road was always locked, but any car—especially a jeep or truck—could have easily driven around it. And then up the hill. Consequently, a gate was more or less a decoration, not a protection. In the daytime, the house felt safe as a church. Only at night did my imagination take over.

Gary's idea about moving to Payson was something that would never have occurred to me. Payson is two hours northeast of Phoenix, at a considerably higher—and cooler—altitude of 5,000 feet. Driving there from New River, via Phoenix, is an extremely circuitous route, to put it mildly—something like traveling two-thirds of the way around a circle.

But it's well worth the trip, as evidenced by the number of Valley residents making plans to not only vacation up there in the pines but to actually build a house there. The scenery en route, as you climb in altitude, is not only mountainous but gorgeous, and people going up for the **second** time make a point of bringing their cameras along. Foster and I had made the trip many times from New River to visit friends of ours in Star Valley, a town east of Payson.

After thinking over all the pros and cons, I made the big decision to at least go up and look it over. I drove up to Payson one day with Diane, one of my best friends, a former court reporter with whom I had worked for years back in our Superior Court days. Gary met us there, list in hand. He had a number of lots to show us, all of which, knowing Payson like the back of his hand, he had carefully selected in advance.

The fourth property we saw—a lot which Gary had actually been saving for last as the **piece de resistance** but which we just happened to get to a little earlier—was the one I liked immediately. All of us explored it for some time, and when we finally left, I told Gary I was pretty sure that was the lot for me.

Most of the properties we had seen were somewhat smaller than those in Phoenix. This lot, however, was three-fifths of an acre—which for Payson would be described as almost huge. Being part of the original pine forest, the trees were mostly all pine, but there were also many cedars, junipers and manzanitas. Some of the trees (as few as possible, I hoped) would have to be removed to fit the house in. Oddly enough, quiet and secluded as the whole area appeared to be, that property was no more than five minutes away from the shopping center in the heart of town.

Another unusual feature—the icing on the cake as far as I was concerned—was that it was directly adjacent to a large empty field. A so-called "wash," owned by the town but which could never be built upon—or indeed used in any way since the ground there went down so much lower than the surrounding area. That field gave the illusion of space. Space which would belong neither to me nor to anyone else, but it made the property which I already considered "mine" even more attractive. In any case, after having had six-and-a-half acres in New River, I wasn't quite ready to be elbow-to-elbow with the house next door.

The longer we looked at that lot, the more I knew I would never find one I liked better, and before Diane and I finally headed back to the Valley, I came up with an offer for Gary to present to the owners. By then, I was nervous about somebody else latching on to it—and somebody certainly would. It was that good a buy.

Two days later, there was a happy phone call from Payson. The owners of the property, both elderly ladies, had decided to accept my offer. Now, there were two projects to get started on—and as things turned out, they were both under way almost simultaneously.

First, of course, was putting the New River house on the market—and once again, Rodney would be coming to the rescue—which was getting to be a well-worn path. Along with his other pursuits, Number One Son was also a real estate broker in Carefree, and obviously the ideal one for me.

Less than a week later, two prospective buyers showed up, seemingly out of nowhere. A man and wife driving by, scanning the properties available in that area, had noticed the For Sale sign down by the road, and pulled over.

They had been hoping to eventually move out of Phoenix and into the country. The New River area being about as rural as it gets, they had finally narrowed their search down to there. However, the gate down by the road being locked as usual, that was as far as they got that day. Still interested, they later called a real estate agent they already knew—who then arranged through Rodney for them to see the house.

At that time, these buyers-to-be were only able to view the house from afar. Not only was it on top of the hill, it was set back quite a bit, but with that amount of acreage you could position a house just about anywhere you wanted it. New River was technically still an unincorporated area—and the "town" was yet to come.

The most famous real estate slogan of all, location-location-location, was never more true. Both Foster and I had loved living in that house. Especially since it was mortgage-free, the Phoenix house having been sold at just the right time. But we also realized the house we put up there was strictly standard, both as to construction and "curb appeal." The location itself was what had also attracted us.

It was always my impression that those people, when they finally got to inspect the house itself, never really looked at it. All they saw was the view—which **was** incomparable, and the size of the property. Plus, where it was on the map, i.e., out of the city and away from the increasing smog in the Phoenix valley. But, most of all, on top of a hill. To quote Rodney (my son, the **Real Estate Broker**), EVERYBODY wants to be up on a hill. Whatever the reason, these people couldn't wait to move in, and when they came up with a fairly attractive offer, we made a deal.

Project Two would be constructing a new house in Payson, and Gary was way ahead of the game even before the New River house was officially sold. He had some time ago shown me a variety of prospective plans, and once we had agreed on the one I liked most, all of Payson seemed to be zooming in on the job.

Gary himself was acting as (unpaid) general contractor, no doubt saving me a bundle in the process. Since he was known far and wide as somewhat of a perfectionist, the various construction people—all of whom knew him well—must have looked forward to the day they would **finish** their jobs on "Gary's Mom's house."

One of the features about Payson, which I most appreciated, was a certain local law concerning trees. When buying residential property which was originally part of the pine forest, still containing trees of whatever description—ponderosa pine, cedar, juniper, even scrub oak—a strictly enforced no-no was the cutting down of any tree which would not interfere with the actual placement of the house.

It's a far-seeing restriction, and fortunately, most people are all for it. The real charm in seeing a home in the middle of a forest is that it's actually in the forest, yet still visible from the road. As for driveways, very often the driveway itself turns out to be very gracefully curved, thanks to avoiding certain trees here and there which would otherwise have to be cut down.

By Payson standards, the lot on which my new home was being built would be considered a fairly good size, so the house itself would still face a forest of beautiful trees, hopefully to remain untouched. Colorful manzanita bushes were all over the place, in between the trees—and manzanitas are bushes that like it just where they are. Even when one is occasionally cut down, unless the roots themselves are removed, manzanitas are fully capable of showing up again wherever they see fit.

Before finally moving away from New River, there remained one rather painful hurdle staring me in the face—and that was, what to do about Buttercup and Jenny, our two burros. Foster and I had had Buttercup since she was practically a baby, and Jenny wasn't much older than that when she joined us. It was very hard to think of parting with either one. Although Payson welcomed almost any type of pet, such as cats and dogs, burros were something else again. As a rule, no welcome mats were put out for burros in most residential areas—unless these parts of town, usually outside town limits, were designated as "horse country."

Gary finally came up with the one solution that was acceptable to all, much as I dreaded the day when I would see the last of Buttercup and Jenny. He had located a family in Pine, a small town north of Payson, who were most anxious to add to their vast collection of animals—and two burros would be the best, according to them. Their ranch already looked like Animal City, but they were reputedly more than happy at the prospect of acquiring Buttercup and Jenny.

The very next morning, the wife and daughter showed up with a horse trailer. The actual transfer of the burros out of the corral and into that trailer turned out to be not only a memorable but time-consuming process—something none of us, including the future owners, could have anticipated.

You would have thought those two burros actually had a premonition their lives were about to change, literally overnight. Buttercup and Jenny made it clear from the very beginning they had no intention whatsoever of leaving their very own corral. Or their very own shed, the only home they could remember. And least of all, with two total strangers.

The ensuing racket was unbelievable. Had all this taken place in the middle of the night, the constant hee-haw, hee-haw protests from both burros would have had everyone in New River calling the S.P.C.A. It took almost two hours, with everyone tugging and pushing (try pushing a burro sometime), to get them up into the trailer. Long before that, I had decided it was just a matter of time before these people would say, "Forget it, you can keep your burros" and I wouldn't have blamed them.

But it never came to that. Both burros had suddenly, for no apparent reason, resigned themselves to their fate. Buttercup and Jenny entered that trailer as calmly as if from the very beginning they'd planned it that way. And who knows?—maybe they just wanted to watch us all going crazy.

The new owners took off, the two burros finally silent in their trailer. A very dear part of my life was going down that road and I suddenly couldn't hold back the tears.

I watched from the corral until the whole procession disappeared around a curve in the road and then walked back up the hill.

One more chapter was closed. Buttercup and Jenny had been very special to Foster and I for many years—and now they, too, were gone.

Seeing them being hauled away by total strangers was something I never thought I'd see.

Jackie, my youngest son, had returned to Arizona from Boston at the time of his father's death. It was the first time in several years that all five boys had been in the same place at the same time—and considering what it had taken to get them all together, the occasion itself was even sadder.

(The nickname "Jackie" is never used outside the family—something I learned very quickly the first time I called him at Northern Arizona University in Flagstaff, shortly after he enrolled there. I had asked to speak to Jackie. Whoever answered the phone replied, "There's no Jackie here"—and hung up. End of conversation. From then on, I was very careful to ask only for John.)

Back in 1990, two years before his father died, Jackie/John had been teaching ESL (English as a Second Language) at Boston University. As a result of a lifelong fascination with France, however, in January of that year he came up with what was probably the best way of getting to know the country of his dreams.

He decided to actually go over to Paris and sign up for a few courses at the Sorbonne (fortunately, he was fluent in French), and hopefully find some kind of a job to keep him going while he tried to discover what France—and Paris—were all about.

After a few months in Gay Paree, Jackie was suggesting the time for me to visit Europe—something I never thought I would ever do—was while he was still in France and could show me the sights—at least the ones in Paris. That was all I had to hear. Jackie himself was predictably entranced with both France and Paris, and he was also becoming more and more adept at finding his way around what is probably the world's most fascinating city.

Me? Go to Paris? **Moi?** I never expected the opportunity to fall from the sky, so to speak, but apparently all I needed was the mere suggestion.

The one and only subject of any and all conversations from that moment on were to be "My Trip to Paris."

When Foster finally got used to the idea of his wife running off to Paris (at first, he thought I was kidding), he was most encouraging. While he had no desire to make the trip himself, he did promise to take TLC of all the animals while I was gone, which would be for two weeks. So, I had the green light as far as he was concerned.

(The only foreign country Foster admitted he might have wanted to visit was Hungry, where his father came from umpteen years ago. Aside from that, living in the States was for him—the preferred one being, of course, Arizona.)

Up until the day I boarded the plane at Sky Harbor with Paris (repeat **PARIS**) as a destination, I can't recall doing much sleeping. Not peacefully, anyway. There were rates to check with travel agencies, deciding what to pack and not pack—**plus** applying for a passport. As for the passport, while it wasn't my first, it would be the only one for which I had personally applied. Back in 1943, when I was headed for Brazil, I was working for the Government and all passport formalities were seen to by Uncle Sam. Details thereof were not even discussed. In effect, what they told me was, get on this plane, fly to Recife, and do your job there.

This time, it was up to me to produce the all-important passport— but there was still no problem. No criminal record was waiting to be uncovered. No notices on a post office wall demanding my capture. Plus, the office personnel in Phoenix handling my application were most cooperative, especially when they noticed my destination: **PARIS**—and then they all looked a little green-eyed.

Meanwhile, Stevie (my son the **Certified Public Accountant**), had caught wind of this mad plan for a European adventure. Happily, for all concerned, he then decided it just might be a great idea to send his son Mark over with me—which it was. I knew Mark would be a lot of fun to have along, his father would be picking up **his** tab, and the trip was looking better and better.

That never-to-be-forgotten day in June when Mark and I took off from Sky Harbor will surely, along with another famous date, go down in infamy. Every thermometer—not only at the airport, but in the city itself—had reached an unheard-of, all-time high of 122 degrees. All previous temperature records were probably destroyed on the spot.

Hot as it was, neither Mark nor I had the remotest idea at the time of how very close we were to not even leaving the ground. (We were all but insulated, anyway, we were so excited—for all we knew it could have been 222 degrees.) Unknown to us, minutes prior to take-off time, official orders had been issued. Due to the record-breaking heat, which was at that very moment causing unrelated problems all over the place, no more planes AFTER ours would be permitted to take off that day. OUR plane would be the very last plane allowed to depart.

Had we been marooned down there on the ground in Phoenix, with the distinct possibility of not being able to make our connecting flight from New York to Paris a day or so later, is something that to this day, I don't even want to think about. With no idea whatsoever at the time of how lucky we were to be taking off at all, we and a few hundred other passengers departed as per scheduled.

The flight to Newark Airport, where Stevie was to meet us, did calm us down a little by the time we landed, which was good. We definitely needed a few quiet hours to get us through whatever the next hectic weeks had to offer.

Two days later, Mark and I took a cab from Stevie's house in Lincoln Park, New Jersey, to JFK in New York—naively assuming we would arrive there in plenty of time. As a native of New Jersey, I should have known that however much time we allowed for the trip, chances were, we would be stopped at least every five minutes en route.

Which is exactly what happened, marking the beginning of a truly crisis-ridden day. From Lincoln Park on down, we ran into one traffic jam after another. At one intersection, the traffic lights weren't working at all and ten minutes of utter chaos ensued. At that point, it was a toss-up as to whether we'd make it to JFK at all, let alone on time.

Both New Jersey and New York being justly famous for horrendous traffic tie-ups, one eventually learns to sit it out, but this one would have tried the patience of a saint—assuming he/she knew how to drive. I was afraid to look at my watch.

With exactly twenty minutes to spare before our plane was to take off for Paris, Mark and I were finally deposited at JFK, suitcases in hand and tickets in our pockets.

The way our luck was running, why it should have surprised us in the least to learn there was a strike going on inside the airport, I don't know. But there was. While normally some ten or twelve ticket agents worked at top speed to take care of some ten or twelve lines of passengers, there were now only TWO ticket agents—both confronted by what must have looked to them like thousands of passengers. Both agents were, needless to say, more frantic by the minute—although not nearly as upset as those waiting in line.

For a few minutes, not yet realizing the situation, Mark and I, each with two suitcases, politely took our places at the end of the nearest line. A moment later, an official working for the airport fortunately selected US to zero in on.

She checked our tickets, and instructed us to immediately push—and she meant PUSH—our way to the very head of any line and demand to be taken care of first.

To put it mildly, pushing people aside and almost knocking them down in the process is not normally my way of life. I had never had occasion to even attempt it before—but here, we had no choice. This official had made it very clear. Get up to the front of the line FAST—or forget about Paris.

That did it. Mark and I grabbed our suitcases and literally shoved our way forward, trying to look neither right nor left. The glares we received cannot be described—and I suddenly didn't even care. I was going to

Paris, **Mark** was going to Paris, and that was all there was to it. We were **NOT** going to miss that plane.

Having won, hands down, the Unpopularity Contest of all time, we finally arrived at the head of the line. After convincing an almost hysterical ticket agent, who by that time couldn't have cared less whose turn it was, that **WE** had to be taken care of first, Mark and I then proceeded with the usual paper work.

On our way back through a now very hostile crowd, Mark and I tried to keep our eyes on the ground, finally making it to the door. Had we not each had suitcases in both hands, we could have also covered our ears—people were actually hissing as we rushed by (and had I been one of them, I would have hated me, too).

Upon reaching the plane, I finally had nerve enough to glance at my watch. There was **ONE MINUTE** left before scheduled take-off, and after finding our seats, we just sat there, catching our breath. The last two hours had been unbelievable.

As it turned out, the plane was half an hour late in taking off—but by then we were up on Cloud 9 anyway, higher than the plane would ever go. We were on the plane, we were officially Paris-bound, and Jackie was on the other side of the Atlantic waiting to meet us. **That** was a great moment.

The Charles De Gaulle airport was also waiting for us, on what was apparently the next morning, Paris time. Neither Mark nor I had been able to sleep on the plane, but we both felt as alert and wide awake as if we'd slept like logs all the way over.

We were looking forward to a fun reunion with Jackie. Mark and I had started to wonder—and then we **worried**—what in the world would we do if we didn't see Jackie anywhere after we landed. Of course, Jackie was the very **first** person we saw, so all worries evaporated on the spot. He was momentarily behind a barricade which separated the "greeters" from the "arrivers," but the barricade was soon down, with everybody rushing across to everybody else. Being with Jackie at last made it all worth while—it was hard to believe three of us from the same family were suddenly now all together in a foreign country.

For Jackie, of course, it was no longer that foreign. While he did say he'd never want to live permanently in Paris—or any other foreign city—he'd been having an even better time there than he had hoped for. Also, he'd been far from idle, having reserved rooms for Mark and I, for our two-week stay, at **SIX** different hotels. We would be spending a day—or two—or three—at each. The idea was we would then have an idea of what all the various "arrondissements" (districts) of Paris were like.

Within ninety minutes, we had checked in at Hotel #1 and left our suitcases. It was so early in the morning—7:30 a.m. Paris time—that the rooms were not yet available—and we wouldn't have wanted to waste time there anyway. We had only two weeks, so time was precious.

As with most first-time visitors, the Eiffel Tower was on the top of our Must-See list. Since our hotel-of-the-day was not too far from the Tower, Jackie, Mark and I had just started walking over there when I suddenly remembered one other, absolutely **obligatory** (in my opinion) stop we had to make. What would have to come before even the world-famous Eiffel Tower was a visit to one of the many equally-famous sidewalk cafes. As far back as I could remember, everyone I ever knew was intrigued by the idea of sitting at a table, located out on the sidewalk, in the midst of a Parisian cafe, casually sipping cafe a la Ernest Hemingway or F. Scott Fitzgerald for all the world to see, with hopefully someone taking my picture for at least my **friends** to see.

Jackie was happy to oblige—we moved not an inch without a camera—and that was the beginning of photos galore for proof we'd really been to Paris.

In time, more than one sidewalk cafe was entertained by the three of us—about as American as they come—doing our very best to look and act like typical Parisians. Naturally, we were fooling no one but ourselves, but it was a lot of fun—and in any case, if enough **francs** were left on the table as we elegantly tried out our **Bon Soirs** on the waiters, everyone was happy.

The closer we got to the Eiffel Tower that day, the more impressive it looked. We were really glad our first choice had been that historical monument—it was truly a work of art and it would have been a shame not to see it. The very top section, the narrowest of all, happened to be closed off at the time for repairs, but we explored all we could of the other two levels below. To us, what was almost as impressive as the Tower itself was something we hadn't expected. Being in the heart of the city, the views from each and every side of the Tower were fantastic, and once again, Jackie's camera was working overtime.

The Eiffel Tower that day was only the beginning. Every morning we looked forward to whatever tour Jackie—who was an ideal guide because he loved the entire city—had decided on the day before, and all three of us enjoyed every minute. Each day would start out about the same—but there the resemblance ended, as our destination for the rest of the day could be just about anywhere. Jackie would appear at an unreasonably early hour, bearing a most welcome thermos of life-saving coffee, and along with that heavenly beverage, which Jackie and I had all to ourselves (Mark, for some strange reason, always preferred soda), we devoured the most delicious croissants to be found any-where in the universe. Jackie would pick up a half-dozen or so of these incomparable goodies at a bakery just down the street—and they were so fresh they were still warm.

(At every bakery, a recipe for **their** very own croissants was report-edly kept under lock and key. Should the head baker, for whatever reason, decide to quit, that particular recipe was guaranteed to be in his pocket as he walked out the door—if he expected to be hired by any other bakery, that is.)

Having a Metro subway available every few blocks (unfortunately not the case in the States) was to come in handy many times, but as a rule we walked whenever possible to whatever historic, or locally famous, or just plain interesting area was on the agenda that day. Later on, when it was time for supper—to which we really looked forward after wearing out our feet all day—we first checked out prices of the various restaurants, looking for the best deal. And it was easy to find one. Sample menus were displayed (presumably by law, since it was the custom with **every** restaurant, expensive or otherwise) on the windows in front of all eating establishments.

More often than not, we settled for Italian food. Many of the other restaurants were known to be rather high-priced, so we seldom bothered to even check them out. Italian places not only had reasonable prices, but the food was always good. Also, the people working there were, without exception, very friendly. Many of them spoke French with an Italian accent—which made things really interesting to Mark and to me, since neither of us spoke either language.

(Jackie, with French as **his** second language, naturally had no trouble in France. Even in Germany, a few days later, his linguistic skills held up. There, the natives listened to his mixture of French and English and somehow figured out what it all meant in German.) We were hardly the best judges of food, anyway. After hoofing it all over the city, almost anything by that time of day would have looked good enough to eat.

Our second week in Paris, having voted on a trip to Germany, we rented a small car. Anywhere in Europe, for anyone not of millionaire status, Junior-size cars—the smaller the better—were the most practical. Not necessarily the most comfortable, but **much** kinder to one's wallet. Buying gasoline in Paris was like buying liquid gold, and the larger the car the bigger the tab.

The trip out of Paris itself and through the formerly peaceful countryside was one neither Mark nor I could have slept through. Jackie was suddenly driving like a typical Parisian in rush hour traffic (not necessarily a compliment). Mark and I, as we tightened our seat belts, wisely made no comment. This being the first four-wheeled vehicle we'd been in all week, Jackie was apparently making up for all the countless miles his poor tired feet had carried him all over the city.

After spending that night at a really spotless German-owned motel in Strasbourg, just over the border, Jackie drove us to Heidelberg. We explored the famous Castle and, just before we left, went outside. We were looking down at what I assumed to be the Rhine, and I felt very proud to be in such an historic spot. We were later advised, however, that particular river was **not** the Rhine, but the "Neckar"—a name I'd never heard before. All thoughts of bragging to my friends that I had finally seen the famous Rhine were G.W.T.W.

What helped to restore my ego, not to mention my appetite, was a really delicious lunch we later enjoyed in the town of Heidelberg itself. Our German waitress there was most charming—particularly when some time later, after we had all finished eating, she brought several samples of items on the menu for us to try—all on the house.

Jackie had been asking, mainly just out of curiosity, about these various entrees—he in his French/English/semi-German and she in half-German, half sign language—but they seemed to understand each other very well. He had also gleaned from her conversation that she was a daughter of the owner of the restaurant—which status apparently entitled her to bestow certain blessings on her customers.

From that restaurant (not caring if we ever ate again), we traveled far enough to reach the border of Switzerland. Jackie drove in just a little way, but enough so we could all later on casually mention to friends, "Oh, of **course** we saw Switzerland."

Viewing the Bavarian countryside in Germany from the famous Autobahn is something I will never forget. It was truly out of a fairy-tale book, and at times the whole scene looked almost unreal. Some distance away from the highway, the most picturesque of villages, one after the other, would periodically appear—and always with the inevitable church tower in the exact center. Everything surrounding it looked, at that distance, like so much doll furniture, which somehow gave you the feeling that if you blinked, it would all vanish from sight.

Why we had to finally run out of film at that phase of the trip, I will never know—possibly a sign we should all return for a second go-round, only this time with beaucoup rolls of film.

The first time we saw the prices for gas in France, we thought—or, rather, **hoped**—they were using some other monetary system, that the prices, when translated, would surely be on a par with American gas prices. But this was not the case. The prices meant what they said and filling up the tank was something everyone did with a rapidly-sinking heart.

We could at least be thankful we didn't have to contend with gas prices like that back in the States. Not yet, anyway. Our rental car—barely large enough for three with Mark crammed into the back seat—at least required less gas than the size car most people would have preferred—IF they could afford it.

Also on the Autobahn, we discovered that speed limits were virtually non-existent—making our first trip on it far more interesting than we ever expected. Mark now had a brand-new job—one he very obviously relished, but which did require his undivided attention. From the back window, he kept track of any and all oncoming speeders doing 100 miles an hour or more (of which there were many) and warning Jackie in time to PULL OUT of the fast lane—FAST.

It was a wonderful vacation, the more so because I had never expected to see anything of Europe, or Paris, in the first place. It was very reluctantly that Mark and I said good-bye to Jackie, and Paris, at the airport.

Many times during those two weeks, as we traveled all over the place, I would say to myself—and yet not really believe it—"I'm here in PARIS!"—then in Heidelberg, "I'm in GERMANY!"—and finally, "Now I'm in SWITZERLAND!" Not once was I mistaken for your typical, suave Parisian.

That day back in 1978 when Foster, Mom and I had moved into the New River house, I had vowed never to move again, but in August, 1993, there were only two days to go before I would be out of the New River house. In the meantime, unknown to them, my five unsuspecting cats and three innocent dogs were scheduled to be checked into a "pet hotel" in Payson by the name of "Furry Friends."

Since to domestic animals, pet hotels are synonymous with pet prisons, I was well aware that every one of my "best friends" would naturally be wondering, throughout their three-week stay there, what sort of doggie/kitty law they must have unknowingly broken. I only hoped all eight of them had enough trust in me to know I would surely be coming back for them.

Once all my belongings were moved out of New River and stored at a local warehouse, I would be staying with Michael and Barbara for those same three weeks, in Mesa. My house in Payson was not quite finished, but my New River buyers were more and more impatient to move into **their** new house, and I was afraid if I didn't get out of the way for them, that sale might somehow bite the dust.

Fortunately for me, Barbara and Michael had some time ago suggested that I stay with them for this interim period. My only alternative would have been nothing short of horrendous, i.e., marching into the desert for three long weeks with eight confused and indignant animals, all of us to reside there in some kind of tent. Within hours, we would have been on "60 Minutes," complete with video cameras and Mike Wallace.

Gary had volunteered to help transport all the animals to Payson, so we split them up. Not numerically, but as to species—Gary took the three dogs, I had the five cats. Fortunately for me, each cat was in his or her own cat-carrier in my car, but Gary wasn't that lucky. His vehicle was a Blazer, and "Cham"—no doubt assuming this would be his position in life from then on—happily rode in the passenger seat. "Pup" and "Jet" sulkily put up with riding on the back seat, which couldn't have been **TOO** uncomfortable, as they both slept soundly from the time we left New River until we arrived in Payson.

Cham, a golden retriever of considerable weight, was not one to waste time on sleeping. Not as long as he could sit up and gaze out both the side window and the front. The problem was, he was constantly turning around and trying to see out the back window as well. Gary finally pulled over and put a leash from Cham's collar over to the side door—which with any **other** dog would have done the trick.

Again we took off—I had been following Gary—and once again we stopped. Cham, not as mindless as golden retrievers are sometimes reputed to be, had just figured out how to slip out of his collar. For the few seconds it took Gary to pull over again, Cham looked like a whirling dervish in there. (At less stressful moments, Cham has a super-gentle disposition. Slightly overweight though he is, the moment you sit down he wants to sit in your lap—and **YOU** don't get up until **HE** gets up.) At one time in his New River back yard, he scooped up a tiny bird from the ground and carried it around in his mouth (his golden retriever ancestors no doubt guiding him from above). We persuaded Cham to let it go, and then took the bird to the vet—who then assured us the poor little thing was totally unharmed. For all we knew, that bird was just enjoying the ride.

As for Jet, our speedier-than-a-bullet whippet, even approaching a bird is totally beyond her. She does bark at them furiously, however, when they fly over the back yard. Apparently, as far as Jet is concerned, that's Jet's **air-space** up there.

Jet's doggie-pal, Pup, female offspring of the long-gone Loner, is approximately three times Jet's size—but Jet's the boss. When food dishes are put out for both dogs, Pup stands back—almost towering over Jet—and politely waits for Jet to make her selection. (Both dishes are identical.) There is no doubt whatsoever in either dog's mind as to who's running the show.

My own feline passengers, in the cat-carriers they detest to this day, had temporarily lost their freedom but not their voices. An outraged chorus of protest went up as soon as we took off from New River. Fortunately for my nerves, within minutes all cats gave up and decided to take a nap, so I could give all my attention to what was going on in Gary's Blazer up ahead.

"Henrietta" was the oldest, a beautiful white cat with a Siamese-sounding voice, who years ago seemed to have come from out of nowhere. Somehow, and this was something I wish I could have seen her doing, she found her way under the house and then couldn't get out. She was making such a racket down there, we could hear it from the living room and went outside to investigate.

Henrietta was finally enticed to come out from under. In desperation, worrying about what would happen if we couldn't get to her, Foster and I finally resorted to waving some catnip back and forth, outside one of the louvered openings in the foundation. Once Henrietta got a whiff of the catnip, she rushed over and we eventually broke the opening itself so she could get through.

Whether Henrietta then adopted us, or vice versa, is a moot question. One look at us and she had our number. She also had a new home.

"Dooley," passenger #2 age-wise, was a (trying to be tactful here) **pleasingly plump** yellowish male cat, a gift to me from Gary. Years ago, Gary, hearing that a very loudly-mewing cat was penned up in someone's abandoned garage, had taken the time-honored step. As per family tradition, Gary—and Dooley—headed for New River.

As for "Stripey," a tiger-striped, perennially scared-looking gray and white cat, she had reason enough to look terrified. All she had to do was recall her own beginnings. As a kitten, Stripey had apparently lived somewhere in Apache Junction, a town about twenty miles east of Phoenix. That is, until the day she became a little too inquisitive for her own good and crawled inside the engine of someone's car. And then, of course, couldn't get out.

The owner of the car happened to work at Michael's company office in Phoenix. Totally unaware he had an unexpected, and certainly uninvited passenger, he drove all the way into Phoenix with Stripey inside the engine. He then left the car in the company parking lot.

Stripey, still inside the engine and undoubtedly having a fully-justified feline fit, was shortly thereafter discovered when the next incoming employee heard loud meows coming out of the car parked next to her. This lady—fortunately for Stripey an animal-lover—ran frantically all over the parking lot looking for someone to help her raise the hood. And when the hood was raised—there was Stripey.

Within minutes, Stripey was the center of attention. Not only was she being petted, consoled and fed by every employee coming through the door of the coffee room, Stripey was the topic of conversation for the day. None of the above making for a smoothly running organization, the attention of all employees was soon drawn to the fact they were there only to **work**. **NOT** to play with a cat. Not on company time.

Fortunately for Stripey's immediate future, Michael happened to stop by the coffee room and saw what was going on. Coming from an animal-oriented background, Michael immediately thought of what would be a much better residence for this still-miserable cat. Stripey's new home was going to be—where else? New River. And with guess-who's Mom and Dad? Michael's. Stripey had become Cat #3.

The fourth oldest (or second youngest?) cat was "Red"—the only name possible considering her coloring. Red was a Persian-appearing cat who turned up on the back porch one day, probably looking for a source of food more reliable than the desert. The Arizona desert is, unfortunately, most inhospitable to domestic cats. To the occasional wild animal out there—who is apparently always hungry—cats even momentarily outside their homes represent potential dinners. As soon as Red had dined with us and discovered what it was like to eat without keeping one eye on the nearest shadow, she not only moved in permanently but never even glanced out the window again. As of that day, we had a cat quartet.

But #5 was soon on the way. One morning, Foster had taken the latest household item to break out to the garage, intending to repair it. Instead, he rushed back into the kitchen saying, "Come on, you've got to see THIS!" When I asked what "this" was, he simply said, "You'll see—come on out" and dashed back to the garage again. Naturally, I dropped everything to see what was going on.

Up on the top shelf over the work bench, trying her best to back into a corner, was "Calico," one of the cutest kittens I'd ever seen. She was actually more or less three-colored, as the name suggests. A very dark gray, a light gray, and an almost reddish tinge here and there. The name came with her.

When our vet (whom we kept fairly busy) eventually looked her over, he informed us Calico was full-grown, well past kittenhood. She had just stopped growing "a little too soon," as he phrased it. Calico to this day still looks and acts like a kitten but, for some unknown reason, runs more like a rabbit than a cat.

Foster and I could only assume one of the dogs—probably mile-a-minute Jet—had playfully chased Calico into the garage, where she went almost straight up the wall to the top shelf. Only there did she evidently feel safe. And from Jet, the one dog in the world totally incapable of attacking **anything.**

However, Calico wasn't all that safe from us. We adopted her then and there, appointed her Cat #5, and later introduced her to Henrietta, Dooley, Stripey and Red. One brother, three sisters.

For me, that last day in New River was truly the end of an era. Fourteen years ago, Foster and I had moved up there as excited and thrilled as two kids—and when we sometimes referred to it as our "rural paradise," we were only half-kidding.

In many ways, it had been. Some of our fondest hopes were realized there, some were not—but moving from the heart of busy, metropolitan

Phoenix to its exact opposite was something we never once regretted. That ranch was everything to us. Watching everything I owned being moved out finally had me wondering after a while if this move was really a good idea. Whether it was or not, I was on my way. It was a little too late to un-sell the New River house, un-build the Payson house, and retrieve all the animals. In other words, go back to Square One. I occasionally felt like running back into the house by then, but Rodney was now checking to make sure that nothing crucial had been left behind, and also that everything supposed to be turned OFF was not still ON. The furniture itself was to be held in storage in Mesa for three weeks, then moved to the Payson house—which hopefully by then would be ready for me and the eight-member zoo.

Finally, the moving van left to start down the hill—a hill still in every way as unmaneuverable as the day we moved in—with these drivers also doubtless cursing each and every curve. Rodney also took off. So far at least, thanks to Number One son's just being there, that day had been a lot less traumatic than I had expected.

The empty garage was waiting to be swept out and that would be it. The very last excuse to put off getting in the car, driving down that hill for the last time, and heading for Mesa. I picked up the extra broom I had planned on leaving in the garage, made a few half-hearted sweeps, and stopped. There was a strange silence all around me, and the world seemed so empty. I suddenly didn't feel like doing **anything**.

I gave up on sweeping altogether—at least my intentions had been good—and slowly walked back into the house. It was high time to pick up the suitcases, get in the car, and drive over to Mesa—which I decided to get started on and get over with as fast as possible. I was definitely not looking forward to walking out the front door in tears from the house I would never see again.

As I picked up the suitcases, the doorbell rang, and for a few seconds I toyed with the idea of slipping out the back door. The last thing I needed at that point was company.

I decided against disappearing out the back door—for which I was later thankful—and finally, very reluctantly, opened the front door. The buyers were standing there. Inasmuch as the official escrow proceedings would not take place until the following day, why these people, knowing I would be moving out within hours, were there at all was totally beyond me—but they hurriedly explained they had noticed the gate was open and decided to drive up. They just couldn't wait to once more check out **their** new house. (Rodney, assuming I would be leaving within minutes after him, had naturally left the gate open for me.)

The owners-to-be (it was still **MY** house, I kept reminding myself for some reason) came in, and we had a most friendly chat. You would have thought we'd known each other for years. Best of all, when I finally walked out that front door for the last time, **EVERY** face, including mine, was wearing a smile. Reason: they had solemnly promised to continue feeding the 1001 wild birds I'd been catering to from the day we moved in. My parting words to them had to be "You've made my day."

Finally en route to Mesa, I hoped for once to be able to locate Michael and Barbara's house without my usual tour of the wrong streets—a problem I'd always had with that particular city. And one my late husband had **never** had. Foster zeroed in immediately on any and all strange cities, almost instantly finding whatever he was looking for. This talent I always assumed was because he'd been driving since the age of ten, and certainly had had enough practice.

I, on the other hand, was all of 28 when I finally learned how to drive. And, for better or for worse, Foster was the teacher. Patient as he may have been in other facets of our lives together, I'm inclined to believe any kid down the street (maybe a ten-year-old?) could have done a better job. Almost immediately, Foster's patience went right out the window. He had pulled over to the side of a busy highway (which to him was no more threatening than a country lane) and was about to turn over the wheel to me. I then suggested (very tactfully, I thought at the time) that it might be easier to learn how to drive on a quieter street.

That was only the first SNAFU. We both calmed down, eventually found an almost deserted street, and changed places again. Now officially behind the wheel, my first accomplishment was to get stuck in the mud. We were eventually towed out by some nearby farmers to higher ground. While I still knew zero about driving, that experience did serve to bring back certain admonitions of some friends of mine—all speaking from sad experience—that having one's husband teach one how to drive was **not** a good idea.

Nevertheless, against all odds, I finally learned to drive, and loved it. All lessons were given in a floor-shift vehicle—which probably **was** a good idea. If you can drive one of those, you're set for life. They're a real pain to learn on, but if somewhere in the unforeseeable future you do have to drive one, all the do's and don'ts will come back to you. Modern cars, which do all your thinking for you, are like toys in comparison.

The third and last crisis—speaking mechanically—was when Foster drove me down to Newark so I could take (and presumably pass) the driver's test. Except that I didn't pass. Not the first time. The one and only skill Foster apparently hadn't given me **enough** instruction on was: how to make a U-turn. Sooner or later, I would certainly have to have some idea of how to do **that** or traffic would be coming at me from all directions and I wouldn't have a clue as to what to do. Unfortunately for family history, what Foster had more or less skimmed over turned out to be the high point of the test. The finer points of U-turns were still beyond me.

At least four times I turned, backed up, turned and backed up—ad nauseum, as far as the gentleman giving the test was concerned. When he had first entered the car, he had made quite a point of fastening his seat belt, but throughout that U-turn phase of the test, he was actually leaning forward with his head in his hands. Which was just as well—I had no desire to see the expression on his face at that particular moment.

Eventually, still saying nothing but obviously having had all he could take of my "driving," he handed me a slip marked "Did Not Pass" and hurriedly escaped from the car.

The day I returned for test #2, however, I had been informed to the nth degree on U-turns. (By that time, I could have given lessons myself.) And, I did pass. What probably helped more than anything else was, this time someone **else** was giving the test. The first words I heard **this** time were, "So, today's the day we get our license, right?" RIGHT.

With only one detour around Mesa this time, I found Michael and Barbara's house and, with suitcases standing by, rang the bell. Barbara had just arrived home from work and opened the door with a big smile. As I walked in, I couldn't help saying, "This has got to be every daughter-in-law's worst nightmare, seeing her mother-in-law walk through the door with suitcases."

We could both laugh, since under the circumstances it was funny. No moving van was out there in the street, waiting to move in tons of furniture. And I was **NOT** staying forever. Living in a room in somebody else's house—no matter who they are and how well we all get along—is not for me. In any case, I think far too much of all my daughters-in-law to inflict any one of them with **ME**.

But for the three weeks I stayed with them, Michael and Barbara were great hosts, and I really enjoyed my visit. They went off to work each morning, of course, at some ungodly hour, but with none of my animals there to worry about, I could sleep as late as I wanted, then get up to explore the various shopping malls. Inept as I was at finding streets in Mesa, zeroing in on the malls was never a problem. (That's what female antennae are for.)

Also, from time to time, I made off with several of Barbara's favorite recipes. As of today, Barbara is a fantastic chef, but when she arrived years ago in Phoenix as a brand new bride, she not only couldn't boil water but—as she herself would confirm—probably didn't even know where the stove was. Or care. Nowadays, Barbara could edit cookbooks for a living and show all the authors where they goofed.

On September 6, 1993, via Beeline Highway, I was at long last on my way to Payson. I soon found myself following a moving van, a very slow-moving van, but as the highway at that point consisted of only two lanes, there was no hope of passing it. Then, taking a closer look at the van, I realized it was the very one containing MY furniture.

Not only furniture, but ALL those boxes and cartons I had spent weeks putting together in New River. There were a total of twenty-seven cartons on their way to Payson—which number was almost unbelievable. For weeks before moving out, I had been stacking all kinds of junk and unusable pieces of furniture out in the driveway, which was collected once a week by the local trash pick-up crew. By the time I could actually start packing everything I wanted to take along, I was convinced there would be nothing left. And yet, along with the furniture, twenty-seven cartons were now heading for my new home—all to be unpacked and put away. (I could hardly wait.)

As for the furniture which had spent the last three weeks in a Mesa warehouse, I only hoped it would at least resemble the way it looked the last time I saw it. However, since the movers fourteen years ago had done such a beautiful job of moving us out of Phoenix and up that incredible hill in New River—losing nothing and breaking nothing—I wasn't really worried about any of the furniture.

Beeline Highway, the most famous highway in the state, is also the most beautiful. Between Mesa and Payson, the scenery is incomparable, something like turning one page after another in a travelogue. The road itself curves constantly right or left, up one hill and down another, with every turn offering a different view of the mountains on all sides. Only the passengers in each vehicle, however, can keep looking at the scenery laid out there before them. For any driver to be equally enthralled could very well be disastrous, but it's still a temptation hard to resist. You have to keep telling yourself **next** time maybe somebody **else** will be driving—and **then** I can look.

From Mesa to Payson, the drive usually takes about an hour and a half—but this time there was something a little different. Despite the many hasty trips I'd made up there in the past few months, now I was going **HOME**. The house was ready, and the animals were undoubtedly more than ready. (If they hadn't written me off altogether, they were probably climbing the walls by now.) Unfortunately, they all had one more long day to mark off on the calendar. Before I picked them up, I'd have to get myself officially moved in, so I wouldn't be coming to their rescue until the following day.

That next morning, as soon as Furry Friends opened its doors, I was there looking for **MY** furry friends. All eight of them. Sadly enough, all of them seemed a little unsure at first as to whether I was **really** picking them up or just visiting again. It took two trips to get eight now hysterically happy animals into their new home (they probably had assumed they were heading back to New River). Overnight, however, one and all adapted to their new surroundings faster than I would have expected— all my faithful, beautiful four-footers. I was finally able to pick up each and every cat and hold him, or her, again. It was a toss-up, however, as to which dog to pat on the head first—all three were literally running around in circles. To all of them, those three weeks probably seemed like an eternity.

Compared to the ranch I'd left behind, the Payson house was like being in another world. In square feet, both houses were almost identical, but everything else was different. The ranch in New River was on top of a hill, surrounded by six-and-a-half acres. Here, the lot size was three-fifths of an acre—which in Payson is a respectable size. (Nearer the center of town where the houses are much smaller, that same space would have accommodated three or four residences.) Also, it was really nice to have visible neighbors on all sides for a change, houses I could actually look over at, instead of telling myself that **some**body must be out there **some**where.

Another "first" for me was having a den. The original house plans had intended it to be a second guest room, but two of those I didn't need. My future guests would be either alone or as a couple, in which case one guest room was plenty. But a den would be a novelty, something I could now escape to for perhaps a computer, a desk, or a sewing machine (listed in order of enjoyment). The computer itself, a Macintosh Plus, was a revelation to me the first day I saw it. I couldn't do much more with it than write letters, make lists and get recipes in some kind of alphabetical order—but I absolutely loved it. Even with no knowledge whatsoever as to "software," "commands" or "hardware," literally overnight I was in the certified computer nut class. From the very first time when, under Michael's tutelage, I tried it out, I knew I would never again insult my fingers with a typewriter keyboard. During my working years, I'd used more than my share of those prehistoric machines and couldn't care less if I never saw another.

Michael had completely taken me by surprise one day by calling up and announcing he was on his way over from Mesa with a computer for me (he had recently graduated to a more elaborate IBM model), as he thought I'd like to try using it. At first, although fascinated by the idea of actually using a **computer**, I was extremely hesitant, as I had always been very envious of **anyone** who could use such a fabulous machine. Computers had been introduced into the courthouse at almost the same time I left there, but I never really expected to see one in front of **me**.

Also, if I couldn't catch on to how this miracle machine worked, I did not want to look like a complete idiot in front of my son. (When children are little, they assume Mommy and Daddy are truly fountains of knowledge, and parents naturally like to preserve that illusion as long as possible.)

I needn't have worried. Michael was the soul of patience and spent as much time as it took to introduce me to the "World of Computerdom." It was so much fun to learn something that fascinating; I was hooked for all time. For some time thereafter, I kept trying to make a deal with Michael. It was only right to pay him for his computer—after all, no one had given it to him—but he kept on stalling, saying, "Wait and see if you like it first. Not everybody hangs in there with computers, they buy one, use it for a while, and then it sits in the closet."

He finally said, "Mom, consider it a Christmas present." It was nowhere near Christmas—but that was one terrific present.

The morning of Day #3 in Payson, everything so far having been very calm and peaceful, I naively assumed Fate was running out of surprises. I soon found out Fate was still way ahead of me.

After feeding the cats in the kitchen, I glanced out the window to check on the three dogs in the back yard. There were only two dogs. I had brought **THREE** dogs. Where was Cham?

The back yard being fully enclosed by a six-foot cedar fence, he couldn't have gone over that. He hadn't. For reasons known only to Cham, he had dug **UNDER** the fence, and somehow squeezed himself through. For any normal dog, this would have been clearly impossible. Cham, being something else again, just went ahead and did it.

Had anyone been standing by with a video camera at that time, my future income would have been greatly enhanced. Any film showing Cham, who is no lightweight, laboriously clawing his way down, under and out, would have won every Pulitzer Prize known to man. Dividends from said film could have put us all on Easy Street. (There actually is an "Easy Street" in the town of Payson, and with a little more help from Fate, I could be living on the real thing.)

The word "frantic" would have been an understatement for my state of mind at that moment. I had no idea what to do. After all the turmoil and upset of the past several months, I had been literally counting the hours until Payson—and a calm new life—became a reality. Now, it was starting out like this.

Fortunately, it occurred to me to call the Humane Society. Under the circumstances, I couldn't even imagine how they could know anything about Cham, but I was desperate to be doing **something.**

Fortunately, the Humane Society was the right place to call. They had all the answers. Earlier that morning, a family living a block away from me had already called them, reporting that some strangely-acting dog (**had** to be Cham) had somehow gotten stuck in their shed the night before, and then howled so loudly it woke them up. These kind souls took him in for the night—no doubt hoping to get some sleep—and eventually phoned the Humane Society.

By that time, just turning on the ignition to start the car took strength I almost didn't have—but I drove there, collected Cham, and fervently thanked those good people.

With a start-up like that, the rest of the day should have been a cinch and, comparatively speaking, it was. However, I should have at least suspected the household was not yet done with crises. Cham changed his evil ways and left the fence alone for about a week. Then, twice again, he was apparently unable to resist the challenge. Two mornings in a row, he created new Dog-Exits under the fence. The fact that he never once got hurt in the process was in itself somewhat of a miracle.

After the third breakout, Gary figured out a way to prevent #4. He strung a heavy overhead wire across the yard, hooked a long leash to Cham's collar with the opposite end circled around the overhead wire, and **Voila!**—fence attacks were a thing of the past. All this had to be puzzling to Cham, who is not exactly the Einstein of dogs. (Cham makes up in personality and disposition what he lacks in gray matter.) But he still had the run of most of the yard—along with Pup and Jet.

Fortunately for all concerned—humans and canines alike—Pup and Jet had no interest whatever in leaving any place where food and drink were served—if not on demand, at least on schedule. And, with no effort whatsoever on their part. Watching Cham trying to dig his way out, they must have thought he was crazy—meals were served on the **inside** of the fence, not outside.

A few weeks later, this new-found peace was just a memory—but for an entirely different reason. A very unusual activity was suddenly going on in the back yard. The two female dogs, Pup and Jet, after all these years, had apparently just awakened to the fact that while there were **TWO** females, Pup and Jet, there was only **ONE** male: Cham.

Almost overnight, this became something for Pup and Jet to fight about—and they fought bitterly. Though all three dogs had been neutered eons ago at the recommended age, the two female dogs now decided they were bitter rivals for Cham's affections. Cham couldn't have cared less. He was totally uninterested in what was going on. As Jet and Pup snarled and fought with each other more and more each day, Cham just kept one eye on them from afar. Finally, as each fight was gradually becoming worse than the last, the vet strongly advised me to separate the two females permanently from each other. And the sooner the better. Otherwise, he predicted, one of these days I would come home and find either or both dogs dead.

That was all I had to hear—and the preventive action consisted of having the side yard closed off for Pup alone. She then had that area all to herself along with her own doghouse and favorite toys. The chain-link fence now separating her from Jet, who was still in the back yard with Cham, seemed to do the trick.

Through the fence, Pup and Jet could still communicate in dog-speak—but with no more physical contact possible, they were reconciled almost immediately. Once more, they were the best of friends.

Unknown to Pup, and certainly to me as well, there were to be only a few more weeks left of Pup's life—but at least those weeks were peaceful. She had been with Foster and me for many years, starting with the day Loner—Pup's paternal parent—had brought her to us in New River, presumably as a "present."

Pup's system, to use the vet's terminology, had been gradually "shutting down" for a long, long time. She became less and less interested in food, seemed to be growing weaker by the day, and the last few days she finally refused to eat at all.

For me, it has always been extremely difficult, next to impossible, to finally admit that for any animal I have taken care of, and loved, the quality of life is no longer there. With Pup, as with all the others, the handwriting on the wall had been there all along. I just didn't want to read it.

Pup eventually had to be put to sleep. I buried her ashes out in the back yard—and once again, she was close to Jet and Cham. That day, for some reason, I had a feeling those other two dogs knew exactly what was going on.

Cham, predictably, took one more shot at trying to put a little excitement into his life—and into mine. Also, into those of nine or ten other people. One stormy afternoon, I could not see Cham anywhere out in the yard. The fence was naturally the first place I checked—and the fence was still intact. Upon further investigation, I noticed Cham's leash disappearing under the back porch.

He had gone all the way under, as far back as he could—presumably to escape the noise of the thunder. The one thing Cham is absolutely paranoid about is thunder. He goes berserk at the faintest rumble—and unfortunately, since dogs seem to hear noises long before people do, he has time to do whatever he thinks he **has** to do. (Cats, on the other hand, simply curl up for a nap during a thunderstorm and consider lightning flashes to be pure entertainment—just something put on for their benefit.)

I tried pulling Cham's leash back, but he was evidently stuck in there somewhere. The depth of the porch is eight feet, as I discovered when I finally quit tugging on the leash and crawled under the porch to find out what was going on. Cham had jammed his head into part of a louvered opening in the foundation, doubtless assuming he could pull the rest of him through as he had done under the fence.

The problem was, when he tried to back out again, having found the rest of him was NOT following, the vents of the louver had reversed themselves. Cham was really stuck—and apparently for all time, the way it looked to me. I ran inside and called Gary, who had just arrived home from work. Within minutes, he was also underneath the porch, trying to do whatever it would take to free Cham.

By this time, Cham was very quiet. We knew he was breathing all right, as we kept checking on him, but he was just not moving. Either he had given up entirely or, hopefully, had great faith in us. Gary finally suggested that I call 9-1-1 and see if anyone there had any ideas as to what we should do. Meanwhile, he managed to crawl under the house from an opening around the side and then made his way over to where Cham's head was sticking through the foundation. I still could not believe all this was actually happening—except that it was.

Once underneath the house and inches away from Cham, Gary continually reassured the dog that help was on the way. The mere fact that Gary was there at all must have been the only real comfort to Cham, who comprehends little, if any, of the English language (with the exception, naturally, of "Come on, it's time to EAT." Gary later said he repeatedly gave thanks, during his 90-minute ordeal under the house, that the foundation itself had been made termite-proof just a few days earlier.

Help was indeed on the way—but it took a while. One of the two policemen who answered my call had likewise crawled under the porch, and from there he used his hand-phone to summon the Fire Department. In a matter of minutes, two members of the Fire Department were also under the porch. It was getting pretty crowded down there.

Next on the scene (and under the porch), was the Animal Control Officer—a very nice lady who brought along her visiting granddaughter to observe this newly-formed Payson Rescue Team in action. Said grand-daughter was only too delighted to join us—also under the porch. The use of a tranquilizer was discussed, for which, according to the Animal Control Officer, some kind of official permission had first to be obtained. Since this was reputedly available by phone, the police officer called and left his number. Everybody stayed where they were—under the porch—waiting for the call-back and meanwhile staring (or glaring) at Cham.

Those five long minutes of silence, crouched under a porch in the middle of the night, with everyone there a total stranger to everyone else, seemed more like five years. Just to pass the time, making polite conversation seemed like the only thing to do—but chances are, no one even heard themselves, let alone anybody else.

Finally, the officer's phone rang. We had the go-ahead for the tranquilizer. When cheers went up on all sides, I think even Cham felt relieved—and he had no idea what was going on.

The person calling advised it would take only fifteen minutes for the tranquilizer to take effect. ONLY fifteen minutes??? Half the town had been crawling around under that porch for what seemed like an eternity, and we had ANOTHER fifteen minutes to go? (The only town official not putting in an appearance that evening was the Mayor, and I can only assume he was out of town.)

A happy, happy ending finally came with Payson's Dog-of-the-Month being pulled out, unhurt, from his three-hour dungeon—slicked down on all sides with the Vaseline that helped to slide him through.

One more cheer went up. Every one of those good-hearted, caring people was applauding—and THEY were the ones who had done all the work.

Ever since the day I buried Pup, I had tried not to even think about losing any more of my pets—but not long afterwards, I could no longer ignore the fact that my beautiful white cat Henrietta was not only losing her appetite but beginning to fade away in much the same way as Pup. It was then I knew her time was all too short.

Henrietta weighed less than five pounds the last time I carried her into the vet's office, and what had to be done there was inevitable. She died in my arms.

I love all my cats, but Henrietta was my "baby," and a little bit of my heart went with her.

Living now in Payson, in the house Gary built for me, is where I and my "furry family" are content and happy. The past was pretty good and sometimes it was absolutely wonderful. I have no complaints—and if I had my life to live over again, **I would probably do every single thing I did the first time.** I would have to say the message from Arizona (my favorite place) would have to be, "**It's been great!**"

THE END